The Excursion *and* The Recluse

Humanities-Ebooks

Humanities-Ebooks publishes primarily in electronic form and its Ebooks (with the facility of word and phrase search, and in some cases both internal and external hyperlinks) are available to private purchasers exclusively from http://www.humanities-ebooks.co.uk and to libraries from EBSCO, Ebrary and Ingram.

The paperback version of this book is available from all booksellers but at a discount from Lulu.com.

William Wordsworth

The Excursion and *The Recluse*

$\mathcal{HEB}$ ☼ Humanities-Ebooks, LLP

© Jared Curtis, 2014

The Author has asserted his right to be identified as the author of this Work in accordance with the Copyright, Designs and Patents Act 1988.

First published by *Humanities-Ebooks, LLP,*
Tirril Hall, Tirril, Penrith CA10 2JE.

Cover image, the Langdale Pikes from above the Solitary's Cottage
© Richard Gravil

The reading texts of Wordsworth's poems used in this volume are from the Cornell Wordsworth series, published by Cornell University Press, Sage House, 512 East State Street, Ithaca, NY 14850. Copyright © Cornell University. Volumes are available at: http://www.cornellpress.cornell.edu

The reading texts are also collected in *The Poems of William Wordsworth: Collected Reading Texts from the Cornell Wordsworth*, 3 vols, edited by Jared Curtis (Humanities-Ebooks, 2009).

A one volume PDF Ebook containing the three volumes and an Addendum is available exclusively from humanities-ebooks.co.uk.

ISBN 978-1-84760-342-5 PDF Ebook
ISBN 978-1-84760-343-2 Paperback

Contents

Preface	6
Hart-leap Well	10

POEMS FROM THE 1798 'RECLUSE'

The Old Cumberland Beggar, A Description	18
A Fragment [A Night-Piece]	24

THE RECLUSE, PART FIRST, BOOK FIRST

Home at Grasmere (1800–1806)	26

FURTHER WRITING FOR THE RECLUSE, PART FIRST

To the Clouds (1808)	56
The Tuft of Primroses (1808)	58
[St. Paul's] (1808)	75
Composed when a probability existed of our being obliged to quit Rydal Mount as a Residence (1826)	77

THE RECLUSE, PART SECOND

The Excursion (1814)	84

[POEMS EXTRACTED FROM THE EXCURSION]

[The Peasant's Life]	354
[The Shepherd of Bield Crag]	357
Wordsworth's Notes	359
Select Bibliography	377

Preface

This book contains all that can be confidently assigned to Wordsworth's final conception of his unfinished philosophical poem, 'The Recluse'. It contents are selected from Jared Curtis's *The Poems of William Wordsworth: Collected Reading Texts from the Cornell Wordsworth*, published by Humanities-Ebooks in 2009.

Writing to James Tobin on 6 March 1798, Wordsworth made his first epistolary reference to 'The Recluse, or Views of Nature, Man and Society' (the poem's working title being bestowed five days later in a letter to Jame Losh):

> I have written 1300 lines of a poem in which I contrive to convey most of the knowledge of which I am possessed. My object is to give pictures of Nature, Man, and Society. Indeed I know not any thing which will not come within the scope of my plan. . . . the work of composition is carved out for me, for at least a year and a half to come.[1]

What became of that grandiose ambition over the next thirty years is too complex a story to follow here. It has been told by John Alban Finch, Mark Reed, James Butler, Jonathan Wordsworth, Sally Bushell, and others in works listed in this book's Select Bibliography.

Essentially, it was to be a poem in three parts, prefaced by a fourth poem of epic length, *The Prelude*. The three Parts of 'The Recluse' proper would have been unified by an attempt to flesh out the remarkable view of mankind's potential outlined in the so-called 'Prospectus to The Recluse', which forms the climax of 'Home at Grasmere' and was published with some revision in the Preface to *The Excursion*.

According to that Preface, 'The Recluse' would have had 'for its principal subject the sensations and opinions of a Poet living in retirement', which account harmonises with Coleridge's judgment,

---

1 *The Letters of William and Dorothy Wordsworth. The Early Years,* 2nd edn, ed. Ernest de Selincourt, rev. Chester L. Shaver (Oxford: Clarendon Press, 1967)., 212.

in 1804, that 'I prophesy immortality to his "Recluse", as the first and finest philosophical poem, if only it be … a faithful transcript of his own most august and innocent life, of his own habitual feelings and modes of seeing and hearing.'[1] 'The Recluse, Part First, Book First', also entitled 'Home at Grasmere', was indubitably such a 'transcript'.[2] It occupied Wordsworth intermittently from 1800 to 1806, spanning most of the period during which *The Prelude* was also composed, which may explain why *The Prelude* pre-empts much of the argument intended for 'The Recluse'. It is, altogether, one of Wordsworth's most ecstatic performances, but it proved a very hard act to follow. It has never been clear to anybody how Wordsworth would have tackled another six, seven, or eight Books of 'The Recluse, Part First'.

In 1808, however, Wordsworth did produce some further pieces of composition, 'To the Clouds', 'The Tuft of Primroses' and 'St. Paul's', which appear to have been intended for one further 'Book' of 'The Recluse, Part First'. Later still, in 1826, having composed some verses on Nab Well ('Composed when a probability existed'), Wordsworth told Henry Crabb Robinson that these lines were 'to be an introduction to a portion of his great poem' containing 'a poetical view of water as an element in the composition of our globe'.[3] All four of these shorter pieces, included in this volume, are as edited by Joseph F. Kishel in *The Tuft of Primroses and other Late Poems for 'The Recluse'* (Ithaca, NY: Cornell University Press, 1986).

To these I have added two further poems. The '1300 lines' referred to in Wordsworth's letter of March 1798 included 'a version of 'The Ruined Cottage', 'A Night Piece', 'The Old Cumberland Beggar', and 'The Discharged Soldier'.[4] Of these, 'The Ruined Cottage' found a place in Wordsworth's masterly tripartite version of Margaret's and

---

[1] *Collected Letters of Samuel Taylor Coleridge, ed.* Earl Leslie Griggs, 6 vols (Oxford: Clarendon Press, 1956–71), 4: 574.
[2] The text of 'Home at Grasmere' presented in this volume is that of the Cornell Wordsworth *Home at Grasmere*, edited by Beth Darlington (Ithaca NY: Cornell University Press, 1977).
[3] Henry Crabb Robinson, *Diary, Reminiscences, and Correspondence*, ed. Thomas Sadler, 3rd edn, 2 vols (London: Macmillan and Co., 1872), 2: 364.
[4] Kenneth R. Johnston, *Wordsworth and 'The Recluse'* (New Haven and London: Yale University Press, 1984), 5–6.

8   Writing for 'The Recluse'

her narrator's tale in Book I of *The Excursion*, while 'The Discharged Soldier' was assigned to Book IV of *The Prelude*. Since, however, Wordsworth's first conception of 'The Recluse' was clearly dominated by a poetry studying human beings in extreme siituations, it seems reasonable to find room in this volume for 'The Old Cumberland Beggar'. And 'A Night Piece', though somewhat extraneous among the '1300 lines', seems like a dress rehearsal for 'To the Clouds' and St Paul's'. I have therefore included both of these 'ur-Recluse' poems under the geneal rubric of 'Poems from the 1798 Recluse'.

'The Recluse, Part Second' was published in 1814 as *The Excursion*. It adopts, as Wordsworth's preface says, 'something of a dramatic form' in narrating, first, the tragedy of Margaret, and then in eight further Books, the attempts of three characters, a Poet (who is and is not Wordsworth), a Wanderer (ditto) and a Pastor, to cure a fourth character, the Solitary (to whom Wordsworth gifts much of his own darkest experience) of his 'dejection' and as the Solitary himself puts it (3: 694), his dependence. In this second 'Part', Wordsworth appears to be responding to Coleridge's somewhat confusing exhortation in September 1799, that apart from, or alongside, or even as part of, writing 'The Recluse', Wordsworth should embark on

> a poem, in blank verse, addressed to those, who in consequence of the complete failure of the French Revolution, have thrown up all hopes of the amelioration of mankind ...It would do great good, and might form a part of 'The Recluse'.[1]

'The Recluse, Part Third' has not even vestigial existence. Wordsworth confessed to George Ticknor in 1838 that all extant composition for 'The Recluse' was intended for 'Part First' and that 'Part Third' was 'untouched'.[2] It would appear logical to suppose that 'Part Third' must have taken up on personal and philosophical grounds the problems left unresolved in the dialogue of 'Part Second', as indeed the concluding lines of *The Excursion* (9: 782–95) suggest, but no sketch is known to have existed. Interestingly, however, Wordsworth

---

1   *Collected Letters of Samuel Taylor Coleridge*, ed. Earl Leslie Griggs, 6 vols (Oxford: Clarendon Press, 1956–71), 1: 527.
2   *The Letters of William and Dorothy Wordsworth: The Later Years*, 2nd edn, ed. Alan G. Hill, 4 vols (Oxford: Clarendon Press, 1978–88), 3: 583n.

excuses himself for publishing Part 2 before Part 1 or Part 3 on the grounds that 'as the second division of the Work was designed to refer more to passing events, and to an existing state of things, than the others were meant to do, more continuous exertion was naturally bestowed upon it, and greater progress made here than in the rest of the Poem'. It may be legitimate to deduce from this way of putting things that 'Part Third' might have set out to portray a better 'state of things' and to justify the optimism about mankind's potential indulged so rapturously in 'Home at Grasmere'. It must also have shown how, as promised in the 'Prospectus', to a mind properly wedded to this world, 'paradise and groves elysian' may be 'a simple produce of the common day'.

'Home at Grasmere' itself appears to ground its optimistic faith in a vision or 'trance' experienced at Hart-Leap Well, while William and Dorothy were journeying to Grasmere. There they received, or so 'Home at Grasmere' claims, 'The intimation of the milder day / Which is to come, the fairer world than this'. For this reason, 'Hart-leap Well', first published in *Lyrical Ballads* (1800), and the only poem mentioned in either 'Home at Grasmere' or *The Excursion*, is included here as a poetical epigraph to 'The Recluse'.

It remains to express my gratitude to Jared Curtis, whose three-volume collection of *The Poems of William Wordsworth: Collected Reading Texts from the Cornell Wordsworth* (Humanities-Ebooks 2009–14) has made possible what is, in effect, this first edition of *The Recluse*, and of course to the editors and publishers of the Cornell Wordsworth. This volume has no 'editor', because it has involved no editing.

Richard Gravil, Tirril, 2014

Hart-leap Well[1]

Hart-leap Well is a small spring of water, about five miles from Richmond in Yorkshire, and near the side of the road which leads from Richmond to Askrigg. Its name is derived from a remarkable chace, the memory of which is preserved by the monuments spoken of in the second Part of the following Poem, which monuments do now exist as I have there described them.

The Knight had ridden down from Wensley Moor
With the slow motion of a summer's cloud;
He turn'd aside towards a Vassal's door,
And, "Bring another Horse," he cried aloud.

"Another Horse."—That shout the Vassal heard, 5
And saddled his best steed, a comely Grey:
Sir Walter mounted him; he was the third
Which he had mounted on that glorious day.

Joy sparkled in the prancing Courser's eyes;
The horse and horseman are a happy pair; 10
But, though Sir Walter like a falcon flies,
There is a doleful silence in the air.

A rout this morning left Sir Walter's Hall,
That as they gallop'd made the echoes roar;
But horse and man are vanish'd, one and all; 15
Such race, I think, was never seen before.

Sir Walter, restless as a veering wind,
Calls to the few tired dogs that yet remain:

---

1   This poem is included in the volume because of its privileged mention in *Home at Grasmere*, lines 236-239. The text is from POems of William Wordswoth, Volume 1, and is that of '*Lyrical Ballads' and other Poems, 1797–1800*, ed. James Butler and Karen Green (Ithaca NY: Cornell University Press, 1992).

Brach, Swift and Music, noblest of their kind,
Follow, and up the weary mountain strain.   20

The Knight halloo'd, he chid and cheer'd them on
With suppliant gestures and upbraidings stern;
But breath and eyesight fail, and, one by one,
The dogs are stretch'd among the mountain fern.

Where is the throng, the tumult of the chace?   25
The bugles that so joyfully were blown?
—This race it looks not like an earthly race;
Sir Walter and the Hart are left alone.

The poor Hart toils along the mountain side;
I will not stop to tell how far he fled,   30
Nor will I mention by what death he died;
But now the Knight beholds him lying dead.

Dismounting then, he lean'd against a thorn;
He had no follower, dog, nor man, nor boy:
He neither smack'd his whip, nor blew his horn,   35
But gaz'd upon the spoil with silent joy.

Close to the thorn on which Sir Walter lean'd
Stood his dumb partner in this glorious act;
Weak as a lamb the hour that it is yean'd,
And foaming like a mountain cataract.   40

Upon his side the Hart was lying stretch'd:
His nose half-touch'd a spring beneath a hill,
And with the last deep groan his breath had fetch'd
The waters of the spring were trembling still.

And now, too happy for repose or rest,   45
Was never man in such a joyful case,
Sir Walter walk'd all round, north, south and west,
And gaz'd, and gaz'd upon that darling place.

And turning up the hill, it was at least
Nine roods of sheer ascent, Sir Walter found   50

Three several marks which with his hoofs the beast
Had left imprinted on the verdant ground.

Sir Walter wiped his face, and cried, 'Till now
Such sight was never seen by living eyes:
Three leaps have borne him from this lofty brow, 55
Down to the very fountain where he lies.

I'll build a Pleasure-house upon this spot,
And a small Arbour, made for rural joy;
'Twill be the traveller's shed, the pilgrim's cot,
A place of love for damsels that are coy. 60

A cunning artist will I have to frame
A bason for that fountain in the dell;
And they, who do make mention of the same,
From this day forth shall call it Hart-leap Well.

And, gallant brute! to make thy praises known, 65
Another monument shall here be rais'd;
Three several pillars, each a rough-hewn stone,
And planted where thy hoofs the turf have graz'd.

And in the summer-time when days are long
I will come hither with my paramour, 70
And with the dancers, and the minstrel's song
We will make merry in that pleasant bower.

Till the foundations of the mountains fail
My mansion with its arbour shall endure;
—The joy of them who till the fields of Swale, 75
And them who dwell among the woods of Ure."

Then home he went, and left the Hart, stone-dead,
With breathless nostrils stretch'd above the spring.
And soon the Knight perform'd what he had said,
The fame whereof through many a land did ring. 80

Ere thrice the moon into her port had steer'd,
A cup of stone receiv'd the living well;

Three pillars of rude stone Sir Walter rear'd,
And built a house of pleasure in the dell.

And near the fountain, flowers of stature tall 85
With trailing plants and trees were intertwin'd,
Which soon compos'd a little sylvan hall,
A leafy shelter from the sun and wind.

And thither, when the summer days were long,
Sir Walter journey'd with his paramour; 90
And with the dancers and a minstrel's song
Made merriment within that pleasant bower.

The Knight Sir Walter died in course of time,
And his bones lie in his paternal vale.—
But there is matter for a second rhyme, 95
And I to this would add another tale.

Part Second.

The moving accident is not my trade,
To curl the blood I have no ready arts;
'Tis my delight, alone in summer shade,
To pipe a simple song to thinking hearts. 100

As I from Hawes to Richmond did repair,
It chanc'd that I saw standing in a dell
Three aspins at three corners of a square,
And one, not four yards distant, near a well.

What this imported I could ill divine, 105
And, pulling now the rein my horse to stop,
I saw three pillars standing in a line,
The last stone pillar on a dark hill-top.

The trees were grey, with neither arms nor head;
Half-wasted the square mound of tawny green; 110
So that you just might say, as then I said,
"Here in old time the hand of man has been."

I look'd upon the hills both far and near;
More doleful place did never eye survey;
It seem'd as if the spring-time came not here,   115
And Nature here were willing to decay.

I stood in various thoughts and fancies lost,
When one who was in Shepherd's garb attir'd
Came up the hollow; him did I accost,
And what this place might be I then inquir'd.   120

The Shepherd stopp'd, and that same story told
Which in my former rhyme I have rehears'd.
"A jolly place," said he, "in times of old,
But something ails it now; the spot is curs'd.

You see these lifeless stumps of aspin wood,   125
Some say that they are beeches, others elms,
These were the Bower; and here a Mansion stood,
The finest palace of a hundred realms.

The arbour does its own condition tell,
You see the stones, the fountain, and the stream,   130
But as to the great Lodge, you might as well
Hunt half a day for a forgotten dream.

There's neither dog nor heifer, horse nor sheep,
Will wet his lips within that cup of stone;
And, oftentimes, when all are fast asleep,   135
This water doth send forth a dolorous groan.

Some say that here a murder has been done,
And blood cries out for blood: but, for my part,
I've guess'd, when I've been sitting in the sun,
That it was all for that unhappy Hart.   140

What thoughts must through the creature's brain have pass'd!
From the stone on the summit of the steep
Are but three bounds, and look, Sir, at this last,
O Master! it has been a cruel leap.

For thirteen hours he ran a desperate race; 145
And in my simple mind we cannot tell
What cause the Hart might have to love this place,
And come and make his death-bed near the well.

Here on the grass perhaps asleep he sank,
Lull'd by this fountain in the summer-tide; 150
This water was perhaps the first he drank
When he had wander'd from his mother's side.

In April here beneath the scented thorn
He heard the birds their morning carols sing,
And he, perhaps, for aught we know, was born 155
Not half a furlong from that self-same spring.

But now here's neither grass nor pleasant shade;
The sun on drearier hollow never shone:
So will it be, as I have often said,
Till trees, and stones, and fountain, all are gone." 160

"Grey-headed Shepherd, thou hast spoken well;
Small difference lies between thy creed and mine;
This beast not unobserv'd by Nature fell,
His death was mourn'd by sympathy divine.

The Being, that is in the clouds and air, 165
That is in the green leaves among the groves,
Maintains a deep and reverential care
For them the quiet creatures whom he loves.

The Pleasure-house is dust:—behind, before,
This is no common waste, no common gloom; 170
But Nature, in due course of time, once more
Shall here put on her beauty and her bloom.

She leaves these objects to a slow decay
That what we are, and have been, may be known;
But, at the coming of the milder day, 175
These monuments shall all be overgrown.

One lesson, Shepherd, let us two divide,
Taught both by what she shews, and what conceals,
Never to blend our pleasure or our pride
With sorrow of the meanest thing that feels." 180

Poems from the 1798 'Recluse'

The Old Cumberland Beggar, A Description[1]

The class of Beggars to which the old man here described belongs, will probably soon be extinct. It consisted of poor, and, mostly, old and infirm persons, who confined themselves to a stated round in their neighbourhood, and had certain fixed days, on which, at different houses, they regularly received charity; sometimes in money, but mostly in provisions.

I saw an aged Beggar in my walk,
And he was seated by the highway side
On a low structure of rude masonry
Built at the foot of a huge hill, that they
Who lead their horses down the steep rough road   5
May thence remount at ease. The aged man
Had placed his staff across the broad smooth stone
That overlays the pile, and from a bag
All white with flour the dole of village dames,
He drew his scraps and fragments, one by one,   10
And scann'd them with a fix'd and serious look
Of idle computation. In the sun,
Upon the second step of that small pile,
Surrounded by those wild unpeopled hills,
He sate, and eat his food in solitude;   15
And ever, scatter'd from his palsied hand,
That still attempting to prevent the waste,
Was baffled still, the crumbs in little showers
Fell on the ground, and the small mountain birds,
Not venturing yet to peck their destin'd meal,   20
Approached within the length of half his staff.

---

[1] The text of this poem is taken from *Poems of William Wordsworth*, volume 1, and from *'Lyrical Ballads' and Other Poems, 1797–1800,* ed. James Butler and Karen Green (Ithaca NY: Cornell Universit Press, 1992).

Him from my childhood have I known, and then
He was so old, he seems not older now;
He travels on, a solitary man,
So helpless in appearance, that for him 25
The sauntering horseman-traveller does not throw
With careless hand his alms upon the ground,
But stops, that he may safely lodge the coin
Within the old Man's hat; nor quits him so,
But still when he has given his horse the rein 30
Towards the aged Beggar turns a look,
Sidelong and half-reverted. She who tends
The toll-gate, when in summer at her door
She turns her wheel, if on the road she sees
The aged Beggar coming, quits her work, 35
And lifts the latch for him that he may pass.
The Post-boy when his rattling wheels o'ertake
The aged Beggar, in the woody lane,
Shouts to him from behind, and, if perchance
The old Man does not change his course, the Boy 40
Turns with less noisy wheels to the road-side,
And passes gently by, without a curse
Upon his lips, or anger at his heart.
He travels on, a solitary Man,
His age has no companion. On the ground 45
His eyes are turn'd, and, as he moves along,
They move along the ground; and evermore,
Instead of common and habitual sight
Of fields with rural works, of hill and dale,
And the blue sky, one little span of earth 50
Is all his prospect. Thus, from day to day,
Bowbent, his eyes for ever on the ground,
He plies his weary journey, seeing still,
And never knowing that he sees, some straw,
Some scatter'd leaf, or marks which, in one track, 55
The nails of cart or chariot wheel have left
Impress'd on the white road, in the same line,

At distance still the same. Poor Traveller!
His staff trails with him, scarcely do his feet
Disturb the summer dust, he is so still 60
In look and motion that the cottage curs,
Ere he have pass'd the door, will turn away
Weary of barking at him. Boys and girls,
The vacant and the busy, maids and youths,
And urchins newly breech'd all pass him by: 65
Him even the slow-pac'd waggon leaves behind.

But deem not this man useless.——Statesmen! ye
Who are so restless in your wisdom, ye
Who have a broom still ready in your hands
To rid the world of nuisances; ye proud, 70
Heart-swoln, while in your pride ye contemplate
Your talents, power, and wisdom, deem him not
A burthen of the earth. 'Tis Nature's law
That none, the meanest of created things,
Of forms created the most vile and brute, 75
The dullest or most noxious, should exist
Divorced from good, a spirit and pulse of good,
A life and soul to every mode of being
Inseparably link'd. While thus he creeps
From door to door, the Villagers in him 80
Behold a record which together binds
Past deeds and offices of charity
Else unremember'd, and so keeps alive
The kindly mood in hearts which lapse of years,
And that half-wisdom half-experience gives 85
Make slow to feel, and by sure steps resign
To selfishness and cold oblivious cares.
Among the farms and solitary huts,
Hamlets, and thinly-scattered villages,
Where'er the aged Beggar takes his rounds, 90
The mild necessity of use compels
To acts of love; and habit does the work
Of reason, yet prepares that after-joy

Which reason cherishes. And thus the soul,
By that sweet taste of pleasure unpursu'd 95
Doth find itself insensibly dispos'd
To virtue and true goodness. Some there are,
By their good works exalted, lofty minds
And meditative, authors of delight
And happiness, which to the end of time 100
Will live, and spread, and kindle; minds like these,
In childhood, from this solitary being,
This helpless wanderer, have perchance receiv'd,
(A thing more precious far than all that books
Or the solicitudes of love can do!) 105
That first mild touch of sympathy and thought,
In which they found their kindred with a world
Where want and sorrow were. The easy man
Who sits at his own door, and like the pear
Which overhangs his head from the green wall, 110
Feeds in the sunshine; the robust and young,
The prosperous and unthinking, they who live
Shelter'd, and flourish in a little grove
Of their own kindred, all behold in him
A silent monitor, which on their minds 115
Must needs impress a transitory thought
Of self-congratulation, to the heart
Of each recalling his peculiar boons,
His charters and exemptions; and perchance,
Though he to no one give the fortitude 120
And circumspection needful to preserve
His present blessings, and to husband up
The respite of the season, he, at least,
And 'tis no vulgar service, makes them felt.

Yet further.——Many, I believe, there are 125
Who live a life of virtuous decency,
Men who can hear the Decalogue and feel
No self-reproach, who of the moral law
Establish'd in the land where they abide

Are strict observers, and not negligent, 130
Meanwhile, in any tenderness of heart
Or act of love to those with whom they dwell,
Their kindred, and the children of their blood.
Praise be to such, and to their slumbers peace!
—But of the poor man ask, the abject poor, 135
Go and demand of him, if there be here,
In this cold abstinence from evil deeds,
And these inevitable charities,
Wherewith to satisfy the human soul.
No—man is dear to man: the poorest poor 140
Long for some moments in a weary life
When they can know and feel that they have been
Themselves the fathers and the dealers out
Of some small blessings, have been kind to such
As needed kindness, for this single cause, 145
That we have all of us one human heart.
—Such pleasure is to one kind Being known
My Neighbour, when with punctual care, each week
Duly as Friday comes, though press'd herself
By her own wants, she from her chest of meal 150
Takes one unsparing handful for the scrip
Of this old Mendicant, and, from her door
Returning with exhilarated heart,
Sits by her fire and builds her hope in heav'n.

Then let him pass, a blessing on his head! 155
And while, in that vast solitude to which
The tide of things has led him, he appears
To breathe and live but for himself alone,
Unblam'd, uninjur'd, let him bear about
The good which the benignant law of heaven 160
Has hung around him, and, while life is his,
Still let him prompt the unletter'd Villagers
To tender offices and pensive thoughts.
Then let him pass, a blessing on his head!
And, long as he can wander, let him breathe 165

The freshness of the vallies, let his blood
Struggle with frosty air and winter snows,
And let the charter'd wind that sweeps the heath
Beat his grey locks against his wither'd face.
Reverence the hope whose vital anxiousness　　　　　170
Gives the last human interest to his heart.
May never House, misnamed of industry,
Make him a captive; for that pent-up din,
Those life-consuming sounds that clog the air,
Be his the natural silence of old age.　　　　　175
Let him be free of mountain solitudes,
And have around him, whether heard or not,
The pleasant melody of woodland birds.
Few are his pleasures; if his eyes, which now
Have been so long familiar with the earth,　　　　　180
No more behold the horizontal sun
Rising or setting, let the light at least
Find a free entrance to their languid orbs.
And let him, *where* and *when* he will, sit down
Beneath the trees, or by the grassy bank　　　　　185
Of high-way side, and with the little birds
Share his chance-gather'd meal, and, finally,
As in the eye of Nature he has liv'd,
So in the eye of Nature let him die.

A Fragment [A Night-Piece][1]

                  The sky is overspread
With a close veil of one continuous cloud
All whitened by the moon, that just appears,
A dim-seen orb, yet chequers not the ground
With any shadow,—plant, or tower, or tree.
At last, a pleasant gleam breaks forth at once,   5
An instantaneous light; the musing [man]
Who walks along with his eyes bent to earth
Is startled. He looks about, the clouds are split
Asunder, and above his head, he views
The clear moon, and the glory of the heavens.   10

There, in a black-blue vault she sails along,
Followed by multitudes of stars, that small,
And bright, and sharp, along the gloomy vault
Drive as she drives. How fast they wheel away!   15
Yet vanish not! The wind is in the trees,
But they are silent; still they roll along
Immeasurably distant, and the vault
Built round by those white clouds, enormous clouds,
Still deepens its interminable depth.   20
At length the vision closes, and the mind
Not undisturbed by the deep joy it feels,
Which slowly settles into peaceful calm,
Is left to muse upon the solemn scene.

---

1 Composed at Alfoxden in 1798 as simply "A Fragment," the poem lay unpublished until Wordsworth revised the first ten lines and included it in *Poems* (1815) as *A Night-Piece*. This text is from the Addendum to *The Poems of William Wordsworth* and from *"Lyrical Ballads," and Other Poems, 1797–1800.* edited by James Butler and Karen Green (Ithaca: Cornell University Press, 1992).

The Recluse, Part First, Book First

Home at Grasmere (1800–1806)[1]

Home at Grasmere

   Once on the brow of yonder Hill I stopped,
While I was yet a School-boy (of what age
I cannot well remember, but the hour
I well remember though the year be gone),
And with a sudden influx overcome   5
At sight of this seclusion, I forgot
My haste—for hasty had my footsteps been,
As boyish my pursuits—[and sighing said],
"What happy fortune were it here to live!
And if I thought of dying, if a thought   10
Of mortal separation could come in
With paradise before me, here to die."
I was no Prophet, nor had even a hope,
Scarcely a wish, but one bright pleasing thought,
A fancy in the heart of what might be   15
The lot of others, never could be mine.
   The place from which I looked was soft and green,
Not giddy yet aerial, with a depth
Of Vale below, a height of Hills above.
Long did I halt; I could have made it even   20
My business and my errand so to halt.
For rest of body 'twas a perfect place;
All that luxurious nature could desire,
But tempting to the Spirit. Who could look
And not feel motions there? I thought of clouds   25

---

[1] For the sources of the reading texts and the editor's commentary see *Home at Grasmere: Part First, Book First, of "The Recluse,"* ed. Beth Darlington (1977).

That sail on winds; of breezes that delight
To play on water, or in endless chase
Pursue each other through the liquid depths
Of grass or corn, over and through and through,
In billow after billow evermore;   30
Of Sunbeams, Shadows, Butterflies, and Birds,
Angels, and winged Creatures that are Lords
Without restraint of all which they behold.
I sate, and stirred in Spirit as I looked,
I seemed to feel such liberty was mine,   35
Such power and joy; but only for this end:
To flit from field to rock, from rock to field,
From shore to island, and from isle to shore,
From open place to covert, from a bed
Of meadow-flowers into a tuft of wood,   40
From high to low, from low to high, yet still
Within the bounds of this huge Concave; here
Should be my home, this Valley be my World.
   From that time forward was the place to me
As beautiful in thought as it had been   45
When present to my bodily eyes; a haunt
Of my affections, oftentimes in joy
A brighter joy, in sorrow (but of that
I have known little), in such gloom, at least,
Such damp of the gay mind as stood to me   50
In place of sorrow, 'twas a gleam of light.
And now 'tis mine for life: dear Vale,
One of thy lowly dwellings is my home!
   Yes, the Realities of Life—so cold,
So cowardly, so ready to betray,   55
So stinted in the measure of their grace,
As we report them, doing them much wrong—
Have been to me more bountiful than hope,
Less timid than desire. Oh bold indeed
They have been! Bold and bounteous unto me,   60
Who have myself been bold, not wanting trust,

Nor resolution, nor at last the hope
Which is of wisdom, for I feel it is.
   And did it cost so much, and did it ask
Such length of discipline, and could it seem   65
An act of courage, and the thing itself
A conquest? Shame that this was ever so,
Not to the Boy or Youth, but shame to thee,
Sage Man, thou Sun in its meridian strength,
Thou flower in its full blow, thou King and crown   70
Of human Nature; shame to thee, sage Man.
Thy prudence, thy experience, thy desires,
Thy apprehensions—blush thou for them all.
But I am safe; yes, one at least is safe;
What once was deemed so difficult is no   75
Smooth, easy, without obstacle; what once
Did to my blindness seem a sacrifice,
The same is now a choice of the whole heart.
If e'er the acceptance of such dower was deemed
A condescension or a weak indulgence   80
To a sick fancy, it is now an act
Of reason that exultingly aspires.
This solitude is mine; the distant thought
Is fetched out of the heaven in which it was.
The unappropriated bliss hath found   85
An owner, and that owner I am he.
The Lord of this enjoyment is on Earth
And in my breast. What wonder if I speak
With fervour, am exalted with the thought
Of my possessions, of my genuine wealth   90
Inward and outward? What I keep have gained,
Shall gain, must gain, if sound be my belief
From past and present rightly understood
That in my day of childhood I was less
The mind of Nature, less, take all in all,   95
Whatever may be lost, than I am now.
For proof behold this Valley and behold

Yon Cottage, where with me my Emma dwells.
   Aye, think on that, my Heart, and cease to stir;
Pause upon that, and let the breathing frame   100
No longer breathe, but all be satisfied.
Oh, if such silence be not thanks to God
For what hath been bestowed, then where, where then
Shall gratitude find rest? Mine eyes did ne'er
Rest on a lovely object, nor my mind   105
Take pleasure in the midst of [happy] thoughts,
But either She whom now I have, who now
Divides with me this loved abode, was there
Or not far off. Where'er my footsteps turned,
Her Voice was like a hidden Bird that sang;   110
The thought of her was like a flash of light
Or an unseen companionship, a breath
Or fragrance independent of the wind;
In all my goings, in the new and old
Of all my meditations, and in this   115
Favorite of all, in this the most of all.
What Being, therefore, since the birth of Man
Had ever more abundant cause to speak
Thanks, and if music and the power of song
Make him more thankful, then to call on these   120
To aid him and with these resound his joy?
The boon is absolute; surpassing grace
To me hath been vouchsafed; among the bowers
Of blissful Eden this was neither given
Nor could be given—possession of the good   125
Which had been sighed for, ancient thought fulfilled,
And dear Imaginations realized
Up to their highest measure, yea, and more.
   Embrace me then, ye Hills, and close me in;
Now in the clear and open day I feel   130
Your guardianship; I take it to my heart;
'Tis like the solemn shelter of the night.
But I would call thee beautiful, for mild

And soft and gay and beautiful thou art,
Dear Valley, having in thy face a smile   135
Though peaceful, full of gladness. Thou art pleased,
Pleased with thy crags and woody steeps, thy Lake,
Its one green Island and its winding shores,
The multitude of little rocky hills,
Thy Church and Cottages of mountain stone—   140
Clustered like stars, some few, but single most,
And lurking dimly in their shy retreats,
Or glancing at each other cheerful looks,
Like separated stars with clouds between.
What want we? Have we not perpetual streams,   145
Warm woods and sunny hills, and fresh green fields,
And mountains not less green, and flocks and herds,
And thickets full of songsters, and the voice
Of lordly birds—an unexpected sound
Heard now and then from morn to latest eve   150
Admonishing the man who walks below
Of solitude and silence in the sky?
These have we, and a thousand nooks of earth
Have also these; but nowhere else is found—
No where (or is it fancy?) can be found—   155
The one sensation that is here; 'tis here,
Here as it found its way into my heart
In childhood, here as it abides by day,
By night, here only; or in chosen minds
That take it with them hence, where'er they go.   160
'Tis (but I cannot name it), 'tis the sense
Of majesty and beauty and repose,
A blended holiness of earth and sky,
Something that makes this individual Spot,
This small abiding-place of many men,   165
A termination and a last retreat,
A Centre, come from wheresoe'er you will,
A Whole without dependence or defect,
Made for itself and happy in itself,

Perfect Contentment, Unity entire. 170
    Long is it since we met to part no more,
Since I and Emma heard each other's call
And were Companions once again, like Birds
Which by the intruding Fowler had been scared,
Two of a scattered brood that could not bear 175
To live in loneliness; 'tis long since we,
Remembering much and hoping more, found means
To walk abreast, though in a narrow path,
With undivided steps. Our home was sweet;
Could it be less? If we were forced to change, 180
Our home again was sweet; but still, for Youth,
Strong as it seems and bold, is inly weak
And diffident, the destiny of life
Remained unfixed, and therefore we were still

                                                                [185–191]

[We will be free, and, as we mean to live[1]
In culture of divinity and truth,
Will choose the noblest Temple that we know.
Not in mistrust or ignorance of the mind 195
And of the power she has within herself
To enoble all things made we this resolve;
Far less from any momentary fit
Of inconsiderate fancy, light and vain;
But that we deemed it wise to take the help 200
Which lay within our reach; and here, we knew,
Help could be found of no mean sort; the spirit
Of singleness and unity and peace.
In this majestic, self-suficing world,
This all in all of Nature, it will suit, 205
We said, no other [   ] on earth so well,
Simplicity of purpose, love intense,
Ambition not aspiring to the prize]
Of outward things, but for the prize within—

---

1 Lines 185–191 are missing altogether. Lines 192–208 have been supplied from an earlier MS. to fill the gap in this MS.

Highest ambition. In the daily walks 210
Of business 'twill be harmony and grace
For the perpetual pleasure of the sense,
And for the Soul—I do not say too much,
Though much be said—an image for the soul,
A habit of Eternity and God. 215
   Nor have we been deceived; thus far the effect
Falls not below the loftiest of our hopes.
Bleak season was it, turbulent and bleak,
When hitherward we journeyed, and on foot,
Through bursts of sunshine and through flying snows, 220
Paced the long vales—how long they were, and yet
How fast that length of way was left behind,
Wensley's long Vale and Sedbergh's naked heights.
The frosty wind, as if to make amends
For its keen breath, was aiding to our course 225
And drove us onward like two Ships at sea.
Stern was the face of nature; we rejoiced
In that stern countenance, for our souls had there
A feeling of their strength. The naked trees,
The icy brooks, as on we passed, appeared 230
To question us. "Whence come ye? To what end?"
They seemed to say. "What would ye?" said the shower,
"Wild Wanderers, whither through my dark domain?"
The Sunbeam said, "Be happy." They were moved,
All things were moved; they round us as we went, 235
We in the midst of them. And when the trance
Came to us, as we stood by Hart-Leap Well—
The intimation of the milder day
Which is to come, the fairer world than this—
And raised us up, dejected as we were 240
Among the records of that doleful place
By sorrow for the hunted beast who there
Had yielded up his breath, the awful trance—
The Vision of humanity and of God
The Mourner, God the Sufferer, when the heart 245

Of his poor Creatures suffers wrongfully—
Both in the sadness and the joy we found
A promise and an earnest that we twain,
A pair seceding from the common world,
Might in that hallowed spot to which our steps   250
Were tending, in that individual nook,
Might even thus early for ourselves secure,
And in the midst of these unhappy times,
A portion of the blessedness which love
And knowledge will, we trust, hereafter give   255
To all the Vales of earth and all mankind.
   Thrice hath the winter Moon been filled with light
Since that dear day when Grasmere, our dear Vale,
Received us. Bright and solemn was the sky
That faced us with a passionate welcoming   260
And led us to our threshold, to a home
Within a home, what was to be, and soon,
Our love within a love. Then darkness came,
Composing darkness, with its quiet load
Of full contentment, in a little shed   265
Disturbed, uneasy in itself, as seemed,
And wondering at its new inhabitants.
It loves us now, this Vale so beautiful
Begins to love us! By a sullen storm,
Two months unwearied of severest storm,   270
It put the temper of our minds to proof,
And found us faithful through the gloom, and heard
The Poet mutter his prelusive songs
With chearful heart, an unknown voice of joy
Among the silence of the woods and hills,   275
Silent to any gladsomeness of sound
With all their Shepherds.
                      But the gates of Spring
Are opened; churlish Winter hath given leave
That she should entertain for this one day,
Perhaps for many genial days to come,   280

His guests and make them happy. They are pleased,
But most of all, the birds that haunt the flood,
With the mild summons, inmates though they be
Of Winter's household. They are jubilant
This day, who drooped or seemed to droop so long; 285
They show their pleasure, and shall I do less?
Happier of happy though I be, like them
I cannot take possession of the sky,
Mount with a thoughtless impulse, and wheel there,
One of a mighty multitude whose way 290
And motion is a harmony and dance
Magnificent. Behold them, how they shape,
Orb after orb, their course, still round and round,
Above the area of the Lake, their own
Adopted region, girding it about 295
In wanton repetition, yet therewith—
With that large circle evermore renewed—
Hundreds of curves and circlets, high and low,
Backwards and forwards, progress intricate,
As if one spirit was in all and swayed 300
Their indefatigable flight. 'Tis done,
Ten times, or more, I fancied it had ceased,
And lo! the vanished company again
Ascending—list again! I hear their wings:
Faint, faint at first, and then an eager sound, 305
Passed in a moment, and as faint again!
They tempt the sun to sport among their plumes;
They tempt the water and the gleaming ice
To show them a fair image. 'Tis themselves,
Their own fair forms upon the glimmering plain, 310
Painted more soft and fair as they descend,
Almost to touch, then up again aloft,
Up with a sally and a flash of speed,
As if they scorned both resting-place and rest.
Spring! for this day belongs to thee, rejoice! 315
Not upon me alone hath been bestowed—

Me, blessed with many onward-looking thoughts—
The sunshine and mild air. Oh, surely these
Are grateful; not the happy Quires of love,
Thine own peculiar family, Sweet Spring, 320
That sport among green leaves so blithe a train.
    But two are missing—two, a lonely pair
Of milk-white Swans. Ah, why are they not here?
These above all, ah, why are they not here 325
To share in this day's pleasure? From afar
They came, like Emma and myself, to live
Together here in peace and solitude,
Choosing this Valley, they who had the choice
Of the whole world. We saw them day by day,
Through those two months of unrelenting storm, 330
Conspicuous in the centre of the Lake,
Their safe retreat. We knew them well—I guess
That the whole Valley knew them—but to us
They were more dear than may be well believed,
Not only for their beauty and their still 335
And placid way of life and faithful love
Inseparable, not for these alone,
But that their state so much resembled ours;
They also having chosen this abode;
They strangers, and we strangers; they a pair, 340
And we a solitary pair like them.
They should not have departed; many days
I've looked for them in vain, nor on the wing
Have seen them, nor in that small open space
Of blue unfrozen water, where they lodged 345
And lived so long in quiet, side by side.
Companions, brethren, consecrated friends,
Shall we behold them yet another year
Surviving, they for us and we for them,
And neither pair be broken? Nay, perchance 350
It is too late already for such hope;
The Shepherd may have seized the deadly tube

And parted them, incited by a prize
Which, for the sake of those he loves at home
And for the Lamb upon the mountain tops, 355
He should have spared; or haply both are gone,
One death, and that were mercy given to both.
 I cannot look upon this favoured Vale
But that I seem, by harbouring this thought,
To wrong it, such unworthy recompence 360
Imagining, of confidence so pure.
Ah! if I wished to follow where the sight
Of all that is before my eyes, the voice
Which is as a presiding Spirit here
Would lead me, I should say unto myself, 365
They who are dwellers in this holy place
Must needs themselves be hallowed. They require
No benediction from the Stranger's lips,
For they are blessed already. None would give
The greeting "peace be with you" unto them, 370
For peace they have; it cannot but be theirs.
And mercy and forbearance—nay, not these;
There is no call for these; that office Love
Performs and charity beyond the bounds
Of charity—an overflowing love, 375
Not for the creature only, but for all
Which is around them, love for every thing
Which in this happy Valley we behold!
 Thus do we soothe ourselves, and when the thought
Is passed we blame it not for having come. 380
What if I floated down a pleasant stream
And now am landed and the motion gone—
Shall I reprove myself? Ah no, the stream
Is flowing and will never cease to flow,
And I shall float upon that stream again. 385
By such forgetfulness the soul becomes—
Words cannot say how beautiful. Then hail!
Hail to the visible Presence! Hail to thee,

Delightful Valley, habitation fair!
And to whatever else of outward form   390
Can give us inward help, can purify
And elevate and harmonize and soothe,
And steal away and for a while deceive
And lap in pleasing rest, and bear us on
Without desire in full complacency,   395
Contemplating perfection absolute
And entertained as in a placid sleep.
   But not betrayed by tenderness of mind
That feared or wholly overlooked the truth
Did we come hither, with romantic hope   400
To find in midst of so much loveliness
Love, perfect love, of so much majesty
A like majestic frame of mind in those
Who here abide, the persons like the place.
Nor from such hope or aught of such belief   405
Hath issued any portion of the joy
Which I have felt this day. An awful voice,
'Tis true, I in my walks have often heard,
Sent from the mountains or the sheltered fields,
Shout after shout—reiterated whoop   410
In manner of a bird that takes delight
In answering to itself, or like a hound
Single at chase among the lonely woods—
A human voice, how awful in the gloom
Of coming night, when sky is dark, and earth   415
Not dark, not yet enlightened, but by snow
Made visible, amid the noise of winds
And bleatings manifold of sheep that know
That summons and are gathering round for food—
That voice, the same, the very same, that breath   420
Which was an utterance awful as the wind,
Or any sound the mountains ever heard.
   That Shepherd's voice, it may have reached mine ear
Debased and under prophanation, made

An organ for the sounds articulate 425
Of ribaldry and blasphemy and wrath,
Where drunkenness hath kindled senseless frays.
I came not dreaming of unruffled life,
Untainted manners; born among the hills,
Bred also there, I wanted not a scale 430
To regulate my hopes; pleased with the good,
I shrink not from the evil in disgust
Or with immoderate pain. I look for man,
The common creature of the brotherhood,
But little differing from the man elsewhere 435
For selfishness and envy and revenge,
Ill neighbourhood—folly that this should be—
Flattery and double-dealing, strife and wrong.
   Yet is it something gained—it is in truth
A mighty gain—that Labour here preserves 440
His rosy face, a Servant only here
Of the fire-side or of the open field,
A Freeman, therefore sound and unenslaved;
That extreme penury is here unknown,
And cold and hunger's abject wretchedness, 445
Mortal to body and the heaven-born mind;
That they who want are not too great a weight
For those who can relieve. Here may the heart
Breathe in the air of fellow-suffering
Dreadless, as in a kind of fresher breeze 450
Of her own native element; the hand
Be ready and unwearied without plea
From task too frequent and beyond its powers,
For languor or indifference or despair.
And as these lofty barriers break the force 455
Of winds—this deep vale as it doth in part
Conceal us from the storm—so here there is
A Power and a protection for the mind,
Dispensed indeed to other solitudes
Favoured by noble privilege like this, 460

Where kindred independence of estate
Is prevalent, where he who tills the field,
He, happy Man! is Master of the field
And treads the mountain which his Father trod.
Hence, and from other local circumstance, 465
In this enclosure many of the old
Substantial virtues have a firmer tone
Than in the base and ordinary world.
   Yon Cottage, would that it could tell a part
Of its own story. Thousands might give ear, 470
Might hear it and blush deep. There few years past
In this his Native Valley dwelt a Man,
The Master of a little lot of ground,
A man of mild deportment and discourse,
A scholar also (as the phrase is here), 475
For he drew much delight from those few books
That lay within his reach, and for this cause
Was by his Fellow-dalesmen honoured more.
A Shepherd and a Tiller of the ground,
Studious withal, and healthy in his frame 480
Of body, and of just and placid mind,
He with his consort and his Children saw
Days that were seldom touched by petty strife,
Years safe from large misfortune, long maintained
That course which men the wisest and most pure 485
Might look on with entire complacency.
Yet in himself and near him were there faults
At work to undermine his happiness
By little and by little. Active, prompt,
And lively was the Housewife, in the Vale 490
None more industrious; but her industry
Was of that kind, 'tis said, which tended more
To splendid neatness, to a showy trim,
And overlaboured purity of house
Than to substantial thrift. He, on his part 495
Generous and easy-minded, was not free

From carelessness, and thus in course of time
These joint infirmities, combined perchance
With other cause less obvious, brought decay
Of worldly substance and distress of mind,   500
Which to a thoughtful man was hard to shun
And which he could not cure. A blooming Girl
Served them, an Inmate of the House. Alas!
Poor now in tranquil pleasure, he gave way
To thoughts of troubled pleasure; he became   505
A lawless Suitor of the Maid, and she
Yielded unworthily. Unhappy Man!
That which he had been weak enough to do
Was misery in remembrance; he was stung,
Stung by his inward thoughts, and by the smiles   510
Of Wife and children stung to agony.
His temper urged him not to seek relief
Amid the noise of revellers nor from draught
Of lonely stupefaction; he himself
A rational and suffering Man, himself   515
Was his own world, without a resting-place.
Wretched at home, he had no peace abroad,
Ranged through the mountains, slept upon the earth,
Asked comfort of the open air, and found
No quiet in the darkness of the night,   520
No pleasure in the beauty of the day.
His flock he slighted; his paternal fields
Were as a clog to him, whose Spirit wished
To fly, but whither? And yon gracious Church,
That has a look so full of peace and hope   525
And love—benignant Mother of the Vale,
How fair amid her brood of Cottages!—
She was to him a sickness and reproach.
I speak conjecturing from the little known,
The much that to the last remained unknown;   530
But this is sure: he died of his own grief,
He could not bear the weight of his own shame.

  That Ridge, which elbowing from the mountain-side
Carries into the Plain its rocks and woods,
Conceals a Cottage where a Father dwells   535
In widowhood, whose Life's Co-partner died
Long since, and left him solitary Prop
Of many helpless Children. I begin
With words which might be prelude to a Tale
Of sorrow and dejection, but I feel—   540
Though in the midst of sadness, as might seem—
No sadness, when I think of what mine eyes
Have seen in that delightful family.
Bright garland make they for their Father's brows,
Those six fair Daughters budding yet, not one,   545
Not one of all the band a full-blown flower.
Go to the Dwelling: There Thou shalt have proof
That He who takes away, yet takes not half
Of what he seems to take, or gives it back
Not to our prayer, but far beyond our prayer,   550
He gives it the boon—produce of a soil
Which Hope hath never watered. Thou shalt see
A House, which at small distance will appear
In no distinction to have passed beyond
Its Fellows, will appear, like them, to have grown   555
Out of the native Rock; but nearer view
Will show it not so grave in outward mien
And soberly arrayed as for the most
Are these rude mountain-dwellings—Nature's care,
Mere friendless Nature's—but a studious work   560
Of many fancies and of many hands,
A play thing and a pride; for such the air
And aspect which the little Spot maintains
In spite of lonely Winter's nakedness.
They have their jasmine resting on the Porch,   565
Their rose-trees, strong in health, that will be soon
Roof-high; and here and there the garden wall
Is topped with single stones, a showy file

Curious for shape or hue—some round, like Balls,
Worn smooth and round by fretting of the Brook　　　570
From which they have been gathered, others bright
And sparry, the rough scatterings of the Hills.
These ornaments the Cottage chiefly owes
To one, a hardy Girl, who mounts the rocks;
Such is her choice; she fears not the bleak wind;　　　575
Companion of her Father, does for him
Where'er he wanders in his pastoral course
The service of a Boy, and with delight
More keen and prouder daring. Yet hath She
Within the garden, like the rest, a bed　　　580
For her own flowers, or favorite Herbs, a space
Holden by sacred charter; and I guess
She also helped to frame that tiny Plot
Of garden ground which one day 'twas my chance
To find among the woody rocks that rise　　　585
Above the House, a slip of smoother earth
Planted with goose-berry bushes, and in one,
Right in the centre of the prickly shrub,
A mimic Bird's-nest, fashioned by the hand,
Was stuck, a staring Thing of twisted hay,　　　590
And one quaint Fir-tree towered above the Whole.
But in the darkness of the night, then most
This Dwelling charms me; covered by the gloom
Then, heedless of good manners, I stop short
And (who could help it?) feed by stealth my sight　　　595
With prospect of the company within,
Laid open through the blazing window. There
I see the eldest Daughter at her wheel,
Spinning amain, as if to overtake
She knows not what, or teaching in her turn　　　600
Some little Novice of the sisterhood
That skill in this or other household work
Which from her Father's honored hands, herself,
While She was yet a Little-one, had learned.

Mild Man! He is not gay, but they are gay, 605
And the whole House is filled with gaiety.
   From yonder grey-stone that stands alone
Close to the foaming Stream, look up and see,
Not less than halfway up the mountain-side,
A dusky Spot, a little grove of firs 610
And seems still smaller than it is. The Dame
Who dwells below, she told me that this grove,
Just six weeks younger than her eldest Boy,
Was planted by her Husband and herself
For a convenient shelter, which in storm 615
Their sheep might draw to. "And they know it well,"
Said she, "for thither do we bear them food
In time of heavy snow." She then began
In fond obedience to her private thoughts
To speak of her dead Husband. Is there not 620
An art, a music, and a stream of words
That shall be life, the acknowledged voice of life?
Shall speak of what is done among the fields,
Done truly there, or felt, of solid good
And real evil, yet be sweet withal, 625
More grateful, more harmonious than the breath,
The idle breath of sweetest pipe attuned
To pastoral fancies? Is there such a stream,
Pure and unsullied, flowing from the heart
With motions of true dignity and grace, 630
Or must we seek these things where man is not?
Methinks I could repeat in tuneful verse
Delicious as the gentlest breeze that sounds
Through that aerial fir-grove, could preserve
Some portion of its human history 635
As gathered from that Matron's lips and tell
Of tears that have been shed at sight of it
And moving dialogues between this Pair,
Who in the prime of wedlock with joint hands
Did plant this grove, now flourishing while they 640

No longer flourish; he entirely gone,
She withering in her loneliness. Be this
A task above my skill; the silent mind
Has its own treasures, and I think of these,
Love what I see, and honour humankind. 645
    No, we are not alone; we do not stand,
My Emma, here misplaced and desolate,
Loving what no one cares for but ourselves.
We shall not scatter through the plains and rocks
Of this fair Vale and o'er its spacious heights 650
Unprofitable kindliness, bestowed
On Objects unaccustomed to the gifts
Of feeling, that were cheerless and forlorn
But few weeks past, and would be so again
If we were not. We do not tend a lamp 655
Whose lustre we alone participate,
Which is dependent upon us alone,
Mortal though bright, a dying, dying flame.
Look where we will, some human heart has been
Before us with its offering; not a tree 660
Sprinkles these little pastures, but the same
Hath furnished matter for a thought, perchance
To some one is as a familiar Friend.
Joy spreads and sorrow spreads; and this whole Vale,
Home of untutored Shepherds as it is, 665
Swarms with sensation, as with gleams of sunshine,
Shadows or breezes, scents or sounds. Nor deem
These feelings—though subservient more than ours
To every day's demand for daily bread,
And borrowing more their spirit and their shape 670
From self-respecting interests—deem them not
Unworthy therefore and unhallowed. No,
They lift the animal being, do themselves
By nature's kind and ever present aid
Refine the selfishness from which they spring, 675
Redeem by love the individual sense

Of anxiousness with which they are combined.
Many are pure, the best of them are pure;
The best, and these, remember, most abound,
Are fit associates of the [worthiest] joy,   680
Joy of the highest and the purest minds;
They blend with it congenially; meanwhile,
Calmly they breathe their own undying life,
Lowly and unassuming as it is,
Through this, their mountain sanctuary (long,   685
Oh long may it remain inviolate!),
Diffusing health and sober chearfulness,
And giving to the moments as they pass
Their little boons of animating thought,
That sweeten labour, make it seem and feel   690
To be no arbitrary weight imposed,
But a glad function natural to Man.
   Fair proof of this, Newcomer though I be,
Already have I seen; the inward frame,
Though slowly opening, opens every day.   695
Nor am I less delighted with the show
As it unfolds itself, now here, now there,
Than is the passing Traveller, when his way
Lies through some region then first trod by him
(Say this fair Valley's self), when low-hung mists   700
Break up and are beginning to recede.
How pleased he is to hear the murmuring stream,
The many Voices, from he knows not where,
To have about him, which way e'er he goes,
Something on every side concealed from view,   705
In every quarter some thing visible,
Half seen or wholly, lost and found again—
Alternate progress and impediment,
And yet a growing prospect in the main.
   Such pleasure now is mine, and what if I—   710
Herein less happy than the Traveller—
Am sometimes forced to cast a painful look

Upon unwelcome things, which unawares
Reveal themselves? Not therefore is my mind
Depressed, nor do I fear what is to come;   715
But confident, enriched at every glance,
The more I see the more is my delight.
Truth justifies herself; and as she dwells
With Hope, who would not follow where she leads?
   Nor let me overlook those other loves   720
Where no fear is, those humbler sympathies
That have to me endeared the quietness
Of this sublime retirement. I begin
Already to inscribe upon my heart
A liking for the small grey Horse that bears   725
The paralytic Man; I know the ass
On which the Cripple in the Quarry maimed
Rides to and fro: I know them and their ways.
The famous Sheep-dog, first in all the vale,
Though yet to me a Stranger, will not be   730
A Stranger long; nor will the blind Man's Guide,
Meek and neglected thing, of no renown.
Whoever lived a Winter in one place,
Beneath the shelter of one Cottage-roof,
And has not had his Red-breast or his Wren?   735
I have them both; and I shall have my Thrush
In spring time, and a hundred warblers more;
And if the banished Eagle Pair return,
Helvellyn's Eagles, to their ancient Hold,
Then shall I see, shall claim with those two Birds   740
Acquaintance, as they soar amid the Heavens.
The Owl that gives the name to Owlet-crag
Have I heard shouting, and he soon will be
A chosen one of my regards. See there,
The Heifer in yon little Croft belongs   745
To one who holds it dear; with duteous care
She reared it, and in speaking of her Charge
I heard her scatter once a word or two,

[A term] domestic, yea, and Motherly,
She being herself a Mother. Happy Beast, 750
If the caresses of a human voice
Can make it so, and care of human hands.
    And Ye as happy under Nature's care,
Strangers to me and all men, or at least
Strangers to all particular amity, 755
All intercourse of knowledge or of love
That parts the individual from the kind;
Whether in large communities ye dwell
From year to year, not shunning man's abode,
A settled residence, or be from far, 760
Wild creatures, and of many homes, that come
The gift of winds, and whom the winds again
Take from us at your pleasure—yet shall ye
Not want for this, your own subordinate place,
According to your claim, an underplace 765
In my affections. Witness the delight
With which ere while I saw that multitude
Wheel through the sky and see them now at rest,
Yet not at rest, upon the glassy lake.
They cannot rest; they gambol like young whelps, 770
Active as lambs and overcome with joy;
They try all frolic motions, flutter, plunge,
And beat the passive water with their wings.
Too distant are they for plain view, but lo!
Those little fountains, sparkling in the sun, 775
Which tell what they are doing, which rise up,
First one and then another silver spout,
As one or other takes the fit of glee—
Fountains and spouts, yet rather in the guise
Of plaything fire-works, which on festal nights 780
Hiss hiss about the feet of wanton boys.
How vast the compass of this theatre,
Yet nothing to be seen but lovely pomp
And silent majesty. The birch tree woods

Are hung with thousand thousand diamond drops 785
Of melted hoar-frost, every tiny knot
In the bare twigs, each little budding-place
Cased with its several bead; what myriads there
Upon one tree, while all the distant grove
That rises to the summit of the steep 790
Is like a mountain built of silver light!
See yonder the same pageant, and again
Behold the universal imagery
At what a depth, deep in the Lake below.
Admonished of the days of love to come, 795
The raven croaks and fills the sunny air
With a strange sound of genial harmony;
And in and all about that playful band,
Incapable although they be of rest,
And in their fashion very rioters, 800
There is a stillness, and they seem to make
Calm revelry in that their calm abode.
I leave them to their pleasure, and I pass,
Pass with a thought the life of the whole year
That is to come—the throngs of mountain flowers 805
And lilies that will dance upon the lake.
   Then boldly say that solitude is not
Where these things are: he truly is alone,
He of the multitude, whose eyes are doomed
To hold a vacant commerce day by day 810
With that which he can neither know nor love—
Dead things, to him thrice dead—or worse than this,
With swarms of life, and worse than all, of men,
His fellow men, that are to him no more
Than to the Forest Hermit are the leaves 815
That hang aloft in myriads—nay, far less,
Far less for aught that comforts or defends
Or lulls or chears. Society is here:
The true community, the noblest Frame
Of many into one incorporate; 820

That must be looked for here; paternal sway,
One Household under God for high and low,
One family and one mansion; to themselves
Appropriate and divided from the world
As if it were a cave, a multitude   825
Human and brute, possessors undisturbed
Of this recess, their legislative Hall,
Their Temple, and their glorious dwelling-place.
   Dismissing therefore all Arcadian dreams,
All golden fancies of the golden age,   830
The bright array of shadowy thoughts from times
That were before all time, or are to be
When time is not, the pageantry that stirs
And will be stirring when our eyes are fixed
On lovely objects and we wish to part   835
With all remembrance of a jarring world—
Give entrance to the sober truth; avow
That Nature to this favourite Spot of ours
Yields no exemption, but her awful rights,
Enforces to the utmost and exacts   840
Her tribute of inevitable pain,
And that the sting is added, man himself
For ever busy to afflict himself.
Yet temper this with one sufficient hope
(What need of more?): that we shall neither droop   845
Nor pine for want of pleasure in the life
Which is about us, nor through dearth of aught
That keeps in health the insatiable mind;
That we shall have for knowledge and for love
Abundance; and that, feeling as we do,   850
How goodly, how exceeding fair, how pure
From all reproach is the aetherial frame
And this deep vale, its earthly counterpart,
By which and under which we are enclosed
To breathe in peace; we shall moreover find   855
(If sound, and what we ought to be ourselves,

If rightly we observe and justly weigh)
The Inmates not unworthy of their home,
The Dwellers of the Dwelling.
      And if this
Were not, we have enough within ourselves,   860
Enough to fill the present day with joy
And overspread the future years with hope—
Our beautiful and quiet home, enriched
Already with a Stranger whom we love
Deeply, a Stranger of our Father's house,   865
A never-resting Pilgrim of the Sea,
Who finds at last an hour to his content
Beneath our roof; and others whom we love
Will seek us also, Sisters of our hearts,
And one, like them, a Brother of our hearts,   870
Philosopher and Poet, in whose sight
These mountains will rejoice with open joy.
Such is our wealth: O Vale of Peace, we are
And must be, with God's will, a happy band!
 But 'tis not to enjoy, for this alone   875
That we exist; no, something must be done.
I must not walk in unreproved delight
These narrow bounds and think of nothing more,
No duty that looks further and no care.
Each Being has his office, lowly some   880
And common, yet all worthy if fulfilled
With zeal, acknowledgement that with the gift
Keeps pace a harvest answering to the seed.
Of ill advised ambition and of pride
I would stand clear, yet unto me I feel   885
That an internal brightness is vouchsafed
That must not die, that must not pass away.
Why does this inward lustre fondly seek
And gladly blend with outward fellowship?
Why shine they round me thus, whom thus I love?   890
Why do they teach me, whom I thus revere?

Strange question, yet it answers not itself.
That humble Roof, embowered among the trees,
That calm fire side—it is not even in them,
Blessed as they are, to furnish a reply 895
That satisfies and ends in perfect rest.
Possessions have I, wholly, solely mine,
Something within, which yet is shared by none—
Not even the nearest to me and most dear—
Something which power and effort may impart. 900
I would impart it; I would spread it wide,
Immortal in the world which is to come.
I would not wholly perish even in this,
Lie down and be forgotten in the dust,
I and the modest partners of my days, 905
Making a silent company in death.
It must not be, if I divinely taught
Am privileged to speak as I have felt
Of what in man is human or divine.
 While yet an innocent little-one, a heart 910
That doubtless wanted not its tender moods,
I breathed (for this I better recollect)
Among wild appetites and blind desires,
Motions of savage instinct, my delight
And exaltation. Nothing at that time 915
So welcome, no temptation half so dear
As that which [urged] me to a daring feat.
Deep pools, tall trees, black chasms, and dizzy crags—
I loved to look in them, to stand and read
Their looks forbidding, read and disobey, 920
Sometimes in act, and evermore in thought.
With impulses which only were by these
Surpassed in strength, I heard of danger met
Or sought with courage, enterprize forlorn,
By one, sole keeper of his own intent, 925
Or by a resolute few, who for the sake
Of glory fronted multitudes in arms.

Yea, to this day I swell with like desire;
I cannot at this moment read a tale
Of two brave Vessels matched in deadly fight 930
And fighting to the death, but I am pleased
More than a wise Man ought to be; I wish,
I burn, I struggle, and in soul am there.
But me hath Nature tamed and bade me seek
For other agitations or be calm, 935
Hath dealt with me as with a turbulent stream—
Some Nurseling of the Mountains which she leads
Through quiet meadows after it has learned
Its strength and had its triumph and its joy,
Its desperate course of tumult and of glee. 940
That which in stealth by nature was performed
Hath Reason sanctioned. Her deliberate Voice
Hath said, "Be mild and love all gentle things;
Thy glory and thy happiness be there.
Yet fear (though thou confide in me) no want 945
Of aspirations which have been—of foes
To wrestle with and victory to complete,
Bounds to be leapt and darkness to explore.
That which enflamed thy infant heart—the love,
The longing, the contempt, the undaunted quest— 950
These shall survive, though changed their office, these
Shall live ; it is not in their power to die."
Then farewell to the Warrior's deeds, farewell
All hope, which once and long was mine, to fill
The heroic trumpet with the muse's breath! 955
Yet in this peaceful Vale we will not spend
Unheard-of days, though loving peaceful thoughts;
A Voice shall speak, and what will be the Theme?
   On Man, on Nature, and on human Life,
Thinking in solitude, from time to time 960
I feel sweet passions traversing my Soul
Like Music; unto these, where'er I may,
I would give utterance in numerous verse.

Of truth, of grandeur, beauty, love, and hope—
Hope for this earth and hope beyond the grave— 965
Of virtue and of intellectual power,
Of blessed consolations in distress,
Of joy in widest commonalty spread,
Of the individual mind that keeps its own
Inviolate retirement, and consists 970
With being limitless the one great Life—
I sing; fit audience let me find though few!
   Fit audience find though few—thus prayed the Bard,
Holiest of Men. Urania, I shall need
Thy guidance, or a greater Muse, if such 975
Descend to earth or dwell in highest heaven!
For I must tread on shadowy ground, must sink
Deep, and, aloft ascending, breathe in worlds
To which the Heaven of heavens is but a veil.
All strength, all terror, single or in bands, 980
That ever was put forth in personal forms—
Jehovah, with his thunder, and the quire
Of shouting angels and the empyreal throne—
I pass them unalarmed. The darkest Pit
Of the profoundest Hell, chaos, night, 985
Nor aught of [blinder] vacancy scooped out
By help of dreams can breed such fear and awe
As fall upon us often when we look
Into our minds, into the mind of Man,
My haunt and the main region of my song. 990
Beauty, whose living home is the green earth,
Surpassing the most fair ideal Forms
The craft of delicate spirits hath composed
From earth's materials, waits upon my steps,
Pitches her tents before me when I move, 995
An hourly Neighbour. Paradise and groves
Elysian, fortunate islands, fields like those of old
In the deep ocean—wherefore should they be
A History, or but a dream, when minds

Once wedded to this outward frame of things
In love, find these the growth of common day?
I, long before the blessed hour arrives,
Would sing in solitude the spousal verse
Of this great consumation, would proclaim—
Speaking of nothing more than what we are—
How exquisitely the individual Mind
(And the progressive powers perhaps no less
Of the whole species) to the external world
Is fitted; and how exquisitely too—
Theme this but little heard of among men—
The external world is fitted to the mind;
And the creation (by no lower name
Can it be called) which they with blended might
Accomplish: this is my great argument.
Such [pleasant haunts] foregoing, if I oft
Must turn elsewhere, and travel near the tribes
And fellowships of men, and see ill sights
Of passions ravenous from each other's rage,
Must hear humanity in fields and groves
Pipe solitary anguish, or must hang
Brooding above the fierce confederate storm
Of Sorrow, barricadoed evermore
Within the walls of cities—may these sounds
Have their authentic comment, that even these
Hearing, I be not heartless or forlorn!
Come, thou prophetic Spirit, Soul of Man,
Thou human Soul of the wide earth that hast
Thy metropolitan Temple in the hearts
Of mighty Poets; unto me vouchsafe
Thy guidance, teach me to discern and part
Inherent things from casual, what is fixed
From fleeting, that my verse may live and be
Even as a Light hung up in heaven to chear
Mankind in times to come! And if with this
I blend more lowly matter—with the thing

Contemplated describe the mind and man
Contemplating, and who and what he was,
The transitory Being that beheld
This vision, when and where and how he lived,
With all his little realities of life—   1040
Be not this labour useless. If such theme
With highest things may [sort],[1] then, Great God,
Thou who art breath and being, way and guide,
And power and understanding, may my life
Express the image of a better time,   1045
More wise desires and simple manners; nurse
My heart in genuine freedom; all pure thoughts
Be with me and uphold me to the end!

---

1   Missing word supplied from 'May sort with highest objects', 'Prospectus' p.89.

Further Writing for The Recluse, Part First

To the Clouds (1808)

Army of clouds, what would ye? Flight of Clouds,
Ascending from behind the motionless brow
Of this tall Rock as from a hidden world,
O whither in this eagerness of speed?
What seek ye? or what shun ye? of the Wind   5
Companions, fear ye to be left behind,
Or racing on your blue ætherial field
Contend ye with each other? of the Sea,
Children, bright Children of the distant sea,
Thus post Ye over dale and mountain height   10
To sink upon your Mother's joyous lap?
Or were Ye rightlier hail'd when first mine eyes
I lifted, for Ye still are sweeping on
Like a wide Army in impetuous march,
Or like a never-ending Flight of Birds   15
Aerial, upon due migration bound,
Embodied Travellers not blindly led
To milder climes? or rather do ye urge
In caravan your hasty pilgrimage,
With hope to pause at last upon the tops   20
Of some remoter mountains more belov'd
Than these, and utter your devotion there
With thunderous voice? or are ye jubilant,
And would ye tracking your proud Lord, the Sun,
Be present at his setting? or the pomp   25
Of Indian mornings would ye fill, and stand,
Yourselves apparell'd in the virgin garb

Of radiance yet unknown, transcendent hues?
O whence, Ye clouds, this eagerness of speed?
Sheer o'er the Rock's gigantic brow Ye cut 30
Your way, each thirsting to reveal himself, athirst,
The coming and the going, to secure
Each for himself an unbelated course?
Ye clouds, the very blood within my veins
Is quickened to your pace, a thousand thoughts, 35
Ten thousand winged Fancies have Ye rais'd,
And not a Thought which is not fleet as Ye are.
Speak, silent Creatures! they are gone, are fled,
All buried in yon mighty mass of gloom
That loads the middle heaven, and clear and bright 40
And vacant does the region of the east
Appear, a calm descent of sky that leads
Down to some unapproachable abyss,
Down to the hidden world from which they came.
But the Wind roars, and toss the rooted Trees 45
As if impatient of yon lofty seat
On which they are enthralled from year to year.
But Lo, the pageant is renew'd, behold,
Another bright Precursor of a band
Perhaps as numerous, from behind the Rock 50
Mounting, the steady Rock that in its pomp
Of sullenness refuses to partake
Of the wild impulse; from a fount of life
Invisible, the long Procession streams,
A rapid multitude of glorious Shapes, 55
Glorious or darksome. Welcome to the Vale
Which they are entering, welcome to mine eye
That sees them, to my Soul that owns in them
And in the bosom of the Firmament
Wherein they move, by which they are contained, 60
An Image, a reflection palpable
Of her capacious self, of what she is
With all her restless Offspring, what she is

And what she doth possess!—
                  An humble walk
Here is my Body doomed to tread, this Path,   65
A little hoary line and faintly traced,
Work shall I call it of the Shepherd's foot,
Or of his sheep?—joint vestige of them both;
I pace it unrepining, for my thoughts
See what they will and through their own wide world   70
Go with the perfect freedom which is theirs.
Where is the Orphean Lyre or Druid Harp
To accompany the Song? the mountain Wind
Shall be our hand of music! it shall sweep
The rocks and quivering trees and billowy lake,   75
And search the fibres of the inner caves, and they
Shall answer: for our Song is of the Clouds,
And the Wind loves them, and the gentle gales
Love them, and every idle breeze in heav'n
Bends to that favorite burthen; and the Sun   80
(That is the daily source of joyous thought,
And Type of Man's far-darting reason, He
Who therefore was esteemed in antient times
The God of Verse, and stood before men's eyes
A blazing intellectual Deity)   85
Loves his own glory in their looks, the Sun
Showers on that unsubstantial Brotherhood
A Vision of beatitude and light.

The Tuft of Primroses (1808)

Once more I welcome Thee, and Thou, fair Plant,
Fair Primrose, hast put forth thy radiant Flowers,
All eager to be welcomed once again.
O pity if the faithful Spring, beguiled
By her accustomed hopes, had come to breathe   5

Upon the bosom of this barren crag
And found thee not; but Thou art here, reviv'd,
And beautiful as ever, like a Queen
Smiling from thy imperishable throne,
And so shalt keep for ages yet untold, 10
Frail as Thou art, if the prophetic Muse
Be rightly trusted, so shalt Thou maintain
Conspicuously thy solitary state,
In splendour unimpaired. For Thou art safe
From most adventurous bound of mountain sheep 15
By keenest hunger press'd, and from approach
Of the wild Goat still bolder, nor more cause,
Though in that sunny and obtrusive [?seat],
Hast thou to dread the desolating grasp
Of Child or school boy, and though hand, perchance, 20
Of taller Passenger may want not power
To win thee, yet a thought would intervene,
Though Thou be tempting, and that thought of love
Would hold him back, check'd in the first conceit
And impulse of such rapine. A benign, 25
A condescending ordonnance as might [?calm],
Hath guarded long and still shall guard thy flowers,
Less for thy beauty's sake, though that might claim
All favour, than for pleasure which Thou shed'st,
Down-looking, and far-looking all day long, 30
Upon the Travellers that do hourly climb
This steep, new gladness yielding to the glad,
And genial promises to those who droop,
Sick, poor, or weary, or disconsolate,
Brightening at once the winter of their souls. 35
—I have a Friend whom seasons as they pass'd[1]
All pleased; they in her bosom damp'd no joy
And from her light step took no liberty,
When suddenly as lightning from a cloud

---

1 The "Friend" is Sara Hutchinson, WW's sister-in-law, who was gravely ill in March and April of 1808.

Came danger with disease; came suddenly 40
And linger'd long, and this commanding Hill,
Which with its rocky chambers heretofore
Had been to her a range of dear resort,
The palace of her freedom, now, sad doom!
Was interdicted ground—a place of fear 45
For her, a melancholy Hill for us,
Constrain'd to think and ponder for her sake.
Fair primrose, lonely and distinguished Flower,
Well worthy of that honourable place
That holds thy beauty up to public view, 50
For ever parted from all neighbourhood,
In a calm course of meditative years,
Oft have I hail'd thee with serene delight,
—This greeting is far more—it is the voice
Of a surpassing joyance!—She herself 55
With her own eyes shall bless thee ere Thou fade;
The Prisoner shall come forth, and all the toil
And labours of this sharp ascent shall melt
Before thy mild assurances, and pain
And weakness shall pass from her like a sleep 60
Chas'd by a bright glimpse of the morning sun.
Farewell! yet turning from thee, happy Flower,
With these Dear thoughts, not therefore are old claims
Unrecognized—not therefore is the sense
Less vivid of that pleasure which to me 65
Thy punctual reappearance would have given
In its pure self. For often when I pass
This Rock, while Thou art in thy winter sleep,
Or the rank summer hides thy flower-like leaf,
I have a thought for thee. Alas how much, 70
Since I beheld and loved Thee first, how much
Is gone, though thou be left; I would not speak
Of best Friends dead, or other deep heart loss
Bewail'd with weeping, but by River sides
And in broad fields how many gentle loves, 75

How many mute memorials pass'd away.
Stately herself, though of a lowly kind,
That little Flower remains and has survived
The lofty band of Firs that overtopp'd
Their antient Neighbour, the old Steeple Tower;　　　80
That consecrated Train which had so oft
Swung in the blast, mingling their solemn strain
Of music with the one determined voice
From the slow funeral bell, a symphony
Most awful and affecting to the ear　　　85
Of him who pass'd beneath: or had dealt forth
Soft murmurs like the cooing of a Dove
Ere first distinguishably heard, and cast
Their dancing shadows on the flowery turf,
While through the Churchyard tripp'd the bridal train　　　90
In festive Ribbands deck'd; and those same trees,
By moonlight, in their stillness and repose,
Deepen'd the silence of a hundred graves.
Ah, what a welcome! when from absence long[1]
Returning, on the centre of the Vale　　　95
I look'd a first glad look and saw them not.
Was it a dream! the aerial grove, no more
Right in the centre of the lovely vale
Suspended like a stationary cloud,
Had vanish'd like a cloud—yet say not so,　　　100
For here and there a straggling Tree was left
To mourn in blanc and monumental grief,
To pine and wither for its fellows gone.
—Ill word that laid them low—unfeeling Heart
Had He who could endure that they should fall,　　　105
Who spared not them nor spar'd that sycamore high,
The universal glory of the Vale,
And did not spare the little avenue
Of lightly stirring Ash-trees, that sufficed

---

1 The Wordsworths had spent the winter in Coleorton, Leicestershire, on the estate of Sir George Beaumont..

To dim the glare of summer, and to blunt 110
The strong Wind turn'd into a gentle breeze,
Whose freshness cheared the paved walk beneath,
That antient walk which from the Vicar's door
Led to the Church-yard gate. Then, Grasmere, then
Thy sabbath mornings had a holy grace, 115
That incommunicable sanctity
Which Time and nature only can bestow,
When from his venerable [?home] the Priest
Did issue forth glistening in best attire,
And down that consecrated visto paced 120
Towards the Churchyard where his ready Flock
Were gathered round in sunshine or in shade,
While Trees and mountains echoed to the Voice
Of the glad bells, and all the murmuring streams
United their soft chorus with the song. 125
Now stands the Steeple naked and forlorn,
And from the spot of sacred ground, the home
To which all change conducts the thought, looks round
Upon the changes of this peaceful Vale.
What sees the old grey Tower through high or low 130
Of his domain, what injury doth he note
Beyond what he himself hath undergone,
What other profanation or despoil
Of fairest things that calls for more regret
Than that small cottage? There it is aloft, 135
And nearest to the flying clouds of three,
Perch'd each above the other on the side
Of the vale's northern outlet—from below
And from afar, yet say not from afar,
For all things in this little world of ours 140
Are in one bosom of close neighbourhood,
The hoary steeple now beholds that roof
Laid open to the glare of common day,
And marks five graves beneath his feet, in which,
Divided by a breadth of smooth green space 145

From all the other hillocks which like waves
Heave close together, they who were erewhile
The Inmates of that Cottage are at rest.
Death to the happy House in which they dwelt
Had given a long reprieve of forty years;   150
Suddenly then they disappeared—not twice
Had Summer scorch'd the fields, not twice had fallen
The first white snow upon Helvellyn's top,
Before the greedy visiting was closed
And the long-priviledg'd House left empty, swept   155
As by a plague; yet no rapacious plague
Had been among them, all was gentle death,
One after one, with intervals of peace,
A Consummation and divine accord,
Though fram'd of sad and melancholy notes,   160
Sweet, perfect, to be wish'd for, save that here
Was something sounding to our mortal sense
Like harshness, that the old greyheaded Sire,
The Oldest, he was taken last, survived
When the dear Partner of his manhood's prime,   165
His Son, and Daughter, then a blooming Wife,
And little smiling Grandchild were no more.
'Twas but a little patience and his term
Of solitude was spent.— The aged one,
(He was our first in eminence of years   170
The Patriarch of the Vale,—a busy Hand,
Yea more, a Burning palm, a flashing eye,
A restless foot, a head that beat at nights
Upon his pillow with a thousand schemes)
"How will he face the remnant of his life,   175
What will become of him?," we said, and mused
In vain conjectures; "Shall we meet him now,
Haunting with rod and line the rocky brooks
And mountain-Tarns; or shall we, as we pass,
Hear him alone, and solacing his ear   180
With music?," for he, in the fitful hours

Of his tranquillity, had not ceas'd to touch
The harp or viol which himself had framed
And fitted to their tasks with perfect skill.
"What Titles will he keep, will he remain 185
Musician, Gardener, Builder, Mechanist,
A Planter and a Rearer from the seed,
A man of hope and forward-looking mind,
Even to the last?"—such was he unsubdued.
But Heaven was gracious; yet a little while, 190
And this old Man, he and his chearful throng
Of open schemes, and all his inward hoard
Of unsunn'd griefs, too many and too keen,
Fell with the body into gentle sleep
In one blest moment, and the family, 195
By yet a higher privilege, once more
Were gathered to each other where they sleep,
For they were strangers, in the realm of death
Divided from all neighbourhood. Yet I own,
Though I can look on their associate graves 200
With nothing but still thought, that I repine,
It costs me something like a pain to feel
That after them so many of their works,
Which round that Dwelling covertly preserv'd
The History of their unambitious lives, 205
Have perish'd, and so soon!—The Cottage-Court,
Spread with blue gravel from the torrent's side
And gay with shrubs, the garden, bed and walk
His own creation, that embattled Host
Of garish tulips, fruit trees chosen and rare, 210
And roses of all colours, which he sought
Most curiously, as generously dispers'd
Their kinds, to beautify his neighbours' grounds;
Trees of the forest, too, a stately fence
Planted for Shelter in his manhood's prime, 215
And Small Flowers watered by his wrinkled hand,
That all are ravaged;—that his Daughter's Bower

Is creeping into shapelessness, self-lost
In the wild wood, like a neglected image
Or fancy which hath ceased to be recalled. 220
The jasmine, her own charge, which she had trained
To deck the wall, and of one flowery spray
Had made an Inmate, luring it from sun
And breezes, and from its fellows, to pervade
The inside of her chamber with its sweet, 225
And be the Comrade of her loneliest thought,—
I grieve to see that Jasmine on the ground
Stretching its desolate length, mourn that these works
Of love and diligence and innocent care
Are sullied and disgrac'd; or that a gulf 230
Hath swallowed them which renders nothing back;
That they, so quickly, in a cave are hidden
Which cannot be unlock'd; upon their bloom
That a perpetual winter should have fallen.
Meanwhile the little Primrose of the rock 235
Remains, in sacred beauty, without taint
Of injury or decay, lives to proclaim
Her charter in the blaze of noon; salutes
Not unobserved the early Shepherd Swain,
Or Labourer plodding at th'accustomed hour 240
Home to his distant hearth; and may be seen,
Long as the fullness of her bloom endures,
With one short instantaneous chear of mind,[1]
By stranger late in travel, as I myself
Have often seen her, when the last lone Thrush 245
Had ceas'd his vesper hymn, piercing the gloom
Of Twilight with the vigor of a star,
Say rather, boldly hung as if in air,
Like the broad Moon, with lustre somewhat dimm'd,
Lonely and bright and as the Moon secure. 250
    Oh for some band of guardian Spirits, prompt

---

[1] Here, and at ll. 329, 358, 477, and 507, the fair copy is interrupted by lengthy passages of drafting or further fair copy before picking up with the line following.

As were those human ministers of old,
Who, daily, nightly, under various names,
With various service stood or walk'd their rounds
Through the wide forest, to protect from harm   255
The wild Beast with her young, and from the touch
Of waste the green-leav'd Thicket to defend,
Their secret couch, and cool umbrageous trees,
Their canopy, and berry-bearing shrub
And grassy lawn, their pasture's open range;   260
Continual and firm peace, from outrage safe
And all annoyance, till the sovereign comes
Heading his train, and through that franchise high
Urges the Chase with clamorous hound and horn.
O grant some wardenship of spirits pure,   265
As duteous in their office to maintain
Inviolate for nobler purposes
These individual precincts, to protect,
Here, if here only, from despoil and wrong
All growth of nature and all frame of Art   270
By, and in which, the blissful pleasures live.
Have not th'incumbent Mountains looks of awe
In which this mandate may be read, the streams
A voice that pleads, beseeches, and implores?
In vain—the deafness of the world is here,   275
Even here, and all too many of the haunts
Of Fancy's choicest pastime, and the best
And Dearest resting places of the heart
Vanish beneath an unrelenting doom.
   What impulse drove the Hermit to his Cell   280
And what detain'd him there his whole life long
Fast anchored in the desart? Not alone
Dread of the persecuting sword, remorse,
Love with despair, or grief in agony;
Not always from intolerable pangs   285
He fled; but in the height of pleasure sigh'd
For independent happiness, craving peace,

The central feeling of all happiness,
Not as a refuge from distress or pain,
A breathing time, vacation, or a truce, 290
But for its absolute self, a life of peace,
Stability without regret or fear,
That hath been, is, and shall be ever more.
Therefore on few external things his heart
Was set, and those his own, or if not his, 295
Subsisting under Nature's stedfast law.
What other yearning was the master tie
Of the monastic brotherhood, upon rock
Aerial or in green secluded vale,
One after one collected from afar, 300
An undissolving fellowship? What but this,
The universal instinct of repose,
The longing for confirm'd tranquillity,
Inward and outward, humble and sublime,
The life where hope and memory are as one, 305
Earth quiet and unchanged, the human soul
Consistent in self rule, and heaven revealed
To meditation in that quietness.
   Thus tempted, thus inspired, St. Basil left
(Man as he was of noble blood, high-born, 310
High-station'd, and elaborately taught)
The vain felicities of Athens, left
Her throng of Sophists glorying in their snares,
Her Poets, and conflicting Orators,
Relinquish'd Alexandria's splendid Halls, 315
Antioch and Cesarea, and withdrew
To his delicious Pontic solitude,
Remembering with deep thankfulness meanwhile
Those exhortations of a female voice
Pathetically urg'd, his Sister's voice, 320
Macrina, pious Maid, most beautiful
And in the gentleness of woman wise,
By whom admonish'd, He while yet a Youth

And a triumphant Scholar, had dismiss'd
That loftiness, and modestly inclined   325
To a strict life of virtuous privacy.
Which sequestration when he chose, erelong
He found the same beyond all promise rich
In dignity, sincere content, and joy.[1]
   Mark, for the Picture to this hour remains,   330
With what luxuriant fondness he pourtrays
The lineaments arid image of that spot,
In which upon a Mount, sylvan and high,
And at the boldest jutting in its side,
His cell was fix'd, a Mount with Towering Hills   335
Fenc'd round and vallies intricate and deep,
Which, leaving one blind Entrance to a plain
Of fertile Meadow ground that lay beneath,
Fronting the cell, had from all quarters else
Forbidden all approach, by rocks abrupt,   340
Or rampart as effectual of huge woods
Neither austere nor gloomy to behold,
But a gay prospect lifting to the sun
Majestic beds of diverse foliage, fruits
And thousand laughing blossoms; and the plain   345
Stretch'd out beneath the high perch'd cell was bright
With herbs and flowers, and tufts of flowering plants,
The choicest which the lavish East pours forth,
And sober-headed Cypress interspers'd,
And grac'd with presence of a famous Stream,   350
The Rapid Iris, journeying from remote
Armenian Mountains to his Euxine bourne,
Sole Traveller by the guarded mount, and He,
To enter there, had leapt with thunderous Voice
Down a steep rock, and through the secret plain,   355
Not without many a lesser bound, advanc'd
Self-chear'd with song, to keep his onward course

---

1 See note to l. 243 above.

Like a belated Pilgrim.[1]
                Come O Friend!
(Thus did St. Basil fervently break forth,
Entreated thus the man he held most dear)   360
Come Nazianzen to these happy fields,
To this enduring Paradise, these walks
Of contemplation, piety, and love,
Coverts serene of bless'd mortality.
What if the Roses and the flowers of Kings,   365
Princes and Emperors, and the crowns and palms
Of all the great are blasted, or decay—
What if the meanest of their subjects, each
Within the narrow region of his cares,
Tremble beneath a sad uncertainty?   370
There is a priviledge to plead, there is,
Renounce, and thou shall find that priviledge, here.
No loss lamenting, no privation felt,
Disturb'd by no vicissitudes, unscarred
By civil faction, by religious broils   375
Unplagu'd, forgetting, and forgotten, here
Mayst thou possess thy own invisible nest,
Like one of those small birds that round us chaunt
In multitudes, their warbling will be thine,
And freedom to unite thy voice with theirs,   380
When they at morn or dewy evening praise
High heaven in sweet and solemn services.
Here mayst thou dedicate thyself to God
And acceptably fill the votive hours,
Not seldom as these Creatures of the grove   385
That need no rule, and live but to enjoy,
Not only lifted often to the calm
Of that entire beatitude in which
The Angels serve, but when thou must descend
From the pure vision, and thy soul admit   390
A salutary glow of hope and fear,

---

1 See note to l. 243 above.

Searching in patience and humility
Among the written mysteries of faith
The will divine, or when thou wouldst assume
The burthen and the seasonable yoke 395
Required by our frail Nature, wouldst be tamed
By vigils, abstinence, and prayer with tears,
What place so fit?—a solitude this deep
Thebais or the Syrian Wilderness
Contains not in its dry and barren round; 400
For not a human form is seen this way,
Unless some straggling Hunter led by chance.
Him, if the graver duties be performed,
Or overwrought with study, if the mind
Be haunted by a vain disquietude 405
And gladly would be taken from itself,
Or if it be the time when thoughts are blithe,
Him mayst Thou follow to the hills, or mount
Alone, as fancy prompts, equipp'd with bow
And shafts and quiver, not for perilous aim 410
At the gaunt wolf, the Lion, or the Pard,
These lurk not in our bounds, but Deer and Goat
And other kinds as peaceable are there
In readiness for inoffensive chase.
The River also owns his harmless tribes 415
And tempts thee to like sport; labour itself
Is pastime here, for generous is the Sun,
And cool airs blowing from the mountain top
Refresh the brow of him who in plain field
Or garden presses his industrious spade. 420
Or if a different exercise thou chuse,
And from boon nature rather wouldst receive
Food for the day; behold the fruits that hang
In the primaeval woods—the wells and springs
Have each a living garland of green herbs, 425
From which they to the rifling hand will yield
Ungrudgingly supply that never fails,

Bestowed as freely as their water—pure
To deck thy temperate board.—
                      From theme to theme
Transported in this sort by fervent zeal   430
That stopp'd not here, the venerable Man,
Holy and great, his invitation breathed.
And Nazianzen fashion'd a reply
Ingenious and rhetorical, with taunts
Of wit and gay good-humour'd ridicule,   435
Directed both against the life itself
And that strong passion for these fortunate isles,
For this Arcadia of a golden dream.
But on her inward council seat, his soul
Was mov'd, was rapt, and fill'd with seriousness;   440
Nor was it long ere broken out from ties
Of the world's business he the call obey'd.
And Amphilochius came, and numbers more,
Men of all tempers, qualities, estates,
Came with one spirit, like a troop of fowl   445
That, single or in clusters, at a sign
Given by their leader, settle on the breast
Of some broad pool, green field, or shady tree,
In harmony and undisturbed repose;
Or as a brood of eager younglings flock,   450
Delighted, to the mother's outspread wings
And shelter there in unity and love.
   An intellectual Champion of the faith,
Accomplish'd above all who then appeared,
Or, haply, since victoriously have stood   455
In opposition to the desperate course
Of Pagan rites or impious heresies,
St. Basil, after lapse of years, went forth
To a station of authority and power,
Upon an urgent summons, and resign'd,   460
Ah, not without regret, the heavenly Mount,
The sheltering Valley, and his lov'd Compeers.

He parted from them, but their common life,
If neither first nor singular, at least
More beautiful than any of like frame   465
That hitherto had been conceived, a life
To which by written institutes and rules
He gave a solid being, did not thence
Depart with him, nor ceas'd when he, and they
Whom he had gather'd to his peaceful Vale   470
In that retirement, were withdrawn from earth.
And afterwards it hung through many an age,
In bright remembrance, like a shining cloud,
O'er the vast regions of the western Church;
Whence those communities of holy men   475
That spread so far, to shrouded quietness
Devoted, and of saintly Virgins pure.[1]

    Fallen, in a thousand vales, the stately Towers
And branching windows gorgeously array'd,
And aisles and roofs magnificent that thrill'd   480
With halleluiahs, and the strong-ribb'd vaults
Are crush'd, and buried under weeds and earth
The cloistral avenues—they that heard the voice
Of some sequester'd brook in Gallia's Vales,
Soft murmuring among woods and olive bowers   485
And tilth and vineyards, and the Piles that rose
On British lawns by Severn, Thames, or Tweed
And saw their pomp reflected in the stream,
As Tintern saw; and, to this day, beholds
Her faded image in the depths of Wye.—   490
Of solemn port, smitten but unsubdued
She stands; nor less tenacious of her rights
Stands Fountains Abbey, glorious in decay,
Before the pious Traveller's lifted eyes,
Threatening to outlive the ravages of Time,   495
And bear the cross till Christ shall come again.
So cleave they to the earth, in monument

---

1 See note to l. 243 above.

Of Revelation, nor in memory less
Of nature's pure religion, as in line
Uninterrupted it hath travelled down 500
From the first man who heard a howling storm,
Or knew a troubled thought or vain desire,
A hope which had deceived, or empty came,
Or, in the very sunshine of his joy
And saddened at a perishable bliss, 505
Or languish'd idly under fond regrets
That might not be subdued.—[1]
                "And is thy doom
Pronounc'd (I said, a Stripling at that time,
Who with a Fellow-pilgrim had been driv'n
Through madding France before a joyous gale, 510
And to the solemn haven of Chartreuse
Repaired for timely rest) and are we twain
The last, perchance, the very last, of men
Who shall be welcom'd here, whose limbs shall find
Repose within these modest cells, whose hearts 515
Receive a comfort from these awful spires?
Alas for what I see, the flash of arms,
O sorrow! and yon military glare,
And hark those voices! let us hide in gloom
Profoundest of St. Bruno's wood, these sighs, 520
These whispers that pursue, or meet me, whence
[   ] are they but a common [   ]
From the two Sister Streams of Life and Death;
Or are they by the parting Genius sent,
Unheard till now, and to be heard no more?" 525
   Yes I was moved and to this hour am moved.
What Man would bring to nothing, if he might,
A natural power or element? and who,
If the ability were his, would dare
To kill a species of insensate life, 530
Or to the bird of meanest wing would say,

---

1 See note to l. 243 above.

Thou, and thy kind, must perish.—Even so,
So consecrated, almost, might he deem
That power, that organ, that transcendent frame
Of social being.— "Stay your impious hand," 535
Such was the vain injunction of that hour,
By Nature uttered from her Alpine throne,
"O leave in quiet this embodied dream,
This substance by which mortal men have clothed,
Humanly cloth'd the ghostliness of things, 540
In silence visible and perpetual calm.
Let this one Temple last—be this one spot
Of earth devoted to Eternity."—
I heard, or seem'd to hear, and thus the Voice
Proceeded— "honour to the Patriot's zeal, 545
Glory and life to new-born liberty—
All hail ye mighty passions of the Time,
The vengeance, and the transport, and the hope,
But spare, if past and present be the wings
On whose support harmoniously conjoined 550
Moves the great Spirit of human knowledge, spare
This House, these courts of mystery, where a step
Between the Portals of the shadowy rocks
Leaves far behind the vanities of life,
Where, if a peasant enter, or a king, 555
One holy thought, a single holy thought
Has power to initiate—let it be redeemed
With all its blameless priesthood—for the sake
Of Heaven-descended truth; and humbler claim
Of these majestic floods, my noblest boast; 560
These shining cliffs, pure as their home, the sky;
These forests unapproachable by death,
That shall endure as long as Man endures
To think, to hope, to worship, and to feel;
To struggle,—to be lost within himself 565
In trepidation,—from the dim abyss
To look with bodily eyes, and be consoled."

Such repetition of that [   ]
My thoughts demanded; now an humbler task
Awaits us, for the unwearied Song will lead   570
Into a lonely Vale, the mild abode
Of female Votaries. No [   ] plain
Blank as the Arabian wilderness defends
This chosen Spot, nor is it [   ]
By rocks like those of Caucasus, or Alps,   575
The untransmuted Shapes of many worlds,
Nor can it boast a massy Structure huge,
Founded and built by hands, with arch and towers,
Pillar and pinnacle and glittering spire
Sublime, as if in Emulation reared   580
Of the eternal Architect—these signs,
These tokens—admonitions to recall,
Curbs to restrain, or stays to lean upon,
Such food to nourish or appease the Soul
The gentle Beings who found harbour here   585
Required not. Them a lowly Edifice
Embrac'd by [?lowly] grounds that did not aim
To overshadow, but to screen and hide,
Contented,—and an unassuming brook
Working between these hills its aimless way   590
Through meadow, chestnut wood, and olive bowers
And tilth and vineyard.——

[St. Paul's] (1808)

Press'd with conflicting thoughts of love and fear,
I parted from thee, Friend! and took my way
Through the great City, pacing with an eye
Down cast, ear sleeping, and feet masterless,
That were sufficient guide unto themselves,   5
And step by step went pensively. Now, mark!

Not how my trouble was entirely hush'd,
(That might not be) but how by sudden gift,
Gift of Imagination's holy power!
My Soul in her uneasiness received   10
An anchor of stability. It chanced
That, while I thus was pacing, I raised up
My heavy eyes and instantly beheld,
Saw at a glance in that familiar spot
A visionary scene: a length of street   15
Laid open in its morning quietness,
Deep, hollow, unobstructed, vacant, smooth,
And white with winter's purest white, as fair,
As fresh and spotless as he ever sheds
On field or mountain. Moving Form was none,   20
Save here and there a shadowy Passenger,
Slow, shadowy, silent, dusky, and beyond
And high above this winding length of street,
This noiseless and unpeopled avenue,
Pure, silent, solemn, beautiful, was seen   25
The huge majestic Temple of St. Paul
In awful sequestration, through a veil,
Through its own sacred veil of falling snow.

Composed when a probability existed of our being obliged to quit Rydal Mount as a Residence

(1826)[1]

   The doubt to which a wavering hope had clung
Is fled; we must depart, willing or not,
Sky-piercing Hills! must bid farewell to you
And all that Ye look down upon with pride,
With tenderness embosom; to your paths,   5
And pleasant dwellings, to familiar trees
And wild flowers known as well as if our hands
Had tended them: and O pellucid Spring!
Insensibly the foretaste of this parting
Hath ruled my steps, and seals me to thy side,   10
Mindful that Thou (ah wherefore by my Muse
So long unthanked) hast cheared a simple board
With beverage pure as ever fixed the choice
Of Hermit, dubious where to scoop his Cell;
Which Persian Kings might envy; and thy meek   15
And gentle aspect oft has ministered
To finer uses. They for me must cease;
Days will pass on, the year, if years be given,
Fade,—and the moralizing mind derive
No lesson from the presence of a Power   20
By the inconstant nature we inherit
Unmatched in delicate beneficence;
For neither unremitting rains avail
To swell Thee into voice; nor longest drought
Thy bounty stints, nor can thy beauty mar,   25
Beauty not therefore wanting change to stir

---

1 A shorter version of this poem appears in *The Poems of William Wordsworth*, vol. II, pp. 294–297. In this version, which appears in the electronic Addendum to the three-volume *Poems*, Wordsworth adds three long sections, the lines on Narcissus, on the muses, and on Joan of Arc, broadening the thematic range of his poem to include ancient myth and more recent history..

The fancy, pleased by spectacles unlooked for.
    Not yet, perchance, translucent Spring! had tolled
The Norman curfew bell when human hands
First offered help that the deficient rock   30
Might overarch Thee, from pernicious heat
Defended, and appropriate to Man's need.
Such ties will not be severed: but, when We
Are gone, what summer Loiterer with regard
Inquisitive, thy countenance will peruse,   35
Pleased to detect the dimpling stir of life,
The breathing faculty with which thou yield'st
(Tho' a mere goblet to the careless eye)
Boons inexhaustible? Who, hurrying on
With a step quickened by November's cold,   40
Shall pause, the skill admiring that can work
Upon thy chance-defilements—withered twigs
That, lodged within thy chrystal depths, seem bright
As if they from a silver tree had fallen—
And oaken leaves that, driven by whirling blasts,   45
Sunk down, and lay immersed in dead repose
For Time's invisible tooth to prey upon—
Unsightly objects and uncoveted,
Till thou with crystal bead-drops didst encrust
Their skeletons turned to brilliant ornaments.   50
But, from thy bosom, should some venturous hand
Abstract those gleaming relics, and uplift them,
However gently, toward the vulgar air,
At once their tender brightness disappears,
Leaving the Intermeddler to upbraid   55
His folly. —Thus (I feel it while I speak)
Thus, with the fibres of these thoughts it fares;
And oh! how much, of all that love creates
Or beautifies, like changes undergoes,
Suffers like loss when drawn out of the Soul,   60
Its silent laboratory! Words should say
(Could they depict the marvels of thy cell)

Composed when a probability existed

How often I have marked a plumy fern
From the live rock with grace inimitable
Bending its apex toward a paler self 65
Reflected all in perfect lineaments—
Shadow and substance kissing point to point
In mutual stillness; or, if some faint breeze
Entering the Cell gave restlessness to one,
The other, glassed in thy unruffled breast, 70
Partook of every motion, met, retired,
And met again, such playful sympathy,
Such delicate caress as in the shape
Of this green Plant had aptly recompensed,
For baffled lips and disappointed arms 75
And hopeless pangs, the Spirit of that Youth,
The fair Narcissus, by some pitying God
Changed to a crimson Flower, when he, whose pride
Provoked a retribution too severe,
Had pined; upon his watery Duplicate 80
Wasting that love the Nymphs implored in vain.
    Thus while my Fancy wanders, Thou, clear Spring—
Moved (shall I say?) like a dear friend who meets
A parting moment with her loveliest look
And seemingly her happiest, look so fair 85
It frustrates its own purpose, and recalls
The grieved One whom it meant to send away—
Dost tempt me by disclosure exquisite
To linger, bending over Thee; for now,
What witchcraft, mild Enchantress, may with thine 90
Compare! thy earthy bed a moment past
Palpable unto sight as the dry ground,
Eludes perception, not by rippling air
Concealed, nor through effect of some impure
Upstirring; but, abstracted by a charm 95
Of thy own cunning, earth mysteriously
From under thee hath vanished, and slant beams,
The silent inquest of a western sun,

Assisting, lucid Well-Spring! Thou revealest
Communion without check of herbs and flowers, 100
And the vault's hoary sides to which they cling,
Imaged in downward shew; the flowrets, herbs—
These not of earthly texture, and the Vault
Not *there* diminutive, but, through a scale
Of vision less and less distinct, descending 105
To gloom impenetrable. So (if Truths
The highest condescend to be set forth
By processes minute) even so—when thought
Wins help from something greater than herself—
Is the firm basis of habitual sense 110
Supplanted, not for treacherous vacancy
And blank dissociation from a world
We love, but that the Residues of flesh,
Mirrored, yet not too strictly, may refine
To Spirit; for the idealizing Soul 115
Time wear the features of Eternity;
And Nature deepen into Nature's God.
   Millions of Kneeling Hindoos at this day
Bow to the watery Element, adored
In their vast Stream, and if an age hath been 120
(As Books and haply votive Altars vouch)
When British Floods were worshipped, some faint trace
Of that Idolatry, through Monkish rites
Transmitted far as living memory,
Might wait on Thee, a silent monitor, 125
On Thee, bright Spring, a bashful little One,
Yet to the measure of thy promises
True, as the mightiest; upon Thee, sequestered
For meditation, nor inopportune
For social interest such as I have shared.— 130
Peace to the sober Matron who shall dip
Her pitcher here at early dawn, by me
No longer greeted—to the tottering Sire,
For whom like service, now and then his choice,

Relieves the tedious holiday of age, 135
Thoughts raised above the Earth while here he sits
Feeding on sunshine—to the blushing Girl
Who here forgets her errand, nothing loth
To be waylaid by her Betrothed, peace
And pleasure sobered down to happiness! 140
   But should these Hills be ranged by One whose Soul,
Scorning love-whispers, shrinks from love itself
As Fancy's snare for female vanity,
Here may the Aspirant find a trysting place
For loftier intercourse. The Muses, crowned 145
With wreaths that have not faded to this hour,
Sprung from high Jove, of sage Mnemosyne
Enamoured, so the fable runs; but they
Certes were self-taught Damsels, scattered Births
Of many a Grecian Vale, who sought not praise 150
And heedless ever of Listeners, warbled out
Their own emotions, given to mountain air
In notes which mountain echoes would take up
Boldly and bear away to softer life;
Hence deified as Sisters they were bound 155
Together in a never-dying choir;
Who, with their Hippocrene and grottoed fount
Of Castaly, attest that woman's heart
Was in the limpid age of this stained World
The most assured seat of fine ecstasy, 160
And new-born Waters deemed the happiest source
Of Inspiration for the conscious lyre.
   Lured by the crystal element in times
Stormy and fierce, the Maid of Arc withdrew
From human converse to frequent alone 165
The Fountain of the Fairies. What to her,
Smooth summer dreams, old favours of the place,
Pageants and revels of blithe Elves—to her
Whose country groaned under a foreign scourge?
She pondered murmurs that attuned her ear 170

For the reception of far other sounds
Than their too happy minstrelsy,—a Voice
Reached her with supernatural mandates charged,
More awful than the chambers of dark earth
Have virtue to send forth. Upon the marge   175
Of the benignant fountain, while she stood
Gazing intensely, the translucent lymph
Darkened beneath the shadow of her thoughts
As if swift clouds swept over it, or caught
War's tincture, mid the forest green and still,   180
Turned into blood before her heart-sick eye.
Erelong, forsaking all her natural haunts,
All her accustomed offices and cares
Relinquishing, but treasuring every law
And grace of feminine humanity,   185
The chosen Rustic urged a war-like Steed
Toward the beleagured City, in the might
Of prophesy, accoutred to fulfil,
At the sword's point, visions conceived in love.
   The cloud of Rooks descending through mid air   190
Softens its evening uproar towards a close
Near and more near; for this protracted strain
A warning not unwelcome. Fare thee well!
Emblem of equanimity and truth,
Farewell!—if thy composure be not ours,   195
Yet as Thou still when we are gone wilt keep
Thy living chaplet of fresh flowers and fern,
Cherished in shade though peeped at by the sun;
So shall our bosoms feel a covert growth
Of grateful recollections, tribute due   200
To thy obscure and modest attributes,
To thee clear Spring, and all-sustaining Heaven!

The Recluse, Part Second

The Excursion (1814)

The Excursion;

BEING A PORTION OF THE RECLUSE,

A POEM

TO THE RIGHT HONORABLE WILLIAM, EARL OF
LONSDALE, K. G. &c. &c.

OFT, through thy fair domains, illustrious Peer!
In youth I roamed, on youthful pleasures bent;
And mused in rocky cell or sylvan tent,
Beside swift-flowing Lowther's current clear.
—Now by thy care befriended, I appear   5
Before thee, LONSDALE, and this Work present,
A token (may it prove a monument!)
Of high respect and gratitude sincere.
Gladly would I have waited till my task
Had reached its close; but Life is insecure,   10
And Hope full oft fallacious as a dream:
Therefore, for what is here produced I ask
Thy favour; trusting that thou wilt not deem
The Offering, though imperfect, premature.

WILLIAM WORDSWORTH.
Rydal Mount, Westmorland,
July 29, 1814.

PREFACE

THE Title-page announces that this is only a Portion of a Poem; and the Reader must be here apprized that it belongs to the second part of a long and laborious Work, which is to consist of three parts.—The Author will candidly acknowledge that, if the first of these had been completed, and in such a manner as to satisfy his own mind, he should have preferred the natural order of publication, and have given that to the World first; but, as the second division of the Work was designed to refer more to passing events, and to an existing state of things, than the others were meant to do, more continuous exertion was naturally bestowed upon it, and greater progress made here than in the rest of the Poem; and as this part does not depend upon the preceding, to a degree which will materially injure its own peculiar interest, the Author, complying with the earnest entreaties of some valued Friends, presents the following Pages to the Public.

It may be proper to state whence the Poem, of which The Excursion is a part, derives its Title of THE RECLUSE.—Several years ago, when the Author retired to his native Mountains, with the hope of being enabled to construct a literary Work that might live, it was a reasonable thing that he should take a review of his own Mind, and examine how far Nature and Education had qualified him for such employment. As subsidiary to this preparation, he undertook to record, in Verse, the origin and progress of his own powers, as far as he was acquainted with them. That Work, addressed to a dear Friend, most distinguished for his knowledge and genius, and to whom the Author's Intellect is deeply indebted, has been long finished; and the result of the investigation which gave rise to it was a determination to compose a philosophical Poem, containing views of Man, Nature, and Society; and to be entitled, The Recluse; as having for its principal subject the sensations and opinions of a Poet living in retirement.—The preparatory Poem is biographical, and conducts the history of the Author's mind to the point when he was emboldened to hope that his faculties were sufficiently matured for entering upon the arduous labour which he had proposed to himself; and the two Works have the same kind of relation to each other, if he may so express himself, as the Anti-chapel has to the body of a gothic Church. Continuing this allusion, he may be permitted to add, that his minor Pieces, which have been long before the Public, when they shall be properly arranged, will be found by the attentive Reader to have such connection with the main Work as may give them claim to be likened to the little Cells, Oratories, and sepulchral Recesses, ordinarily included in those Edifices.

The Author would not have deemed himself justified in saying, upon this occasion, so much of performances either unfinished, or unpublished, if he had not thought that the labour bestowed by him upon what he has heretofore and now laid before the Public, entitled him to candid attention for such a statement as he thinks necessary to throw light upon his endeavours to please, and he would hope, to benefit his countrymen. —Nothing further need be added, than that the first and third parts of the Recluse will consist chiefly of meditations in the Author's own Person; and that in the intermediate part (The Excursion) the intervention of Characters speaking is employed, and something of a dramatic form adopted.

It is not the Author's intention formally to announce a system: it was more animating to him to proceed in a different course; and if he shall succeed in conveying to the mind clear thoughts, lively images, and strong feelings, the Reader will have no difficulty in extracting the system for himself. And in the mean time the following passage, taken from the conclusion of the first Book of the Recluse, may be acceptable as a kind of *Prospectus* of the design and scope of the whole Poem.

> "*On Man, on Nature, and on Human Life*
> *Musing in Solitude, I oft perceive*
> *Fair trains of imagery before me rise,*
> *Accompanied by feelings of delight*
> *Pure, or with no unpleasing sadness mixed;* 5
> *And I am conscious of affecting thoughts*
> *And dear remembrances, whose presence soothes*
> *Or elevates the Mind, intent to weigh*
> *The good and evil of our mortal state.*
> *—To these emotions, whencesoe'er they come,* 10

Whether from breath of outward circumstance,
Or from the Soul—an impulse to herself,
I would give utterance in numerous Verse.
—Of Truth, of Grandeur, Beauty, Love, and Hope—
And melancholy Fear subdued by Faith; 15
Of blessed consolations in distress;
Of moral strength, and intellectual power;
Of joy in widest commonalty spread;
Of the individual Mind that keeps her own
Inviolate retirement, subject there 20
To Conscience only, and the law supreme
Of that Intelligence which governs all;
I sing: —"fit audience let me find though few!"

   So prayed, more gaining than he asked, the Bard,
Holiest of Men.—Urania, I shall need 25
Thy guidance, or a greater Muse, if such
Descend to earth or dwell in highest heaven!
For I must tread on shadowy ground, must sink
Deep—and, aloft ascending, breathe in worlds
To which the heaven of heavens is but a veil. 30
All strength—all terror, single or in bands,
That ever was put forth in personal form;
Jehovah—with his thunder, and the choir
Of shouting Angels, and the empyreal thrones,
I pass them, unalarmed. Not Chaos, not 35
The darkest pit of lowest Erebus,
Nor aught of blinder vacancy—scooped out
By help of dreams, can breed such fear and awe
As fall upon us often when we look
Into our Minds, into the Mind of Man, 40
My haunt, and the main region of my Song.
—Beauty—a living Presence of the earth,
Surpassing the most fair ideal Forms
Which craft of delicate Spirits hath composed
From earth's materials—waits upon my steps; 45
Pitches her tents before me as I move,

*An hourly neighbour. Paradise, and groves
Elysian, Fortunate Fields—like those of old
Sought in the Atlantic Main, why should they be
A history only of departed things,
Or a mere fiction of what never was?
For the discerning intellect of Man,
When wedded to this goodly universe
In love and holy passion, shall find these
A simple produce of the common day.
—I, long before the blissful hour arrives,
Would chaunt, in lonely peace, the spousal verse
Of this great consummation:—and, by words
Which speak of nothing more than what we are,
Would I arouse the sensual from their sleep
Of Death, and win the vacant and the vain
To noble raptures; while my voice proclaims
How exquisitely the individual Mind
(And the progressive powers perhaps no less
Of the whole species) to the external World
Is fitted:—and how exquisitely, too,
Theme this but little heard of among Men,
The external World is fitted to the Mind;
And the creation (by no lower name
Can it be called) which they with blended might
Accomplish:—this is our high argument.
—Such grateful haunts foregoing, if I oft
Must turn elsewhere—to travel near the tribes
And fellowships of men, and see ill sights
Of madding passions mutually inflamed;
Must hear Humanity in fields and groves
Pipe solitary anguish; or must hang
Brooding above the fierce confederate storm
Of sorrow, barricadoed evermore
Within the walls of Cities; may these sounds
Have their authentic comment,—that, even these
Hearing, I be not downcast or forlorn!*

—Come thou prophetic Spirit, that inspir'st
The human Soul of universal earth,[1]
Dreaming on things to come; and dost possess   85
A metropolitan Temple in the hearts
Of mighty Poets; upon me bestow
A gift of genuine insight; that my Song
With star-like virtue in its place may shine;
Shedding benignant influence,—and secure,   90
Itself, from all malevolent effect
Of those mutations that extend their sway
Throughout the nether sphere!—And if with this
I mix more lowly matter; with the thing
Contemplated, describe the Mind and Man   95
Contemplating; and who, and what he was,
The transitory Being that beheld
This Vision,—when and where, and how he lived;—
Be not this labour useless. If such theme
May sort with highest objects, then, dread Power,   100
Whose gracious favour is the primal source
Of all illumination, may my Life
Express the image of a better time,
More wise desires, and simpler manners;—nurse
My Heart in genuine freedom:—all pure thoughts   105
Be with me;—so shall thy unfailing love
Guide, and support, and cheer me to the end!"

---

[1] "'Come thou prophetic Spirit, that inspir'st
The human soul, &c.'
Not mine own fears, nor the prophetic Soul
Of the wide world dreaming on things to come.
Shakespeare's Sonnets." WW

SUMMARY OF CONTENTS

BOOK FIRST
THE WANDERER

A summer forenoon—The Author reaches a ruined Cottage upon a Common, and there meets with a revered Friend, the Wanderer, of whom he gives an account—The Wanderer while resting under the shade of the Trees that surround the Cottage relates the History of its last Inhabitant.

BOOK SECOND
THE SOLITARY

The Author describes his travels with the Wanderer, whose character is further illustrated—Morning scene, and view of a Village Wake—Wanderer's account of a Friend whom he purposes to visit—View, from an eminence, of the Valley which his Friend had chosen for his retreat—feelings of the Author at the sight of it—Sound of singing from below—a funeral procession—Descent into the Valley—Observations drawn from the Wanderer at sight of a Book accidentally discovered in a recess in the Valley—Meeting with the Wanderer's friend, the Solitary—Wanderer's description of the mode of burial in this mountainous district—Solitary contrasts with this, that of the Individual carried a few minutes before from the Cottage—Brief conversation—The Cottage entered—description of the Solitary's apartment—repast there—View from the Window of two mountain summits—and the Solitary's description of the Companionship they afford him—account of the departed Inmate of the Cottage—description of a grand spectacle upon the mountains, with its effect upon the Solitary's mind—Quit the House.

BOOK THIRD
DESPONDENCY

Images in the Valley—Another Recess in it entered and described—Wanderer's sensations—Solitary's excited by the same objects—Contrast between these—Despondency of the Solitary gently reproved—Conversation exhibiting the Solitary's past and present opinions and feelings, till he enters upon his own History at length—His domestic felicity—afflictions—dejection—roused by the French Revolution—Disappointment and disgust—Voyage to America—disappointment and disgust pursue him—his return—His languor and depression of mind, from want of faith in the great truths of Religion, and want of confidence in the virtue of Mankind.

BOOK FOURTH

DESPONDENCY CORRECTED

State of feeling produced by the foregoing Narrative—A belief in a superintending Providence the only adequate support under affliction—Wanderer's ejaculation to the supreme Being—Account of his own devotional feelings in youth involved in it—Implores that he may retain in age the power to find repose among enduring and eternal things—What these latter are—Acknowledges the difficulty of a lively faith—Hence immoderate sorrow—but doubt or despondence not therefore to be inferred—And proceeds to administer consolation to the Solitary—Exhortations—How these are received—Wanderer resumes—and applies his discourse to that other cause of dejection in the Solitary's mind—the disappointment of his expectations from the French Revolution—States the rational grounds of hope—and insists on the necessity of patience and fortitude with respect to the course of the great revolutions of the world—Knowledge the source of tranquility—Rural life and Solitude particularly favourable to a knowledge of the inferior Creatures—Study of their habits and ways recommended for its influence on the affections and the imagination—Exhortation to bodily exertion and an active Communion with Nature—Morbid Solitude a pitiable thing—If the elevated imagination cannot be exerted—try the humbler fancy—Superstition better than apathy—Apathy and destitution unknown in the infancy of society—The various modes of Religion prevented it—this illustrated in the Jewish, Persian, Babylonian, Chaldean and Grecian modes of belief—Solitary interposes—Wanderer, in answer, points out the influence of religious and imaginative feeling on the mind in the humble ranks of society, in rural life especially—This illustrated from present and past times—Observation that these principles tend to recal exploded superstitions and popery—Wanderer rebuts this charge, and contrasts the dignities of the Imagination with the presumptive littleness of certain modern Philosophers, whom the Solitary appears to esteem—Recommends to him other lights and guides—Asserts the power of the Soul to regenerate herself—Solitary agitated, and asks how—Reply—Personal appeal—Happy for us that the imagination and affections in our own despite mitigate the evils of that state of intellectual Slavery which the calculating understanding is so apt to produce—Exhortation to activity of Body renewed—How Nature is to be communed with—Wanderer concludes with a prospect of a legitimate union of the imagination, the affections, the understanding, and the reason—Effect of the Wanderer's discourse—Evening—Return to the Cottage.

BOOK FIFTH

THE PASTOR

Farewell to the Valley—Reflections—Sight of a large and populous Vale—Solitary consents to go forward—Vale described—The Pastor's Dwelling, and some account of him—The Church-yard—Church and Monuments—The Solitary musing, and where—Roused—In the Church-yard the Solitary communicates the thoughts which had recently passed through his mind—Lofty tone of the Wanderer's discourse of yesterday adverted to—Rite of Baptism, and the professions accompanying it, contrasted with the real state of human life—Inconsistency of the best men—Acknowledgement that practice falls far below the injunctions of duty as existing in the mind—General complaint of a falling-off in the value of life after the time of youth—Outward appearances of content and happiness in degree illusive—Pastor approaches—Appeal made to him—His answer—Wanderer in sympathy with him—Suggestion that the least ambitious Inquirers may be most free from error—The Pastor is desired to give some Portraits of the living or dead from his own observation of life among these Mountains—and for what purpose—Pastor consents—Mountain cottage—Excellent qualities of its Inhabitants—Solitary expresses his pleasure; but denies the praise of virtue to worth of this kind—Feelings of the Priest before he enters upon his account of Persons interred in the Church-yard—Graves of unbaptized Infants—What sensations they excite—Funereal and sepulchral Observances—Whence—Ecclesiastical Establishments—Whence derived—Profession of Belief in the doctrine of Immortality.

BOOK SIXTH

THE CHURCH-YARD AMONG
THE MOUNTAINS

Poet's Address to the State and Church of England—The Pastor not inferior to the ancient Worthies of the Church—He begins his Narratives with an Instance of unrequited love—Anguish of mind subdued—and how—The lonely Miner, an Instance of Perseverance, which leads by contrast to an Example of abused talents, irresolution, and weakness—Solitary, applying this covertly to his own case, asks for an Instance of some Stranger, whose dispositions may have led him to end his days here—Pastor, in answer, gives an account of the harmonizing influence of Solitude upon two Men of opposite principles, who had encountered agitations in public life—The Rule by which Peace may be obtained expressed—and where—Solitary hints at an overpowering Fatality—Answer of the Pastor—What subjects he will exclude from his Narratives—Conversation upon this—Instance of an unamiable Character, a Female—

and why given—Contrasted with this, a meek Sufferer, from unguarded and betrayed Love—Instance of heavier guilt—and its consequences to the Offender—With this Instance of a Marriage Contract broken is contrasted one of a Widower, evidencing his faithful affection towards his deceased Wife by his care of their female Children—Second Marriage of a Widower prudential and happy.

BOOK SEVENTH

THE CHURCH-YARD AMONG THE MOUNTAINS,

CONTINUED

Impression of these Narratives upon the Author's mind—Pastor invited to give account of certain Graves that lie apart—Clergyman and his Family—Fortunate influence of change of situation—Activity in extreme old age—Another Clergyman, a character of resolute Virtue—Lamentations over misdirected applause—Instance of less exalted excellence in a deaf Man—Elevated character of a blind Man—Reflection upon Blindness—Interrupted by a Peasant who passes—his animal cheerfulness and careless vivacity—He occasions a digression on the fall of beautiful and interesting Trees—A female Infant's Grave—Joy at her Birth—Sorrow at her Departure—A youthful Peasant—his patriotic enthusiasm—distinguished qualities—and untimely Death—Exultation of the Wanderer, as a patriot, in this Picture—Solitary how affected—Monument of a Knight—Traditions concerning him—Peroration of Wanderer on the transitoriness of things and the revolutions of society—Hints at his own past Calling—Thanks the Pastor.

BOOK EIGHTH

THE PARSONAGE

Pastor's apprehensions that he might have detained his Auditors too long—Invitation to his House—Solitary disinclined to comply—rallies the Wanderer; and somewhat playfully draws a comparison between his itinerant profession and that of the Knight-errant—which leads to Wanderer's giving an account of changes in the Country from the manufacturing spirit—Favourable effects—The other side of the picture, and chiefly as it has affected the humbler classes—Wanderer asserts the hollowness of all national grandeur if unsupported by moral worth—gives Instances—Physical science unable to support itself—Lamentations over an excess of manufacturing industry among the humbler Classes of Society—Picture of a Child employed in a Cotton-mill—Ignorance and degradation of Children among the agricultural Population reviewed—Conversation broken off by a renewed Invitation from the Pastor—Path leading to his House—Its appearance described—His Daughter—His Wife—His Son (a Boy) enters with his Companion—Their happy appearance—The Wanderer how affected by the sight of them.

BOOK NINTH

DISCOURSE OF THE WANDERER, &c.

Wanderer asserts that an active principle pervades the Universe—Its noblest seat the human soul—How lively this principle is in Childhood—Hence the delight in old age of looking back upon childhood—The dignity, powers, and privileges of Age asserted—These not to be looked for generally but under a just government—Right of a human Creature to be exempt from being considered as a mere Instrument—Vicious inclinations are best kept under by giving good ones an opportunity to shew themselves—The condition of multitudes deplored from want of due respect to this truth on the part of their superiors in society—Former conversation recurred to, and the Wanderer's opinions set in a clearer light—Genuine principles of equality—Truth placed within reach of the humblest—Happy state of the two Boys again adverted to—Earnest wish expressed for a System of National Education established universally by Government—Glorious effects of this foretold—Wanderer breaks off—Walk to the Lake—embark—Description of scenery and amusements—Grand spectacle from the side of a hill—Address of Priest to the Supreme Being—in the Course of which he contrasts with ancient Barbarism the present appearance of the scene before him—The change ascribed to Christianity—Apostrophe to his Flock, living and dead—Gratitude to the Almighty—Return over the Lake—Parting with the Solitary—Under what circumstances.

BOOK THE FIRST

THE WANDERER

'Twas summer, and the sun had mounted high:
Southward, the landscape indistinctly glared
Through a pale steam; but all the northern downs,
In clearest air ascending, shew'd far off
A surface dappled o'er with shadows, flung   5
From many a brooding cloud; far as the sight
Could reach, those many shadows lay in spots
Determined and unmoved, with steady beams
Of bright and pleasant sunshine interposed.
Pleasant to him who on the soft cool moss   10
Extends his careless limbs along the front
Of some huge cave, whose rocky ceiling casts
A twilight of its own, an ample shade,
Where the wren warbles; while the dreaming Man,
Half conscious of the soothing melody,   15
With side-long eye looks out upon the scene,
By that impending covert made more soft,
More low and distant! Other lot was mine;
Yet with good hope that soon I should obtain
As grateful resting-place, and livelier joy.   20
Across a bare wide Common I was toiling
With languid feet, which by the slippery ground
Were baffled; nor could my weak arm disperse
The host of insects gathering round my face,
And ever with me as I paced along.   25
    Upon that open level stood a Grove,
The wished-for Port to which my steps were bound.
Thither I came, and there—amid the gloom
Spread by a brotherhood of lofty elms—
Appeared a roofless Hut; four naked walls   30
That stared upon each other! I looked round,
And to my wish and to my hope espied
Him whom I sought; a Man of reverend age,

But stout and hale, for travel unimpaired.
There was he seen upon the Cottage bench,   35
Recumbent in the shade, as if asleep;
An iron-pointed staff lay at his side.

   Him had I marked the day before—alone
And in the middle of the public way
Stationed, as if to rest himself, with face   40
Turned tow'rds the sun then setting, while that staff
Afforded to his Figure, as he stood,
Detained for contemplation or repose,
Graceful support; the countenance of the Man
Was hidden from my view, and he himself   45
Unrecognized; but, stricken by the sight,
With slacken'd footsteps I advanced, and soon
A glad congratulation we exchanged
At such unthought-of meeting.—For the night
We parted, nothing willingly; and now   50
He by appointment waited for me here,
Beneath the shelter of these clustering elms.

   We were tried Friends: I from my Childhood up
Had known him.—In a little Town obscure,
A market-village, seated in a tract   55
Of mountains, where my school-day time was pass'd,
One room he owned, the fifth part of a house,
A place to which he drew, from time to time,
And found a kind of home or harbour there.

   He loved me; from a swarm of rosy Boys   60
Singled out me, as he in sport would say,
For my grave looks—too thoughtful for my years.
As I grew up it was my best delight
To be his chosen Comrade. Many a time,
On holidays, we wandered through the woods,   65
A pair of random travellers; we sate—
We walked; he pleas'd me with his sweet discourse

Of things which he had seen; and often touch'd
Abstrusest matter, reasonings of the mind
Turned inward; or at my request he sang 70
Old songs—the product of his native hills;
A skilful distribution of sweet sounds,
Feeding the soul, and eagerly imbibed
As cool refreshing Water, by the care
Of the industrious husbandman, diffused 75
Through a parched meadow-ground, in time of drought.
Still deeper welcome found his pure discourse:
How precious when in riper days I learn'd
To weigh with care his words, and to rejoice
In the plain presence of his dignity! 80

   Oh! many are the Poets that are sown
By Nature; Men endowed with highest gifts,
The vision and the faculty divine,
Yet wanting the accomplishment of Verse,
(Which in the docile season of their youth 85
It was denied them to acquire, through lack
Of culture and the inspiring aid of books,
Or haply by a temper too severe,
Or a nice backwardness afraid of shame),
Nor having e'er, as life advanced, been led 90
By circumstance to take unto the height
The measure of themselves, these favored Beings,
All but a scattered few, live out their time,
Husbanding that which they possess within,
And go to the grave, unthought of. Strongest minds 95
Are often those of whom the noisy world
Hears least; else surely this Man had not left
His graces unrevealed and unproclaimed.
But, as the mind was filled with inward light,
So not without distinction had he lived, 100
Beloved and honoured—far as he was known.
And some small portion of his eloquent speech,
And something that may serve to set in view

The feeling pleasures of his loneliness,
The doings, observations, which his mind   105
Had dealt with—I will here record in verse;
Which, if with truth it correspond, and sink
Or rise, as venerable Nature leads,
The high and tender Muses shall accept
With gracious smile, deliberately pleased,   110
And listening Time reward with sacred praise.

   Among the hills of Athol he was born:
There, on a small hereditary Farm,
An unproductive slip of rugged ground,
His Father dwelt; and died in poverty;   115
While He, whose lowly fortune I retrace,
The youngest of three sons, was yet a babe,
A little One—unconscious of their loss.
But ere he had outgrown his infant days
His widowed Mother, for a second Mate,   120
Espoused the Teacher of the Village School;
Who on her offspring zealously bestowed
Needful instruction; not alone in arts
Which to his humble duties appertained,
But in the lore of right and wrong, the rule   125
Of human kindness, in the peaceful ways
Of honesty, and holiness severe.
A virtuous Household though exceeding poor!
Pure Livers were they all, austere and grave,
And fearing God; the very Children taught   130
Stern self-respect, a reverence for God's word,
And an habitual piety, maintained
With strictness scarcely known on English ground.

   From his sixth year, the Boy of whom I speak,
In summer, tended cattle on the Hills;   135
But, through the inclement and the perilous days
Of long-continuing winter, he repaired
To his Step-father's School, that stood alone,

Sole Building on a mountain's dreary edge,
Far from the sight of City spire, or sound 140
Of Minster clock! From that bleak Tenement
He, many an evening to his distant home
In solitude returning, saw the Hills
Grow larger in the darkness, all alone
Beheld the stars come out above his head, 145
And travelled through the wood, with no one near
To whom he might confess the things he saw.
So the foundations of his mind were laid.
In such communion, not from terror free,
While yet a Child, and long before his time, 150
He had perceived the presence and the power
Of greatness; and deep feelings had impress'd
Great objects on his mind, with portraiture
And colour so distinct, that on his mind
They lay like substances, and almost seemed 155
To haunt the bodily sense. He had received
(Vigorous in native genius as he was)
A precious gift; for, as he grew in years,
With these impressions would he still compare
All his remembrances, thoughts, shapes, and forms; 160
And, being still unsatisfied with aught
Of dimmer character, he thence attained
An active power to fasten images
Upon his brain; and on their pictured lines
Intensely brooded, even till they acquired 165
The liveliness of dreams. Nor did he fail,
While yet a Child, with a Child's eagerness
Incessantly to turn his ear and eye
On all things which the moving seasons brought
To feed such appetite: nor this alone 170
Appeased his yearning:—in the after day
Of Boyhood, many an hour in caves forlorn,
And 'mid the hollow depths of naked crags
He sate, and even in their fix'd lineaments,

    Or from the power of a peculiar eye,   175
    Or by creative feeling overborne,
    Or by predominance of thought oppress'd,
    Even in their fix'd and steady lineaments
    He traced an ebbing and a flowing mind,
    Expression ever varying!
                       Thus informed,   180
    He had small need of books; for many a Tale
    Traditionary, round the mountains hung,
    And many a Legend, peopling the dark woods,
    Nourished Imagination in her growth,
    And gave the Mind that apprehensive power   185
    By which she is made quick to recognize
    The moral properties and scope of things.
    But eagerly he read, and read again,
    Whate'er the Minister's old Shelf supplied;
    The life and death of Martyrs, who sustained,   190
    With will inflexible, those fearful pangs
    Triumphantly displayed in records left
    Of Persecution, and the Covenant—Times
    Whose echo rings through Scotland to this hour!
    And there by lucky hap had been preserved   195
    A straggling volume, torn and incomplete,
    That left half-told the preternatural tale,
    Romance of Giants, chronicle of Fiends
    Profuse in garniture of wooden cuts
    Strange and uncouth; dire faces, figures dire,   200
    Sharp-knee'd, sharp-elbowed, and lean-ankled too,
    With long and ghostly shanks—forms which once seen
    Could never be forgotten!
                           In his heart
    Where Fear sate thus, a cherished visitant,
    Was wanting yet the pure delight of love   205
    By sound diffused, or by the breathing air,
    Or by the silent looks of happy things,
    Or flowing from the universal face

Of earth and sky. But he had felt the power
Of Nature, and already was prepared,   210
By his intense conceptions, to receive
Deeply the lesson deep of love which he,
Whom Nature, by whatever means, has taught
To feel intensely, cannot but receive.

   From early childhood, even, as hath been said,   215
From his sixth year, he had been sent abroad
In summer to tend herds: such was his task
Thenceforward 'till the later day of youth.
O then what soul was his, when, on the tops
Of the high mountains, he beheld the sun   220
Rise up, and bathe the world in light! He looked—
Ocean and earth, the solid frame of earth
And ocean's liquid mass, beneath him lay
In gladness and deep joy. The clouds were touch'd,
And in their silent faces did he read   225
Unutterable love. Sound needed none,
Nor any voice of joy; his spirit drank
The spectacle; sensation, soul, and form
All melted into him; they swallowed up
His animal being; in them did he live,   230
And by them did he live; they were his life.
In such access of mind, in such high hour
Of visitation from the living God,
Thought was not; in enjoyment it expired.
No thanks he breathed, he proffered no request;   235
Rapt into still communion that transcends
The imperfect offices of prayer and praise,
His mind was a thanksgiving to the power
That made him; it was blessedness and love!

   A Herdsman on the lonely mountain tops,   240
Such intercourse was his, and in this sort
Was his existence oftentimes *possessed*.
Oh then how beautiful, how bright appeared

The written Promise! He had early learned
To reverence the Volume which displays 245
The mystery, the life which cannot die:
But in the mountains did he feel his faith;
There did he see the writing;—all things there
Breathed immortality, revolving life
And greatness still revolving; infinite; 250
There littleness was not; the least of things
Seemed infinite; and there his spirit shaped
Her prospects, nor did he believe,—he saw.
What wonder if his being thus became
Sublime and comprehensive! Low desires, 255
Low thoughts had there no place; yet was his heart
Lowly; for he was meek in gratitude,
Oft as he called those extacies to mind,
And whence they flowed; and from them he acquired
Wisdom, which works through patience; thence he learned 260
In many a calmer hour of sober thought
To look on Nature with a humble heart,
Self-questioned where it did not understand,
And with a superstitious eye of love.

    So passed the time; yet to a neighbouring town 265
He duly went with what small overplus
His earnings might supply, and brought away
The Book which most had tempted his desires
While at the Stall he read. Among the hills
He gazed upon that mighty Orb of Song 270
The divine Milton. Lore of different kind,
The annual savings of a toilsome life,
His Step-father supplied; books that explain
The purer elements of truth involved
In lines and numbers, and, by charm severe, 275
(Especially perceived where nature droops
And feeling is suppressed,) preserve the mind
Busy in solitude and poverty.
These occupations oftentimes deceived

The listless hours, while in the hollow vale, 280
Hollow and green, he lay on the green turf
In pensive idleness. What could he do
With blind endeavours, in that lonesome life,
Thus thirsting daily? Yet still uppermost
Nature was at his heart as if he felt, 285
Though yet he knew not how, a wasting power
In all things which from her sweet influence
Might tend to wean him. Therefore with her hues,
Her forms, and with the spirit of her forms,
He clothed the nakedness of austere truth. 290
While yet he lingered in the rudiments
Of science, and among her simplest laws,
His triangles—they were the stars of heaven,
The silent stars! Oft did he take delight
To measure th' altitude of some tall crag 295
Which is the eagle's birth-place, or some peak
Familiar with forgotten years, that shews
Inscribed, as with the silence of the thought,
Upon it's bleak and visionary sides,
The history of many a winter storm,— 300
Or obscure records of the path of fire.

   And thus, before his eighteenth year was told,
Accumulated feelings pressed his heart
With an increasing weight; he was o'erpower'd
By Nature, by the turbulence subdued 305
Of his own mind; by mystery and hope,
And the first virgin passion of a soul
Communing with the glorious Universe.
Full often wished he that the winds might rage
When they were silent; far more fondly now 310
Than in his earlier season did he love
Tempestuous nights—the conflict and the sounds
That live in darkness:—from his intellect
And from the stillness of abstracted thought
He asked repose; and I have heard him say 315

That often, failing at this time to gain
The peace required, he scanned the laws of light
Amid the roar of torrents, where they send
From hollow clefts up to the clearer air
A cloud of mist, which in the sunshine frames   320
A lasting tablet—for the observer's eye
Varying it's rainbow hues. But vainly thus,
And vainly by all other means, he strove
To mitigate the fever of his heart.

   In dreams, in study, and in ardent thought,   325
Thus, even from Childhood upward, was he reared;
For intellectual progress wanting much,
Doubtless, of needful help—yet gaining more;
And every moral feeling of his soul
Strengthened and braced, by breathing in content   330
The keen, the wholesome air of poverty,
And drinking from the well of homely life.
—But, from past liberty, and tried restraints,
He now was summoned to select the course
Of humble industry which promised best   335
To yield him no unworthy maintenance.
The Mother strove to make her Son perceive
With what advantage he might teach a School
In the adjoining Village; but the Youth,
Who of this service made a short essay,   340
Found that the wanderings of his thought were then
A misery to him; that he must resign
A task he was unable to perform.

   That stern yet kindly spirit, Who constrains
The Savoyard to quit his naked rocks,   345
The free-born Swiss to leave his narrow vales,
(Spirit attached to regions mountainous
Like their own stedfast clouds)—did now impel
His restless Mind to look abroad with hope.
—An irksome drudgery seems it to plod on,   350

Through dusty ways, in storm, from door to door,
A vagrant Merchant bent beneath his load!
Yet do such Travellers find their own delight;
And their hard service, deemed debasing now,
Gained merited respect in simpler times;   355
When Squire, and Priest, and they who round them dwelt
In rustic sequestration, all, dependant
Upon the Pedlar's toil—supplied their wants,
Or pleased their fancies, with the wares he brought.
Not ignorant was the Youth that still no few   360
Of his adventurous Countrymen were led
By perseverance in this Track of life
To competence and ease;—for him it bore
Attractions manifold;—and this he chose.
He asked his Mother's blessing; and, with tears   365
Thanking his second Father, asked from him
Paternal blessings. The good Pair bestowed
Their farewell benediction, but with hearts
Foreboding evil. From his native hills
He wandered far; much did he see of Men,[1]   370
Their manners, their enjoyments, and pursuits,
Their passions, and their feelings; chiefly those
Essential and eternal in the heart,
Which, mid the simpler forms of rural life,
Exist more simple in their elements,   375
And speak a plainer language. In the woods,
A lone Enthusiast, and among the fields,
Itinerant in this labour, he had passed
The better portion of his time; and there

---

1 "In Heron's Tour in Scotland is given an intelligent account of the qualities by which this class of men used to be, and still are, in some degree, distinguished, and of the benefits which Society derives from their labours. Among their characteristics, he does not omit to mention that, from being obliged to pass so much of their time in solitary wandering among rural objects, they frequently acquire meditative habits of mind, and are strongly disposed to enthusiasm poetical and religious. I regret that I have not the book at hand to quote the passage, as it is interesting on many accounts." WW refers to Robert Heron's *Observations Made in a Journey Through the Western Counties of Scotland* (1793)

Spontaneously had his affections thriven 380
Upon the bounties of the year, and felt
The liberty of Nature; there he kept
In solitude and solitary thought
His mind in a just equipoise of love.
Serene it was, unclouded by the cares 385
Of ordinary life; unvexed, unwarped
By partial bondage. In his steady course
No piteous revolutions had he felt,
No wild varieties of joy and grief.
Unoccupied by sorrow of it's own 390
His heart lay open; and, by Nature tuned
And constant disposition of his thoughts
To sympathy with Man, he was alive
To all that was enjoyed where'er he went;
And all that was endured; for in himself 395
Happy, and quiet in his chearfulness,
He had no painful pressure from without
That made him turn aside from wretchedness
With coward fears. He could *afford* to suffer
With those whom he saw suffer. Hence it came 400
That in our best experience he was rich,
And in the wisdom of our daily life.
For hence, minutely, in his various rounds,
He had observed the progress and decay
Of many minds, of minds and bodies too; 405
The History of many Families;
How they had prospered; how they were o'erthrown
By passion or mischance; or such misrule
Among the unthinking masters of the earth
As makes the nations groan.—This active course, 410
Chosen in youth, through manhood he pursued,
Till due provision for his modest wants
Had been obtained;—and, thereupon, resolved
To pass the remnant of his days—untasked
With needless services,—from hardship free. 415

His Calling laid aside, he lived at ease:
But still he loved to pace the public roads
And the wild paths; and, when the summer's warmth
Invited him, would often leave his home
And journey far, revisiting those scenes 420
Which to his memory were most endeared.
—Vigorous in health, of hopeful spirits, untouched
By worldly-mindedness or anxious care;
Observant, studious, thoughtful, and refreshed
By knowledge gathered up from day to day;— 425
Thus had he lived a long and innocent life.

   The Scottish Church, both on himself and those
With whom from childhood he grew up, had held
The strong hand of her purity; and still
Had watched him with an unrelenting eye. 430
This he remembered in his riper age
With gratitude, and reverential thoughts.
But by the native vigour of his mind,
By his habitual wanderings out of doors,
By loneliness, and goodness, and kind works, 435
Whate'er in docile childhood or in youth
He had imbibed of fear or darker thought
Was melted all away: so true was this
That sometimes his religion seemed to me
Self-taught, as of a dreamer in the woods; 440
Who to the model of his own pure heart
Framed his belief, as grace divine inspired,
Or human reason dictated with awe.
—And surely never did there live on earth
A Man of kindlier nature. The rough sports 445
And teazing ways of Children vexed not him,
Nor could he bid them from his presence, tired
With questions and importunate demands:
Indulgent listener was he to the tongue
Of garrulous age; nor did the sick man's tale, 450
To his fraternal sympathy addressed,

Obtain reluctant hearing.
                Plain his garb
Such as might suit a rustic sire, prepared
For sabbath duties; yet he was a Man
Whom no one could have passed without remark.   455
Active and nervous was his gait; his limbs
And his whole figure breathed intelligence.
Time had compressed the freshness of his cheek
Into a narrower circle of deep red
But had not tamed his eye; that under brows   460
Shaggy and grey had meanings which it brought
From years of youth; which, like a Being made
Of many Beings, he had wondrous skill
To blend with knowledge of the years to come,
Human, or such as lie beyond the grave.   465

So was He framed; and such his course of life
Who now, with no Appendage but a Staff,
The prized memorial of relinquish'd toils,
Upon that Cottage bench reposed his limbs,
Screened from the sun. Supine the Wanderer lay,   470
His eyes as if in drowsiness half shut,
The shadows of the breezy elms above
Dappling his face. He had not heard my steps
As I approached; and near him did I stand
Unnotic'd in the shade, some minutes' space.   475
At length I hailed him, seeing that his hat
Was moist with water-drops, as if the brim
Had newly scooped a running stream. He rose,
And ere the pleasant greeting that ensued
Was ended, "'Tis," said I, "a burning day;   480
My lips are parched with thirst, but you, I guess,
Have somewhere found relief." He, at the word,
Pointing towards a sweet-briar, bade me climb
The fence hard by, where that aspiring shrub
Looked out upon the road. It was a plot   485

Of garden-ground run wild, it's matted weeds
Marked with the steps of those, whom, as they pass'd,
The gooseberry trees that shot in long lank slips,
Or currants hanging from their leafless stems
In scanty strings, had tempted to o'erleap   490
The broken wall. I looked around, and there,
Where two tall hedge-rows of thick alder boughs
Joined in a cold damp nook, espied a Well
Shrouded with willow-flowers and plumy fern.
My thirst I slaked, and from the chearless spot   495
Withdrawing, straightway to the shade returned
Where sate the Old Man on the Cottage bench;
And, while, beside him, with uncovered head,
I yet was standing, freely to respire,
And cool my temples in the fanning air,   500
Thus did he speak. "I see around me here
Things which you cannot see: we die, my Friend,
Nor we alone, but that which each man loved
And prized in his peculiar nook of earth
Dies with him, or is changed; and very soon   505
Even of the good is no memorial left.
—The Poets, in their elegies and songs
Lamenting the departed, call the groves,
They call upon the hills and streams to mourn,
And senseless rocks; nor idly; for they speak,   510
In these their invocations, with a voice
Obedient to the strong creative power
Of human passion. Sympathies there are
More tranquil, yet perhaps of kindred birth,
That steal upon the meditative mind,   515
And grow with thought. Beside yon Spring I stood,
And eyed its waters till we seemed to feel
One sadness, they and I. For them a bond
Of brotherhood is broken: time has been
When, every day, the touch of human hand   520
Dislodged the natural sleep that binds them up

In mortal stillness; and they minister'd
To human comfort. As I stooped to drink,
Upon the slimy foot-stone I espied
The useless fragment of a wooden bowl, 525
Green with the moss of years; a pensive sight
That moved my heart!—recalling former days
When I could never pass that road but She
Who lived within these walls, at my approach,
A Daughter's welcome gave me; and I loved her 530
As my own child. O Sir! the good die first,
And they whose hearts are dry as summer dust
Burn to the socket. Many a Passenger
Hath blessed poor Margaret for her gentle looks,
When she upheld the cool refreshment drawn 535
From that forsaken Spring; and no one came
But he was welcome; no one went away
But that it seemed she loved him. She is dead,
The light extinguished of her lonely Hut,
The Hut itself abandoned to decay, 540
And She forgotten in the quiet grave!

   "I speak," continued he, "of One whose stock
Of virtues bloom'd beneath this lowly roof.
She was a Woman of a steady mind,
Tender and deep in her excess of love, 545
Not speaking much, pleased rather with the joy
Of her own thoughts: by some especial care
Her temper had been framed, as if to make
A Being—who by adding love to peace
Might live on earth a life of happiness. 550
Her wedded Partner lacked not on his side
The humble worth that satisfied her heart:
Frugal, affectionate, sober, and withal
Keenly industrious. She with pride would tell
That he was often seated at his loom, 555
In summer, ere the Mower was abroad
Among the dewy grass,—in early spring,

Ere the last Star had vanished.—They who passed
At evening, from behind the garden fence
Might hear his busy spade, which he would ply,   560
After his daily work, until the light
Had failed, and every leaf and flower were lost
In the dark hedges. So their days were spent
In peace and comfort; and a pretty Boy
Was their best hope,—next to the God in Heaven.   565

   Not twenty years ago, but you I think
Can scarcely bear it now in mind, there came
Two blighting seasons when the fields were left
With half a harvest. It pleased heaven to add
A worse affliction in the plague of war;   570
This happy Land was stricken to the heart!
A Wanderer then among the Cottages
I, with my freight of winter raiment, saw
The hardships of that season; many rich
Sank down, as in a dream, among the poor;   575
And of the poor did many cease to be
And their place knew them not. Meanwhile abridg'd
Of daily comforts, gladly reconciled
To numerous self-denials, Margaret
Went struggling on through those calamitous years   580
With chearful hope: but ere the second autumm
Her life's true Help-mate on a sick-bed lay,
Smitten with perilous fever. In disease
He lingered long; and when his strength return'd,
He found the little he had stored, to meet   585
The hour of accident or crippling age,
Was all consumed. Two children had they now,
One newly born. As I have said, it was
A time of trouble; shoals of Artisans
Were from their daily labour turn'd adrift   590
To seek their bread from public charity,
They, and their wives and children—happier far
Could they have lived as do the little birds

That peck along the hedges, or the Kite
That makes his dwelling on the mountain Rocks! 595

   A sad reverse it was for Him who long
Had filled with plenty, and possess'd in peace,
This lonely Cottage. At his door he stood,
And whistled many a snatch of merry tunes
That had no mirth in them; or with his knife 600
Carved uncouth figures on the heads of sticks—
Then, not less idly, sought, through every nook
In house or garden, any casual work
Of use or ornament; and with a strange,
Amusing, yet uneasy novelty, 605
He blended, where he might, the various tasks
Of summer, autumn, winter, and of spring.
But this endured not; his good humour soon
Became a weight in which no pleasure was:
And poverty brought on a petted mood 610
And a sore temper: day by day he drooped,
And he would leave his work—and to the Town,
Without an errand, would direct his steps,
Or wander here and there among the fields.
One while he would speak lightly of his Babes, 615
And with a cruel tongue: at other times
He toss'd them with a false unnatural joy:
And 'twas a rueful thing to see the looks
Of the poor innocent children. "Every smile,"
Said Margaret to me, here beneath these trees, 620
"Made my heart bleed."
                At this the Wanderer paused;
And, looking up to those enormous Elms,
He said, "'Tis now the hour of deepest noon.—
At this still season of repose and peace,
This hour, when all things which are not at rest 625
Are chearful; while this multitude of flies
Is filling all the air with melody;
Why should a tear be in an Old Man's eye?

Why should we thus, with an untoward mind,
And in the weakness of humanity, 630
From natural wisdom turn our hearts away,
To natural comfort shut our eyes and ears,
And, feeding on disquiet, thus disturb
The calm of nature with our restless thoughts?"

———————

He spake with somewhat of a solemn tone: 635
But, when he ended, there was in his face
Such easy chearfulness, a look so mild,
That for a little time it stole away
All recollection, and that simple Tale
Passed from my mind like a forgotten sound. 640
A while on trivial things we held discourse,
To me soon tasteless. In my own despite
I thought of that poor Woman as of one
Whom I had known and loved. He had rehearsed
Her homely Tale with such familiar power, 645
With such an active countenance, an eye
So busy, that the things of which he spake
Seemed present; and, attention now relax'd,
There was a heart-felt chillness in my veins.—
I rose; and, turning from the breezy shade, 650
Went forth into the open air, and stood
To drink the comfort of the warmer sun.
Long time I had not staid, ere, looking round
Upon that tranquil Ruin, I return'd,
And begged of the Old Man that, for my sake, 655
He would resume his story.—
                    He replied,
"It were a wantonness, and would demand
Severe reproof, if we were Men whose hearts
Could hold vain dalliance with the misery
Even of the dead; contented thence to draw 660
A momentary pleasure, never marked
By reason, barren of all future good.

But we have known that there is often found
In mournful thoughts, and always might be found,
A power to virtue friendly; were't not so, 665
I am a Dreamer among men, indeed
An idle Dreamer! 'Tis a common Tale,
An ordinary sorrow of Man's life,
A tale of silent suffering, hardly clothed
In bodily form.—But, without further bidding, 670
I will proceed.—
              While thus it fared with them,
To whom this Cottage, till those hapless years,
Had been a blessed home, it was my chance
To travel in a Country far remote.
And glad I was, when, halting by yon gate 675
That leads from the green lane, once more I saw
These lofty elm-trees. Long I did not rest:
With many pleasant thoughts I chear'd my way
O'er the flat Common.—Having reached the door
I knock'd,—and, when I entered with the hope 680
Of usual greeting, Margaret looked at me
A little while; then turn'd her head away
Speechless,—and sitting down upon a chair
Wept bitterly. I wist not what to do,
Or how to speak to her. Poor Wretch! at last 685
She rose from off her seat, and then,—O Sir!
I cannot *tell* how she pronounced my name.—
With fervent love, and with a face of grief
Unutterably helpless, and a look
That seemed to cling upon me, she enquired 690
If I had seen her Husband. As she spake
A strange surprize and fear came to my heart,
Nor had I power to answer ere she told
That he had disappear'd—not two months gone.
He left his House: two wretched days had pass'd, 695
And on the third, as wistfully she rais'd
Her head from off her pillow, to look forth,

Like one in trouble, for returning light,
Within her chamber-casement she espied
A folded paper, lying as if placed 700
To meet her waking eyes. This tremblingly
She open'd—found no writing, but therein
Pieces of money carefully enclosed,
Silver and gold.—"I shuddered at the sight,"
Said Margaret, "for I knew it was his hand 705
Which placed it there: and ere that day was ended,
That long and anxious day! I learned from One
Sent hither by my Husband to impart
The heavy news,—that he had joined a Troop
Of Soldiers, going to a distant Land. 710
—He left me thus—he could not gather heart
To take a farewell of me; for he fear'd
That I should follow with my Babes, and sink
Beneath the misery of that wandering Life."

    This Tale did Margaret tell with many tears: 715
And when she ended I had little power
To give her comfort, and was glad to take
Such words of hope from her own mouth as served
To chear us both:—but long we had not talked
Ere we built up a pile of better thoughts, 720
And with a brighter eye she look'd around
As if she had been shedding tears of joy.
We parted.—'Twas the time of early spring;
I left her busy with her garden tools;
And well remember, o'er that fence she looked, 725
And, while I paced along the foot-way path,
Called out, and sent a blessing after me,
With tender chearfulness; and with a voice
That seem'd the very sound of happy thoughts.

    I roved o'er many a hill and many a dale, 730
With my accustomed load; in heat and cold,
Through many a wood, and many an open ground,

In sunshine and in shade, in wet and fair,
Drooping, or blithe of heart, as might befal;
My best companions now the driving winds, 735
And now the "trotting brooks" and whispering trees,
And now the music of my own sad steps,
With many a short-lived thought that pass'd between,
And disappeared.—I journey'd back this way
Towards the wane of Summer; when the wheat 740
Was yellow; and the soft and bladed grass
Springing afresh had o'er the hay-field spread
Its tender verdure. At the door arrived,
I found that she was absent. In the shade,
Where now we sit, I waited her return. 745
Her Cottage, then a chearful Object, wore
Its customary look,—only, I thought,
The honeysuckle, crowding round the porch,
Hung down in heavier tufts: and that bright weed,
The yellow stone-crop, suffered to take root 750
Along the window's edge, profusely grew,
Blinding the lower panes. I turned aside,
And strolled into her garden. It appeared
To lag behind the season, and had lost
Its pride of neatness. From the border lines 755
Composed of daisy and resplendent thrift,
Flowers straggling forth had on those paths encroached
Which they were used to deck:—Carnations, once
Prized for surpassing beauty, and no less
For the peculiar pains they had required, 760
Declined their languid heads—without support.
The cumbrous bind-weed, with its wreaths and bells,
Had twined about her two small rows of pease,
And dragged them to the earth.—Ere this an hour
Was wasted.—Back I turned my restless steps, 765
And, as I walked before the door, it chanced
A Stranger passed; and, guessing whom I sought,
He said that she was used to ramble far.—

The sun was sinking in the west; and now
I sate with sad impatience. From within   770
Her solitary Infant cried aloud;
Then, like a blast that dies away self-stilled,
The voice was silent. From the bench I rose;
But neither could divert nor soothe my thoughts.
The spot, though fair, was very desolate—   775
The longer I remained more desolate.
And, looking round, I saw the corner stones,
Till then unnotic'd, on either side the door
With dull red stains discolour'd, and stuck o'er
With tufts and hairs of wool, as if the Sheep,   780
That fed upon the Common, thither came
Familiarly; and found a couching-place
Even at her threshold. Deeper shadows fell
From these tall elms;—the Cottage-clock struck eight;—
I turned, and saw her distant a few steps.   785
Her face was pale and thin, her figure too
Was changed. As she unlocked the door, she said,
"It grieves me you have waited here so long,
But, in good truth, I've wandered much of late,
And, sometimes,—to my shame I speak, have need   790
Of my best prayers to bring me back again."
While on the board she spread our evening meal
She told me,—interrupting not the work
Which gave employment to her listless hands,
That she had parted with her elder Child;   795
To a kind Master on a distant farm
Now happily apprenticed—"I perceive
You look at me, and you have cause; to-day
I have been travelling far; and many days
About the fields I wander, knowing this   800
Only, that what I seek I cannot find.
And so I waste my time: for I am changed;
And to myself, said she, have done much wrong
And to this helpless Infant. I have slept

Weeping, and weeping I have waked; my tears 805
Have flowed as if my body were not such
As others are; and I could never die.
But I am now in mind and in my heart
More easy; and I hope," said she, "that heaven
Will give me patience to endure the things 810
Which I behold at home." It would have grieved
Your very soul to see her; Sir, I feel
The story linger in my heart: I fear
'Tis long and tedious; but my spirit clings
To that poor Woman:—so familiarly 815
Do I perceive her manner, and her look,
And presence, and so deeply do I feel
Her goodness, that, not seldom, in my walks
A momentary trance comes over me;
And to myself I seem to muse on One 820
By sorrow laid asleep;—or borne away,
A human being destined to awake
To human life, or something very near
To human life, when he shall come again
For whom she suffered. Yes, it would have grieved 825
Your very soul to see her: evermore
Her eyelids drooped, her eyes were downward cast;
And, when she at her table gave me food,
She did not look at me. Her voice was low,
Her body was subdued. In every act 830
Pertaining to her house affairs, appeared
The careless stillness of a thinking mind
Self-occupied; to which all outward things
Are like an idle matter. Still she sighed,
But yet no motion of the breast was seen, 835
No heaving of the heart. While by the fire
We sate together, sighs came on my ear,
I knew not how, and hardly whence they came.

   Ere my departure to her care I gave,
For her Son's use, some tokens of regard, 840

Which with a look of welcome She received;
And I exhorted her to have her trust
In God's good love, and seek his help by prayer.
I took my staff, and when I kissed her babe
The tears stood in her eyes. I left her then 845
With the best hope and comfort I could give;
She thanked me for my wish;—but for my hope
Methought she did not thank me.
        I returned,
And took my rounds along this road again
Ere on its sunny bank the primrose flower 850
Peeped forth, to give an earnest of the Spring.
I found her sad and drooping; she had learned
No tidings of her Husband; if he lived
She knew not that he lived; if he were dead
She knew not he was dead. She seem'd the same 855
In person and appearance; but her House
Bespake a sleepy hand of negligence.
The floor was neither dry nor neat, the hearth
Was comfortless, and her small lot of books,
Which, in the Cottage window, heretofore 860
Had been piled up against the corner panes
In seemly order, now, with straggling leaves
Lay scattered here and there, open or shut,
As they had chanced to fall. Her Infant Babe
Had from its Mother caught the trick of grief, 865
And sighed among its playthings. Once again
I turned towards the garden gate, and saw,
More plainly still, that poverty and grief
Were now come nearer to her: weeds defaced
The harden'd soil, and knots of wither'd grass; 870
No ridges there appeared of clear black mold,
No winter greenness; of her herbs and flowers,
It seemed the better part were gnawed away
Or trampled into earth; a chain of straw,
Which had been twined about the slender stem 875

Of a young apple-tree, lay at its root;
The bark was nibbled round by truant Sheep.
—Margaret stood near, her Infant in her arms,
And, noting that my eye was on the tree,
She said, "I fear it will be dead and gone   880
Ere Robert come again." Towards the House
Together we returned; and she enquired
If I had any hope:—but for her Babe
And for her little orphan Boy, she said,
She had no wish to live, that she must die   885
Of sorrow. Yet I saw the idle loom
Still in its place; his Sunday garments hung
Upon the self-same nail; his very staff
Stood undisturbed behind the door. And when,
In bleak December, I retraced this way,   890
She told me that her little Babe was dead,
And she was left alone. She now, released
From her maternal cares, had taken up
The employment common through these Wilds, and gain'd
By spinning hemp a pittance for herself;   895
And for this end had hired a neighbour's Boy
To give her needful help. That very time
Most willingly she put her work aside,
And walked with me along the miry road
Heedless how far; and, in such piteous sort   900
That any heart had ached to hear her, begged
That, wheresoe'er I went, I still would ask
For him whom she had lost. We parted then,
Our final parting; for from that time forth
Did many seasons pass ere I return'd   905
Into this tract again.
     Nine tedious years;
From their first separation, nine long years,
She lingered in unquiet widowhood;
A Wife and Widow. Needs must it have been
A sore heart-wasting! I have heard, my Friend,   910

That in yon arbour oftentimes she sate
Alone, through half the vacant Sabbath-day,
And if a dog passed by she still would quit
The shade, and look abroad. On this old Bench
For hours she sate; and evermore her eye 915
Was busy in the distance, shaping things
That made her heart beat quick. You see that path,
Now faint,—the grass has crept o'er its grey line;
There, to and fro, she paced through many a day
Of the warm summer, from a belt of hemp 920
That girt her waist, spinning the long drawn thread
With backward steps. Yet ever as there pass'd
A man whose garments shewed the Soldier's red,
Or crippled Mendicant in Sailor's garb,
The little Child who sate to turn the wheel 925
Ceas'd from his task; and she with faultering voice
Made many a fond enquiry; and when they,
Whose presence gave no comfort, were gone by,
Her heart was still more sad. And by yon gate,
That bars the Traveller's road, she often stood, 930
And when a stranger Horseman came the latch
Would lift, and in his face look wistfully;
Most happy, if, from aught discovered there
Of tender feeling, she might dare repeat
The same sad question. Meanwhile her poor Hut 935
Sank to decay: for he was gone—whose hand,
At the first nipping of October frost,
Closed up each chink, and with fresh bands of straw
Chequered the green-grown thatch. And so she lived
Through the long winter, reckless and alone; 940
Until her House by frost, and thaw, and rain,
Was sapped; and while she slept the nightly damps
Did chill her breast; and in the stormy day
Her tattered clothes were ruffled by the wind;
Even at the side of her own fire. Yet still 945
She loved this wretched spot, nor would for worlds

Have parted hence; and still that length of road,
   And this rude bench, one torturing hope endeared,
   Fast rooted at her heart: and here, my Friend,
   In sickness she remained; and here she died, 950
   Last human Tenant of these ruined Walls."

   The Old Man ceased: he saw that I was moved;
From that low Bench, rising instinctively
I turn'd aside in weakness, nor had power
To thank him for the Tale which he had told. 955
I stood, and leaning o'er the Garden wall,
Reviewed that Woman's sufferings; and it seemed
To comfort me while with a Brother's love
I bless'd her—in the impotence of grief.
At length towards the Cottage I returned 960
Fondly,—and traced, with interest more mild,
That secret spirit of humanity
Which, mid the calm oblivious tendencies
Of Nature, mid her plants, and weeds, and flowers,
And silent overgrowings, still survived. 965
The Old Man, noting this, resumed, and said,
"My Friend! enough to sorrow you have given,
The purposes of wisdom ask no more;
Be wise and chearful; and no longer read
The forms of things with an unworthy eye. 970
She sleeps in the calm earth, and peace is here.
I well remember that those very plumes,
Those weeds, and the high spear-grass on that wall,
By mist and silent rain-drops silver'd o'er,
As once I passed, did to my heart convey 975
So still an image of tranquillity,
So calm and still, and looked so beautiful
Amid the uneasy thoughts which filled my mind,
That what we feel of sorrow and despair
From ruin and from change, and all the grief 980
The passing shews of Being leave behind,
Appeared an idle dream, that could not live

Where meditation was. I turned away
And walked along my road in happiness."

He ceased. Ere long the sun declining shot 985
A slant and mellow radiance, which began
To fall upon us, while beneath the trees
We sate on that low Bench: and now we felt,
Admonished thus, the sweet hour coming on.
A linnet warbled from those lofty elms, 990
A thrush sang loud, and other melodies,
At distance heard, peopled the milder air.
The Old Man rose, and, with a sprightly mien
Of hopeful preparation, grasped his Staff:
Together casting then a farewell look 995
Upon those silent walls, we left the Shade;
And, ere the Stars were visible, had reached
A Village Inn,—our Evening resting-place.

END OF THE FIRST BOOK

BOOK THE SECOND

THE SOLITARY

In days of yore how fortunately fared
The Minstrel! wandering on from Hall to Hall,
Baronial Court or Royal; cheered with gifts
Munificent, and love, and Ladies' praise;
Now meeting on his road an armed Knight, 5
Now resting with a Pilgrim by the side
Of a clear brook;—beneath an Abbey's roof
One evening sumptuously lodged; the next
Humbly, in a religious Hospital;
Or with some merry Outlaws of the wood; 10
Or haply shrouded in a Hermit's cell.
Him, sleeping or awake, the Robber spared;

He walked—protected from the sword of war
By virtue of that sacred Instrument
His Harp, suspended at the Traveller's side; 15
His dear Companion wheresoe'er he went
Opening from Land to Land an easy way
By melody, and by the charm of verse.
Yet not the noblest of that honoured Race
Drew happier, loftier, more empassioned thoughts 20
From his long journeyings and eventful life,
Than this obscure Itinerant (an obscure,
But a high-souled and tender-hearted Man)
Had skill to draw from many a ramble, far
And wide protracted, through the tamer ground 25
Of these our unimaginative days;
Both while he trod the earth in humblest guise
Accoutred with his burthen and his staff;
And now, when free to move with lighter pace.

    What wonder, then, if I, whose favourite School 30
Hath been the fields, the roads, and rural lanes,
And pathways winding on from farm to farm,
Looked on this Guide with reverential love?
Each with the other pleased, we now pursued
Our journey—beneath favourable skies. 35
Turn wheresoe'er we would, he was a light
Unfailing: not a Hamlet could we pass,
Rarely a House, which did not yield to him
Remembrances; or from his tongue call forth
Some way-beguiling tale. Nor less regard 40
Accompanied those strains of apt discourse,
Which Nature's various objects might supply:
And in the silence of his face I read
His overflowing spirit. Birds and beasts,
And the mute fish that glances in the stream, 45
And harmless reptile coiling in the sun,
And gorgeous insect hovering in the air,
The fowl domestic, and the household dog,

In his capacious mind—he loved them all:
Their rights acknowledging he felt for all.   50
Oft was occasion given me to perceive
How the calm pleasures of the pasturing Herd
To happy contemplation soothed his walk
Along the field, and in the shady grove;
How the poor Brute's condition, forced to run   55
Its course of suffering in the public road,
Sad contrast! all too often smote his heart
With unavailing pity. Rich in love
And sweet humanity, he was, himself,
To the degree that he desired, beloved.   60
—Greetings and smiles we met with all day long
From faces that he knew; we took our seats
By many a cottage hearth, where he received
The welcome of an Inmate come from far.
—Nor was he loth to enter ragged Huts,   65
Wherein his charity was blessed; his voice
Heard as the voice of an experienced Friend.
And, sometimes, where the Poor Man held dispute
With his own mind, unable to subdue
Impatience, through inaptness to perceive   70
General distress in his particular lot;
Or cherishing resentment, or in vain
Struggling against it, with a soul perplexed,
And finding in itself no steady power
To draw the line of comfort that divides   75
Calamity, the chastisement of heaven,
From the injustice of our brother men;
To Him appeal was made as to a judge;
Who, with an understanding heart, allayed
The perturbation; listened to the plea;   80
Resolved the dubious point; and sentence gave
So grounded, so applied, that it was heard
With softened spirit,—even when it condemned.

    Such intercourse I witnessed, while we roved

Now as his choice directed, now as mine; 85
Or both, with equal readiness of will,
Our course submitting to the changeful breeze
Of accident. But when the rising sun
Had three times called us to renew our walk,
My Fellow Traveller said with earnest voice, 90
As if the thought were but a moment old,
That I must yield myself without reserve
To his disposal. Glad was I of this:
We started—and he led towards the hills;
Up through an ample vale, with higher hills 95
Before us, mountains stern and desolate;
But in the majesty of distance now
Set off, and to our ken appearing fair
Of aspect, with aerial softness clad,
And beautified with morning's purple beams. 100

   The Wealthy, the Luxurious, by the stress
Of business roused, or pleasure, ere their time,
May roll in chariots, or provoke the hoofs
Of the fleet coursers they bestride, to raise
From earth the dust of morning, slow to rise; 105
And They, if blessed with health and hearts at ease,
Shall lack not their enjoyment:—but how faint
Compared with our's! who, pacing side by side,
Could with an eye of leisure look on all
That we beheld; and lend the listening sense 110
To every grateful sound of earth and air,
Pausing at will; our spirits braced, our thoughts
Pleasant as roses in the thickets blown,
And pure as dew bathing their crimson leaves.

   Mount slowly Sun! and may our journey lie 115
Awhile within the shadow of this hill,
This friendly hill, a shelter from thy beams!
Such is the summer Pilgrim's frequent wish;
And as that wish, with prevalence of thanks

For present good o'er fear of future ill, 120
Stole in among the morning's blither thoughts,
'Twas chased away: for, tow'rds the western side
Of the broad Vale, casting a casual glance,
We saw a throng of People;—wherefore met?
Blithe notes of music, suddenly let loose 125
On the thrilled ear, did to the question yield
Prompt answer: they proclaim the annual Wake,
Which the bright season favours.—Tabor and Pipe
In purpose join to hasten and reprove
The laggard Rustic; and repay with boons 130
Of merriment a party-coloured Knot,
Already formed upon the Village green.
—Beyond the limits of the shadow cast
By the broad hill, glistened upon our sight
That gay Assemblage. Round them and above, 135
Glitter, with dark recesses interposed,
Casement, and cottage-roof, and stems of trees
Half-veiled in vapoury cloud, the silver steam
Of dews fast melting on their leafy boughs
By the strong sun-beams smitten. Like a mast 140
Of gold, the Maypole shines; as if the rays
Of morning, aided by exhaling dew,
With gladsome influence could reanimate
The faded garlands dangling from its sides.

   Said I, "the music and the sprightly scene 145
Invite us; shall we quit our road and join
These festive matins?"—He replied, "Not loth
Here would I linger, and with you partake,
Not one hour merely, but till evening's close,
The simple pastimes of the day and place. 150
By the fleet Racers, ere the Sun be set,
The turf of yon large pasture will be skimmed:
There, too, the lusty Wrestlers will contend:—
But know we not that he, who intermits
The appointed task and duties of the day, 155

Untunes full oft the pleasures of the day;
Checking the finer spirits that refuse
To flow, when purposes are lightly changed?
We must proceed—a length of journey yet
Remains untraced." Then, pointing with his staff   160
Towards those craggy summits, his intent
He thus imparted.
                    "In a spot that lies
Among yon mountain fastnesses concealed,
You will receive, before the hour of noon,
Good recompence, I hope, for this day's toil—   165
From sight of One who lives secluded there,
Lonesome and lost: of whom, and whose past life,
(Not to forestal such knowledge as may be
More faithfully collected from himself,)
This brief communication shall suffice.   170

   Though now sojourning there, he, like myself,
Sprang from a stock of lowly parentage
Among the wilds of Scotland; in a tract
Where many a sheltered and well-tended plant,
Upon the humblest ground of social life,   175
Doth at this day, I trust, the blossoms bear
Of piety and simple innocence.
Such grateful promises his youth displayed:
And, as he shewed in study forward zeal,
All helps were sought, all measures strained, that He,   180
By due scholastic discipline prepared,
Might to the Ministry be called: which done,
Partly through lack of better hopes—and part
Perhaps incited by a curious mind,
In early life he undertook the charge   185
Of Chaplain to a Military Troop
Cheered by the Highland Bagpipe, as they marched
In plaided vest,—his Fellow-countrymen.
This Office filling, and, by native power
And force of native inclination, made   190

An intellectual Ruler in the haunts
Of social vanity—he walked the World,
Gay, and affecting graceful gaiety;
Lax, buoyant—less a Pastor with his Flock
Than a Soldier among Soldiers—lived and roamed   195
Where Fortune led:—and Fortune, who oft proves
The careless wanderer's Friend, to him made known
A blooming Lady—a conspicuous Flower,
Admired for beauty, for her sweetness praised;
Whom he had sensibility to love,   200
Ambition to attempt, and skill to win.

   For this fair Bride, most rich in gifts of mind,
Nor sparingly endowed with worldly wealth,
His Office he relinquished; and retired
From the world's notice to a rural Home.   205
Youth's season yet with him was scarcely past,
And she was in youth's prime. How full their joy,
How free their love! nor did their love decay;
Nor joy abate, till, pitiable doom!
In the short course of one undreaded year   210
Death blasted all.—Death suddenly o'erthrew
Two lovely Children—all that they possessed!
The Mother followed:—miserably bare
The one Survivor stood; he wept, he prayed
For his dismissal; day and night, compelled   215
By pain to turn his thoughts towards the grave,
And face the regions of Eternity.
An uncomplaining apathy displaced
This anguish; and, indifferent to delight,
To aim and purpose, he consumed his days,   220
To private interest dead, and public care.
So lived he; so he might have died.
                              But now,
To the wide world's astonishment, appeared
The glorious opening, the unlooked-for dawn,
That promised everlasting joy to France!   225

That sudden light had power to pierce the gloom
In which his Spirit, friendless upon earth,
In separation dwelt, and solitude.
The voice of social transport reached even him!
He broke from his contracted bounds, repaired   230
To the great City, an Emporium then
Of golden expectations, and receiving
Freights every day from a new world of hope.
Thither his popular talents he transferred;
And from the Pulpit zealously maintained   235
The cause of Christ and civil liberty,
As one; and moving to one glorious end.
Intoxicating service! I might say
A happy service; for he was sincere
As vanity and fondness for applause,   240
And new and shapeless wishes, would allow.

    That righteous Cause of freedom did, we know,
Combine, for one hostility, as friends,
Etherial Natures and the worst of Slaves;
Was served by rival Advocates that came   245
From regions opposite as heaven and hell.
One courage seemed to animate them all:
And, from the dazzling conquests daily gained
By their united efforts, there arose
A proud and most presumptuous confidence   250
In the transcendent wisdom of the age,
And its discernment; not alone in rights,
And in the origin and bounds of power,
Social and temporal; but in laws divine,
Deduced by reason, or to faith revealed.   255
An overweening trust was raised; and fear
Cast out,—alike of person and of thing.
Plague from this union spread, whose subtle bane
The strongest did not easily escape;
And He, what wonder! took a mortal taint.   260
How shall I trace the change, how bear to tell

That he broke faith with those whom he had laid
In earth's dark chambers, with a Christian's hope!
An infidel contempt of holy writ
Stole by degrees upon his mind; and hence 265
Life, like that Roman Janus, double-faced;
Vilest hypocrisy, the laughing, gay
Hypocrisy, not leagued with fear, but pride.
Smooth words he had to wheedle simple souls;
But, for disciples of the inner school, 270
Old freedom was old servitude, and they
The wisest, whose opinions stooped the least
To known restraints: and who most boldly drew
Hopeful prognostications from a creed,
Which, in the light of false philosophy, 275
Spread like a halo round a misty moon,
Widening its circle as the storms advance.

    His sacred function was at length renounced;
And every day and every place enjoyed
The unshackled Layman's natural liberty; 280
Speech, manners, morals, all without disguise.
I do not wish to wrong him;—though the course
Of private life licentiously displayed
Unhallowed actions—planted like a crown
Upon the insolent aspiring brow 285
Of spurious notions—worn as open signs
Of prejudice subdued—he still retained,
'Mid such abasement, what he had received
From nature—an intense and glowing mind.
Wherefore, when humbled Liberty grew weak 290
And mortal sickness on her face appeared,
He coloured objects to his own desire
As with a Lover's passion. Yet his moods
Of pain were keen as those of better men,
Nay keener—as his fortitude was less. 295
And he continued, when worse days were come,
To deal about his sparkling eloquence,

Struggling against the strange reverse with zeal
That showed like happiness; but, in despite
Of all this outside bravery, within, 300
He neither felt encouragement nor hope.
For moral dignity, and strength of mind,
Were wanting; and simplicity of Life;
And reverence for himself; and, last and best,
Confiding thoughts, and love and fear of Him 305
Before whose sight the troubles of this world
Are vain as billows in a tossing sea.

    The glory of the times fading away,
The splendor, which had given a festal air
To self-importance, hallowed it, and veiled 310
From his own sight,—this gone, therewith he lost
All joy in human nature; was consumed,
And vexed, and chased, by levity and scorn,
And fruitless indignation; galled by pride;
Made desperate by contempt of Men who throve 315
Before his sight in power or fame, and won,
Without desert, what he desired; weak men,
Too weak even for his envy or his hate!
—And thus beset, and finding in himself
Nor pleasure nor tranquillity, at last, 320
After a wandering course of discontent
In foreign Lands, and inwardly oppressed
With malady—in part, I fear, provoked
By weariness of life, he fixed his Home,
Or, rather say, sate down by very chance, 325
Among these rugged hills; where now he dwells,
And wastes the sad remainder of his hours
In self-indulging spleen, that doth not want
Its own voluptuousness;—on this resolved,
With this content, that he will live and die 330
Forgotten,—at safe distance from a "world
Not moving to his mind."
                    These serious words

Closed the preparatory notices
With which my Fellow-traveller had beguiled
The way, while we advanced up that wide Vale. 335
Now, suddenly diverging, he began
To climb upon its western side a Ridge
Pathless and smooth, a long and steep ascent;
As if the object of his quest had been
Some secret of the Mountains, Cavern, Fall 340
Of water—or some boastful Eminence,
Renowned for splendid prospect far and wide.
We clomb without a track to guide our steps;
And, on the summit, reached a heathy plain,
With a tumultuous waste of huge hill tops 345
Before us; savage region! and I walked
In weariness: when, all at once, behold!
Beneath our feet, a little lowly Vale,
A lowly Vale, and yet uplifted high
Among the mountains; even as if the spot 350
Had been, from eldest time by wish of theirs,
So placed,—to be shut out from all the world!
Urn-like it was in shape, deep as an Urn;
With rocks encompassed, save that to the South
Was one small opening, where a heath-clad ridge 355
Supplied a boundary less abrupt and close.
A quiet treeless nook, with two green fields,
A liquid pool that glittered in the sun,
And one bare Dwelling; one Abode, no more!
It seemed the home of poverty and toil 360
Though not of want: the little fields, made green
By husbandry of many thrifty years,
Paid cheerful tribute to the moorland House.
—There crows the Cock, single in his domain:
The small birds find in spring no thicket there 365
To shroud them; only from the neighbouring Vales
The Cuckoo straggling up to the hill tops
Shouteth faint tidings of some gladder place.

Ah! what a sweet Recess, thought I, is here!
Instantly throwing down my limbs at ease 370
Upon a bed of heath;—full many a spot
Of hidden beauty have I chanced to espy
Among the mountains; never one like this;
So lonesome, and so perfectly secure:
Not melancholy—no, for it is green, 375
And bright, and fertile, furnished in itself
With the few needful things which life requires.
—In rugged arms how soft it seems to lie,
How tenderly protected! Far and near
We have an image of the pristine earth, 380
The planet in its nakedness; were this
Man's only dwelling, sole appointed seat,
First, last, and single in the breathing world,
It could not be more quiet: peace is here
Or no where; days unruffled by the gale 385
Of public news or private; years that pass
Forgetfully; uncalled upon to pay
The common penalties of mortal life,
Sickness, or accident, or grief, or pain.

  On these and other kindred thoughts intent, 390
In silence by my Comrade's side I lay,
He also silent: when from out the heart
Of that profound Abyss a solemn Voice,
Or several Voices in one solemn sound,
Was heard—ascending: mournful, deep, and slow 395
The cadence, as of Psalms—a funeral dirge!
We listened, looking down towards the Hut,
But seeing no One: meanwhile from below
The strain continued, spiritual as before;
And now distinctly could I recognize 400
These words;—*"Shall in the Grave thy love be known,
In Death thy faithfulness?"*—"God rest his Soul,"
The Wanderer cried, abruptly breaking silence,
"He is departed, and finds peace at last!"

This scarcely spoken, and those holy strains　　　405
Not ceasing, forth appeared in view a band
Of rustic Persons, from behind the hut
Bearing a Coffin in the midst, with which
They shaped their course along the sloping side
Of that small Valley; singing as they moved;　　　410
A sober company and few, the Men
Bare-headed, and all decently attired!
Some steps when they had thus advanced, the dirge
Ended; and, from the stillness that ensued
Recovering, to my Friend I said, "You spake,　　　415
Methought, with apprehension that these rites
Are paid to Him upon whose shy retreat
This day we purposed to intrude."—"I did so.
But let us hence, that we may learn the truth:
Perhaps it is not he but some One else　　　420
For whom this pious service is performed;
Some other Tenant of the Solitude."

　　So, to a steep and difficult descent
Trusting ourselves, we wound from crag to crag,
Where passage could be won; and, as the last　　　425
Of the mute train, upon the heathy top
Of that off-sloping Outlet, disappeared,
I, more impatient in the course I took,
Had landed upon easy ground; and there
Stood waiting for my Comrade. When behold　　　430
An object that enticed my steps aside!
It was an Entry, narrow as a door;
A passage whose brief windings opened out
Into a platform; that lay, sheepfold-wise,
Enclosed between a single mass of rock　　　435
And one old moss-grown wall;—a cool Recess,
And fanciful! For, where the rock and wall
Met in an angle, hung a tiny roof,
Or penthouse, which most quaintly had been framed
By thrusting two rude sticks into the wall　　　440

And overlaying them with mountain sods;
To weather-fend a little turf-built seat
Whereon a full-grown man might rest, nor dread
The burning sunshine, or a transient shower;
But the whole plainly wrought by Children's hands! 445
Whose simple skill had thronged the grassy floor
With work of frame less solid, a proud show
Of baby-houses, curiously arranged;
Nor wanting ornament of walks between,
With mimic trees inserted in the turf, 450
And gardens interposed. Pleased with the sight
I could not choose but beckon to my Guide,
Who, having entered, carelessly looked round,
And now would have passed on; when I exclaimed,
"Lo! what is here?" and, stooping down, drew forth 455
A Book, that, in the midst of stones and moss
And wreck of party-coloured earthen-ware,
Aptly disposed, had lent its help to raise
One of those petty structures. "Gracious Heaven!"
The Wanderer cried, "it cannot but be his, 460
And he is gone!" The Book, which in my hand
Had opened of itself, (for it was swoln
With searching damp, and seemingly had lain
To the injurious elements exposed
From week to week,) I found to be a work 465
In the French Tongue, a Novel of Voltaire,
His famous Optimist. "Unhappy Man!"
Exclaimed my Friend; "here then has been to him
Retreat within retreat, a sheltering-place
Within how deep a shelter! He had fits, 470
Even to the last, of genuine tenderness,
And loved the haunts of Children; here no doubt
He sometimes played with them; and here hath sate
Far oftener by himself. This Book, I guess,
Hath been forgotten in his careless way; 475
Left here when he was occupied in mind;

And by the Cottage Children has been found.
Heaven bless them, and their inconsiderate work;
To what odd purpose have the Darlings turned
This sad memorial of their hapless Friend!" 480

"Me, said I, most doth it surprize, to find
Such Book in such a place!" "A Book it is,"
He answered, "to the Person suited well,
Though little suited to surrounding things;
Nor, with the knowledge which my mind possessed, 485
Could I behold it undisturbed: 'tis strange,
I grant, and stranger still had been to see
The Man, who was its Owner, dwelling here,
With one poor Shepherd, far from all the world!
Now, if our errand hath been thrown away 490
As from these intimations I forebode,
Grieved shall I be—less for my sake than your's;
And least of all for Him who is no more."

By this the Book was in the Old Man's hand;
And he continued, glancing on the leaves 495
An eye of scorn. "The Lover," said he, "doomed
To love when hope hath failed him—whom no depth
Of privacy is deep enough to hide,
Hath yet his bracelet or his lock of hair,
And that is joy to him. When change of times 500
Hath summoned Kings to scaffolds, do but give
The faithful Servant, who must hide his head
Henceforth in whatsoever nook he may,
A kerchief sprinkled with his Master's blood,
And he too hath his comforter. How poor, 505
Beyond all poverty how destitute,
Must that Man have been left, who, hither driven,
Flying or seeking, could yet bring with him
No dearer relique, and no better stay,
Than this dull product of a Scoffer's pen, 510
Impure conceits discharging from a heart

Hardened by impious pride!—I did not fear
To tax you with this journey;"—mildly said
My venerable Friend, as forth we stepped
Into the presence of the cheerful light—   515
"For I have knowledge that you do not shrink
From moving spectacles;—but let us on."
So speaking, on he went, and at the word
I followed, till he made a sudden stand:
For full in view, approaching through the gate   520
That opened from the enclosure of green fields
Into the rough uncultivated ground,
Behold the Man whom he had fancied dead!
I knew, from the appearance and the dress,
That it could be no other; a pale face,   525
A tall and meagre person, in a garb
Not rustic, dull and faded like himself!
He saw us not, though distant but few steps;
For he was busy, dealing, from a store
Which on a leaf he carried in his hand,   530
Strings of ripe currants; gift by which he strove,
With intermixture of endearing words,
To soothe a Child, who walked beside him, weeping
As if disconsolate.—"They to the Grave
Are bearing him, my little One," he said,   535
"To the dark pit; but he will feel no pain;
His body is at rest, his soul in Heaven."

    Glad was my Comrade now, though he at first,
I doubt not, had been more surprized than glad.
But now, recovered from the shock and calm,   540
He soberly advanced; and to the Man
Gave cheerful greeting.—Vivid was the light
Which flashed at this from out the Other's eyes;
He was all fire: the sickness from his face
Passed like a fancy that is swept away;   545
Hands joined he with his Visitant,—a grasp,
An eager grasp; and, many moments' space,

When the first glow of pleasure was no more,
And much of what had vanished was returned,
An amicable smile retained the life 550
Which it had unexpectedly received,
Upon his hollow cheek. "How kind," he said,
"Nor could your coming have been better timed;
For this, you see, is in our little world
A day of sorrow. I have here a charge"— 555
And, speaking thus, he patted tenderly
The sun-burnt forehead of the weeping Child—
"A little Mourner whom it is my task
To comfort;—but how came Ye?—if yon track
(Which doth at once befriend us and betray) 560
Conducted hither your most welcome feet
Ye could not miss the Funeral Train—they yet
Have scarcely disappeared." "This blooming Child,"
Said the Old Man, "is of an age to weep
At any grave or solemn spectacle, 565
Inly distressed, or overpowered with awe,
He knows not why;—but he, perchance, this day,
Is shedding Orphan's tears; and you yourself
Must have sustained a loss."—"The hand of Death,"
He answered, "has been here; but could not well 570
Have fallen more lightly, if it had not fallen
Upon myself."—The Other left these words
Unnoticed, thus continuing.—
       "From yon Crag,
Down whose steep sides we dropped into the Vale,
We heard the hymn they sang—a solemn sound 575
Heard anywhere, but in a place like this
'Tis more than human! Many precious rites
And customs of our rural ancestry
Are gone, or stealing from us; this, I hope,
Will last for ever. Often have I stopped 580
When on my way, I could not chuse but stop,
So much I felt the awfulness of Life,

In that one moment when the Corse is lifted
In silence, with a hush of decency,
Then from the threshold moves with song of peace, 585
And confidential yearnings, to its home,
Its final home in earth. What Traveller—who—
(How far soe'er a Stranger) does not own
The bond of brotherhood, when he sees them go,
A mute Procession, on the houseless road, 590
Or passing by some single tenement
Or clustered dwellings, where again they raise
The monitory voice? But most of all
It touches, it confirms, and elevates,
Then, when the Body, soon to be consigned 595
Ashes to ashes, dust bequeathed to dust,
Is raised from the church-aisle, and forward borne
Upon the shoulders of the next in love,
The nearest in affection or in blood;
Yea by the very Mourners who had knelt 600
Beside the Coffin, resting on its lid
In silent grief their unuplifted heads,
And heard meanwhile the Psalmist's mournful plaint,
And that most awful scripture which declares
We shall not sleep, but we shall all be changed! 605
—Have I not seen?—Ye likewise may have seen
Son, Husband, Brothers—Brothers side by side,
And Son and Father also side by side,
Rise from that posture:—and in concert move,
On the green turf following the vested Priest, 610
Four dear Supporters of one senseless Weight,
From which they do not shrink, and under which
They faint not, but advance towards the grave
Step after step—together, with their firm
Unhidden faces; he that suffers most 615
He outwardly, and inwardly perhaps,
The most serene, with most undaunted eye!
Oh! blest are they who live and die like these,

Loved with such love, and with such sorrow mourned!"

"That poor Man taken hence to day," replied 620
The Solitary, with a faint sarcastic smile
Which did not please me, "must be deemed, I fear,
Of the unblest; for he will surely sink
Into his mother earth without such pomp
Of grief, depart without occasion given 625
By him for such array of fortitude.
Full seventy winters hath he lived, and mark!
This simple Child will mourn his one short hour,
And I shall miss him; scanty tribute! yet,
This wanting, he would leave the sight of men, 630
If love were his sole claim upon their care,
Like a ripe date which in the desert falls
Without a hand to gather it." At this
I interposed, though loth to speak, and said,
"Can it be thus among so small a band 635
As ye must needs be here? in such a place
I would not willingly, methinks, lose sight
Of a departing cloud."—"'Twas not for love"—
Answered the sick man with a careless voice—
"That I came hither; neither have I found 640
Among Associates who have power of speech,
Nor in such other converse as is here,
Temptation so prevailing as to change
That mood, or undermine my first resolve."—
Then, speaking in like careless sort, he said 645
To my benign Companion,—"Pity 'tis
That fortune did not guide you to this house
A few days earlier; then would you have seen
What stuff the Dwellers in this Solitude,
(That seems by Nature framed to be the seat 650
And very bosom of pure innocence)
Are made of; an ungracious matter this!
Which for truth's sake, yet in remembrance too
Of past discussions with this zealous Friend

And Advocate of humble life, I now 655
Will force upon his notice; undeterred
By the example of his own pure course,
And that respect and deference which a soul
May fairly claim, by niggard age enriched
In what it values most—the love of God 660
And his frail creature Man;—but ye shall hear.
I talk—and ye are standing in the sun
Without refreshment!"
               Saying this he led
Towards the Cottage;—homely was the spot;
And, to my feeling, ere we reached the door, 665
Had almost a forbidding nakedness;
Less fair, I grant, even painfully less fair,
Than it appeared when from the Valley's brink
We had looked down upon it. All within,
As left by that departed company, 670
Was silent; and the solitary clock
Ticked, as I thought, with melancholy sound.—
Following our Guide we clomb the cottage stairs
And reached a small apartment dark and low,
Which was no sooner entered than our Host 675
Said gaily, "This is my domain, my cell,
My hermitage, my cabin, what you will.—
I love it better than a snail his house.
But now Ye shall be feasted with our best."
So, with more ardour than an unripe girl 680
Left one day mistress of her mother's stores,
He went about his hospitable task.
My eyes were busy, and my thoughts no less,
And pleased I looked upon my grey-haired Friend
As if to thank him; he returned that look, 685
Cheered plainly, and yet serious. What a wreck
We had around us! scattered was the floor,
And, in like sort, chair, window-seat, and shelf,
With books, maps, fossils, withered plants and flowers,

And tufts of mountain moss; and here and there 690
Lay, intermixed with these, mechanic tools,
And scraps of paper,—some I could perceive
Scribbled with verse: a broken angling-rod
And shattered telescope, together linked
By cobwebs, stood within a dusty nook; 695
And instruments of music, some half-made,
Some in disgrace, hung dangling from the walls.
—But speedily the promise was fulfilled,
A feast before us, and a courteous Host
Inviting us in glee to sit and eat. 700
A napkin, white as foam of that rough brook
By which it had been bleached, o'erspread the board;
And was itself half-covered with a load
Of dainties,—oaten bread, curds, cheese, and cream,
And cakes of butter curiously embossed, 705
Butter that had imbibed a golden tinge,
A hue like that of yellow meadow flowers
Reflected faintly in a silent pool.
Nor lacked, for more delight on that warm day,
Our Table, small parade of garden fruits, 710
And whortle-berries from the mountain-sides.
The Child, who long ere this had stilled his sobs,
Was now a help to his late Comforter,
And moved a willing Page, as he was bid,
Ministering to our need.
                      In genial mood 715
While at our pastoral banquet thus we sate
Fronting the window of that little Cell,
I could not ever and anon forbear
To glance an upward look on two huge Peaks,
That from some other Vale peered into this. 720
"Those lusty Twins on which your eyes are cast,"
Exclaimed our Host, "if here you dwelt, would be
Your prized Companions.—Many are the notes
Which in his tuneful course the wind draws forth

From rocks, woods, caverns, heaths, and dashing shores;   725
And well those lofty Brethren bear their part
In the wild concert—chiefly when the storm
Rides high; then all the upper air they fill
With roaring sound, that ceases not to flow,
Like smoke, along the level of the blast   730
In mighty current; theirs, too, is the song
Of stream and headlong flood that seldom fails;
And, in the grim and breathless hour of noon,
Methinks that I have heard them echo back
The thunder's greeting:—nor have Nature's laws   735
Left them ungifted with a power to yield
Music of finer frame; a harmony,
So do I call it, though it be the hand
Of silence, though there be no voice;—the clouds,
The mist, the shadows, light of golden suns,   740
Motions of moonlight, all come thither—touch,
And have an answer—thither come, and shape
A language not unwelcome to sick hearts
And idle spirits:—there the sun himself
At the calm close of summer's longest day   745
Rests his substantial Orb;—between those heights
And on the top of either pinnacle,
More keenly than elsewhere in night's blue vault,
Sparkle the Stars as of their station proud.
Thoughts are not busier in the mind of man   750
Than the mute Agents stirring there:—alone
Here do I sit and watch.—"
                              With brightening face
The Wanderer heard him speaking thus, and said,
"Now for the Tale with which you threatened us!"
"In truth the threat escaped me unawares   755
And was forgotten. Let this challenge stand
For my excuse, if what I shall relate
Tire your attention.—Outcast and cut off
As we seem here, and must have seemed to you

When ye looked down upon us from the crag, 760
Islanders of a stormy Mountain sea,
We are not so;—perpetually we touch
Upon the vulgar ordinance of the world,
And he, whom this our Cottage hath to-day
Relinquished, was dependant for his bread 765
Upon the laws of public charity.
The Housewife, tempted by such slender gains
As might from that occasion be distilled,
Opened, as she before had done for me,
Her doors to admit this homeless Pensioner; 770
The portion gave of coarse but wholesome fare
Which appetite required—a blind dull nook
Such as she had—the *kennel* of his rest!
This, in itself not ill, would yet have been
Ill borne in earlier life; but his was now 775
The still contentedness of seventy years.
Calm did he sit beneath the wide-spread tree
Of his old age; and yet less calm and meek,
Winningly meek or venerably calm,
Than slow and torpid; paying in this wise 780
A penalty, if penalty it were,
For spendthrift feats, excesses of his prime.
I loved the Old Man, for I pitied him!
A task it was, I own, to hold discourse
With One so slow in gathering up his thoughts, 785
But he was a cheap pleasure to my eyes;
Mild, inoffensive, ready in *his* way,
And useful to his utmost power: and there
Our Housewife knew full well what she possess'd!
He was her Vassal of all labour, tilled 790
Her garden, from the pasture fetched her Kine;
And, one among the orderly array
Of Hay-makers, beneath the burning sun
Maintained his place; or heedfully pursued
His course, on errands bound, to other vales, 795

Leading sometimes an inexperienced Child
Too young for any profitable task.
So moved he like a Shadow that performed
Substantial service. Mark me now, and learn
For what reward! The Moon her monthly round   800
Hath not completed since our Dame, the Queen
Of this one cottage and this lonely dale,
Into my little sanctuary rushed,
Voice to a rueful treble humanized,
And features in deplorable dismay.—   805
I treat the matter lightly, but alas!
It is most serious: from mid-noon the rain
Had fallen in torrents; all the mountain tops
Were hidden, and black vapours coursed their sides;
This had I seen and saw; but, till she spake,   810
Was wholly ignorant that my ancient Friend,
Who at her bidding, early and alone,
Had clomb aloft to delve the mountain turf
For winter fuel, to his noontide meal
Came not, and now perchance upon the Heights   815
Lay at the mercy of this raging storm.
"Inhuman!"—said I, "was an Old Man's life
Not worth the trouble of a thought?—alas!
This notice comes too late." With joy I saw
Her Husband enter—from a distant Vale.   820
We sallied forth together; found the tools
Which the neglected Veteran had dropped,
But through all quarters looked for him in vain.
We shouted—but no answer! Darkness fell
Without remission of the blast or shower,   825
And fears for our own safety drove us home.
I, who weep little, did, I will confess,
The moment I was seated here alone,
Honour my little Cell with some few tears
Which anger or resentment could not dry.   830
All night the storm endured; and, soon as help
Had been collected from the neighbouring Vale,

With morning we renewed our quest: the wind
Was fallen, the rain abated, but the hills
Lay shrouded in impenetrable mist; 835
And long and hopelessly we sought in vain.
Till, chancing by yon lofty ridge to pass
A heap of ruin, almost without walls
And wholly without roof (in ancient time
It was a Chapel, a small Edifice 840
In which the Peasants of these lonely Dells
For worship met upon that central height)—
Chancing to pass this wreck of stones, we there
Espied at last the Object of our search,
Couched in a nook, and seemingly alive. 845
It would have moved you, had you seen the guise
In which he occupied his chosen bed,
Lying full three parts buried among tufts
Of heath-plant, under and above him strewn,
To baffle, as he might, the watery storm: 850
And there we found him breathing peaceably,
Snug as a Child that hides itself in sport
Mid a green hay-cock in a sunny field.
We spake—he made reply, but would not stir
At our entreaty; less from want of power 855
Than apprehension and bewildering thoughts.
So was he lifted gently from the ground,
And with their freight the Shepherds homeward moved
Through the dull mist, I following—when a step,
A single step, that freed me from the skirts 860
Of the blind vapour, opened to my view
Glory beyond all glory ever seen
By waking sense or by the dreaming soul!
—Though I am conscious that no power of words
Can body forth, no hues of speech can paint 865
That gorgeous spectacle—too bright and fair
Even for remembrance; yet the attempt may give
Collateral interest to this homely Tale.
The Appearance, instantaneously disclosed,
Was of a mighty City—boldly say 870

A wilderness of building, sinking far
And self-withdrawn into a wondrous depth,
Far sinking into splendor—without end!
Fabric it seemed of diamond and of gold,
With alabaster domes, and silver spires; 875
And blazing terrace upon terrace high
Uplifted; here, serene pavilions bright,
In avenues disposed; there, towers begirt
With battlements that on their restless fronts
Bore stars—illumination of all gems! 880
By earthly nature had the effect been wrought
Upon the dark materials of the storm
Now pacified; on them, and on the coves
And mountain-steeps and summits, whereunto
The vapours had receded, taking there 885
Their station under a cerulean sky.
O, 'twas an unimaginable sight!
Clouds, mists, streams, watery rocks and emerald turf,
Clouds of all tincture, rocks and sapphire sky,
Confused, commingled, mutually inflamed, 890
Molten together, and composing thus,
Each lost in each, that marvellous array
Of temple, palace, citadel, and huge
Fantastic pomp of structure without name,
In fleecy folds voluminous, enwrapp'd. 895
Right in the midst, where interspace appeared
Of open court, an object like a throne
Beneath a shining canopy of state
Stood fixed; and fixed resemblances were seen
To implements of ordinary use, 900
But vast in size, in substance glorified;
Such as by Hebrew Prophets were beheld
In vision—forms uncouth of mightiest power,
For admiration and mysterious awe.
Below me was the earth; this little Vale 905
Lay low beneath my feet; 'twas visible—

I saw not, but I felt that it was there.
That which I *saw* was the revealed abode
Of Spirits in beatitude: my heart
Swelled in my breast.—"I have been dead," I cried, 910
"And now I live! Oh! wherefore do I live?"
And with that pang I prayed to be no more!—
—But I forget our Charge, as utterly
I then forgot him:—there I stood and gazed;
The apparition faded not away, 915
And I descended.—Having reached the House
I found its rescued Inmate safely lodged,
And in serene possession of himself,
Beside a genial fire; that seemed to spread
A gleam of comfort o'er his pallid face. 920
Great shew of joy the Housewife made, and truly
Was glad to find her conscience set at ease;
And not less glad, for sake of her good name,
That the poor Sufferer had escaped with life.
But, though he seemed at first to have received 925
No harm, and uncomplaining as before
Went through his usual tasks, a silent change
Soon shewed itself; he lingered three short weeks;
And from the Cottage hath been borne to-day.

  So ends my dolorous Tale, and glad I am 930
That it is ended." At these words he turned—
And, with blithe air of open fellowship,
Brought from the Cupboard wine and stouter cheer,
Like one who would be merry. Seeing this
My grey-haired Friend said courteously—"Nay, nay, 935
You have regaled us as a Hermit ought;
Now let us forth into the sun!"—Our Host
Rose, though reluctantly, and forth we went.

END OF THE SECOND BOOK.

BOOK THE THIRD

DESPONDENCY

A humming Bee—a little tinkling Rill—
A pair of Falcons, wheeling on the wing,
In clamorous agitation, round the crest
Of a tall rock, their airy Citadel—
By each and all of these the pensive ear   5
Was greeted, in the silence that ensued,
When through the Cottage-threshold we had passed,
And, deep within that lonesome Valley, stood
Once more, beneath the concave of the blue
And cloudless sky.—Anon! exclaimed our Host,   10
Triumphantly dispersing with the taunt
The shade of discontent which on his brow
Had gathered,—"Ye have left my Cell,—but see
How Nature hems you in with friendly arms!
And by her help ye are my Prisoners still.   15
But which way shall I lead you?—how contrive,
In Spot so parsimoniously endowed,
That the brief hours, which yet remain, may reap
Some recompence of knowledge or delight?"
So saying, round he looked, as if perplexed;   20
And, to remove those doubts, my grey-haired Friend
Said—"Shall we take this pathway for our guide?—
Upwards it winds, as if, in summer heats,
Its line had first been fashioned by the flock
A place of refuge seeking at the root   25
Of yon black yew-tree; whose protruded boughs
Darken the silver bosom of the crag,
From which it draws its meagre sustenance.
There in commodious shelter may we rest.
Or let us trace this Streamlet to its source;   30
Feebly it tinkles with an earthy sound,
And a few steps may bring us to the spot
Where, haply, crowned with flowerets and green herbs,

The mountain Infant to the sun comes forth,
Like human Life from darkness."—At the word   35
We followed where he led:—a sudden turn
Through a strait passage of encumbered ground,
Proved that such hope was vain:—for now we stood
Shut out from prospect of the open Vale,
And saw the water, that composed this Rill,   40
Descending, disembodied, and diffused
O'er the smooth surface of an ample Crag,
Lofty, and steep, and naked as a Tower.
All further progress here was barred;—And who,
Thought I, if master of a vacant hour,   45
Here would not linger, willingly detained?
Whether to such wild objects he were led
When copious rains have magnified the stream
Into a loud and white-robed Waterfall,
Or introduced at this more quiet time.   50

   Upon a semicirque of turf-clad ground,
The hidden nook discovered to our view
A Mass of rock, resembling, as it lay
Right at the foot of that moist precipice,
A stranded Ship, with keel upturned,—that rests   55
Fearless of winds and waves. Three several Stones
Stood near, of smaller size, and not unlike
To monumental pillars: and, from these
Some little space disjoined, a pair were seen,
That, with united shoulders bore aloft   60
A Fragment, like an Altar, flat and smooth.
Barren the tablet, yet thereon appeared,
Conspicuously stationed, one fair Plant,
A tall and shining Holly, which had found
A hospitable chink, and stood upright,   65
As if inserted by some human hand,
In mockery, to wither in the sun,
Or lay its beauty flat before a breeze,
The first that entered. But no breeze did now

Find entrance;—high, or low, appeared no trace 70
Of motion, save the Water that descended,
Diffused adown that Barrier of steep rock,
And softly creeping, like a breath of air,
Such as is sometimes seen, and hardly seen,
To brush the still breast of a chrystal Lake. 75

   "Behold a Cabinet for Sages built,
Which Kings might envy!"—Praise to this effect
Broke from the happy Old Man's reverend lip;
Who to the Solitary turned, and said,
"In sooth, with love's familiar privilege, 80
You have decried, in no unseemly terms
Of modesty, that wealth which is your own.
Among these Rocks and Stones, methinks, I see
More than the heedless impress that belongs
To lonely Nature's casual work: they bear 85
A semblance strange of power intelligent,
And of design not wholly worn away.
Boldest of plants that ever faced the wind,
How gracefully that slender Shrub looks forth
From its fantastic birth-place! And I own, 90
Some shadowy intimations haunt me here,
I cannot but incline to a belief
That in these shows a chronicle survives
Of purposes akin to those of Man,
But wrought with mightier arm than now prevails. 95
—Voiceless the Stream descends into the gulph
With timid lapse;—and lo! while in this Strait
I stand—the chasm of sky above my head
Is heaven's profoundest azure; no domain
For fickle, short-lived clouds to occupy, 100
Or to pass through, but rather an Abyss
In which the everlasting Stars abide;
And whose soft gloom, and boundless depth, might tempt
The curious eye to look for them by day.
—Hail Contemplation! from the stately towers, 105

Reared by the industrious hand of human Art
To lift thee high above the misty air,
And turbulence, of murmuring cities vast;
From academic groves, that have for thee
Been planted, hither come and find a Lodge 110
To which thou mayest resort for holier peace,—
From whose calm centre Thou, through height or depth,
Mayest penetrate, wherever Truth shall lead;
Measuring through all degrees, until the scale
Of time and conscious Nature disappear, 115
Lost in unsearchable Eternity!"[1]

   A pause ensued; and with minuter care
We scanned the various features of the scene:
And soon the Tenant of that lonely Vale
With courteous voice thus spake—
                            "I should have grieved 120
Hereafter, should perhaps have blamed myself,
If from my poor Retirement ye had gone
Leaving this Nook unvisited: but, in sooth,
Your unexpected presence had so roused
My spirits, that they were bent on enterprize; 125
And, like an ardent Hunter, I forgot,
Or, shall I say?—disdained, the game that lurked
At my own door. The shapes before our eyes,
And their arrangement, doubtless must be deemed
The sport of Nature, aided by blind Chance 130
Rudely to mock the works of toiling Man.
And hence, this upright Shaft of unhewn stone,
From Fancy, willing to set off her stores
By sounding Titles, hath acquired the name
Of Pompey's Pillar; that I gravely style 135

---

1 "Since this paragraph was composed I have read with so much pleasure, in Burnet's Theory of the Earth, a passage expressing correspondent sentiments, excited by objects of a similar nature, that I cannot forbear to transcribe it." WW. WW gave the passage from Thomas Burnet's *Telluris Theoria Sacra* (2nd ed., 1688–1689) in the original Latin. See the notes to this line in the Cornell edition of *The Excursion* (2008) for the quotation and a translation.

My Theban Obelisk; and, there, behold
A Druid Cromlech!—thus I entertain
The antiquarian humour, and am pleased
To skim along the surfaces of things,
Beguiling harmlessly the listless hours.   140
But, if the spirit be oppressed by sense
Of instability, revolt, decay,
And change, and emptiness, these freaks of Nature
And her blind helper Chance, do *then* suffice
To quicken, and to aggravate, to feed   145
Pity and scorn, and melancholy pride,
Not less than that huge Pile (from some abyss
Of mortal power unquestionably sprung)
Whose hoary Diadem of pendant rocks
Confines the shrill-voiced whirlwind, round and round   150
Eddying within its vast circumference,
On Sarum's naked plain;—than Pyramid
Of Egypt, unsubverted, undissolved;
Or Syria's marble Ruins towering high
Above the sandy Desart, in the light   155
Of sun or moon.—Forgive me, if I say
That an appearance, which hath raised your minds
To an exalted pitch, (the self-same cause
Different effect producing) is for me
Fraught rather with depression than delight,   160
Though shame it were, could I not look around me,
By the reflection of your pleasure, pleased.
Yet happier, in my judgment, even than you,
With your bright transports, fairly may be deemed,
Is He (if such have ever entered here)   165
The wandering Herbalist,—who, clear alike
From vain, and, that worse evil, vexing thoughts,
Casts on these uncouth Forms a slight regard
Of transitory interest, and peeps round
For some rare Floweret of the hills, or Plant   170
Of craggy fountain; what he hopes for wins,

Or learns, at least, that 'tis not to be won:
Then, keen and eager, as a fine-nosed Hound
By soul-engrossing instinct driven along
Through wood or open field, the harmless Man 175
Departs, intent upon his onward quest!
Nor is that Fellow-wanderer, so deem I,
Less to be envied (you may trace him oft
By scars which his activity has left
Beside our roads and pathways, though, thank heaven! 180
This covert nook reports not of his hand)
He, who with pocket hammer smites the edge
Of every luckless rock or stone that stands
Before his sight, by weather-stains disguised,
Or crusted o'er with vegetation thin, 185
Nature's first growth, detaching by the stroke
A chip, or splinter,—to resolve his doubts;
And, with that ready answer satisfied,
Doth to the substance give some barbarous name,
Then hurries on; or from the fragments picks 190
His specimen, if haply interveined
With sparkling mineral, or should chrystal cube
Lurk in its cells—and thinks himself enriched,
Wealthier, and doubtless wiser, than before!
Entrusted safely—each to his pursuit, 195
This earnest Pair may range from hill to hill,
And, if it please them, speed from clime to clime;
The mind is full—no pain is in their sport."

"Then," said I, interposing, "One is near
Who cannot but possess in your esteem 200
Place worthier still of envy. May I name,
Without offence, that fair-faced Cottage-boy?
Dame Nature's Pupil of the lowest Form,
Youngest Apprentice in the School of Art!
Him, as we entered from the open Glen, 205
You might have noticed, busily engaged,
Heart, soul, and hands,—in mending the defects

Left in the fabric of a leaky dam,
Framed for enabling this penurious stream
To turn a slender mill (that new-made plaything)   210
For his delight—the happiest he of all!"

   "Far happiest," answered the desponding Man,
"If, such as now he is, he might remain!
Ah! what avails Imagination high
Or Question deep? what profits all that Earth,   215
Or Heaven's blue Vault, is suffered to put forth
Of impulse or allurement, for the Soul
To quit the beaten track of life, and soar
Far as she finds a yielding element
In past or future; far as she can go   220
Through time or space; if neither in the one
Nor in the other region, nor in aught
That Fancy, dreaming o'er the map of things,
Hath placed beyond these penetrable bounds,
Words of assurance can be heard; if no where   225
A habitation, for consummate good,
Or for progressive virtue, by the search
Can be attained, a better sanctuary
From doubt and sorrow, than the senseless grave?"

   "Is this," the grey-haired Wanderer mildly said,   230
"The voice, which we so lately overheard,
To that same Child, addressing tenderly
The Consolations of a hopeful mind?
'His body is at rest, his soul in heaven.'
These were your words; and, verily, methinks   235
Wisdom is oft-times nearer when we stoop
Than when we soar."—
                      The Other, not displeased,
Promptly replied—"My notion is the same.
And I, without reluctance, could decline
All act of inquisition whence we rise,   240
And what, when breath hath ceased, we may become.

Here are we, in a bright and breathing World!
Our origin, what matters it? In lack
Of worthier explanation, say at once
With the American (a thought which suits   245
The place where now we stand) that certain Men
Leapt out together from a rocky Cave;
And these were the first Parents of Mankind!
Or, if a different image be recalled
By the warm sunshine, and the jocund voice   250
Of insects—chirping out their careless lives
On these soft beds of thyme-besprinkled turf,
Chuse, with the gay Athenian, a conceit
As sound; with that blithe race who wore ere-while
Their golden Grasshoppers, in sign that they 255
Had sprung from out the soil whereon they dwelt.
But stop!—these theoretic fancies jar
On serious minds; for doubtless, in one sense,
The theme is serious; then, as Hindoos draw
Their holy Ganges from a skiey fount,   260
Even so deduce the Stream of human Life
From seats of Power divine; and hope, or trust,
That our Existence winds its stately course
Beneath the Sun, like Ganges, to make part
Of a living Ocean: or, if such may seem   265
Its tendency, to be engulphed and lost
Like Niger, in impenetrable sands
And utter darkness: thought which may be faced,
Though comfortless!—Not of myself I speak;
Such acquiescence neither doth imply,   270
In me, a meekly-bending spirit—soothed
By natural piety; nor a lofty mind,
By philosophic discipline prepared
For calm subjection to acknowledged law;
Pleased to have been, contented not to be.   275
Such palms I boast not:—no! to me, who find,
Reviewing my past way, much to condemn,

Little to praise, and nothing to regret
(Save some remembrances of dream-like joys
That scarcely seem to have belonged to me) 280
If I must take my choice between the pair
That rule alternately the weary hours,
Night is than day more acceptable;—sleep
Doth, in my estimate of good, appear
A better state than waking; death than sleep: 285
Feelingly sweet is stillness after storm,
Though under covert of the wormy ground!

    Yet be it said, in justice to myself,
That in more genial times, when I was free
To explore the destiny of human kind; 290
Not as an intellectual game pursued
With curious subtilty, thereby to cheat
Irksome sensations; but by love of truth
Urged on, or haply by intense delight
In feeding thought, wherever thought could feed; 295
I did not rank with those (too dull or nice,
For to my judgment such they then appeared,
Or too aspiring, thankless at the best)
Who, in this frame of human life, perceive
An object whereunto their souls are tied 300
In discontented wedlock; nor did e'er,
From me, those dark, impervious shades, that hang
Upon the region whither we are bound,
Exclude a power to enjoy the vital beams
Of present sunshine.—Deities that float 305
On wings, angelic Spirits, I could muse
O'er what from eldest time we have been told
Of your bright forms and glorious faculties,
And with the imagination be content,
Not wishing more; repining not to tread 310
The little sinuous path of earthly care,
By flowers embellished, and by springs refreshed.
—"Blow winds of Autumn!—let your chilling breath

"Take the live herbage from the mead, and strip
"The shady forest of its green attire,— 315
"And let the bursting Clouds to fury rouse
"The gentle Brooks!—Your desolating sway,"
Thus I exclaimed, "no sadness sheds on me,
"And no disorder in your rage I find.
"What dignity, what beauty, in this change 320
"From mild to angry, and from sad to gay,
"Alternate and revolving! How benign,
"How rich in animation and delight,
"How bountiful these elements—compared
"With aught, as more desirable and fair, 325
"Devised by Fancy for the Golden Age;
"Or the perpetual warbling that prevails
"In Arcady, beneath unaltered skies,
"Through the long year in constant quiet bound,
"Night hush'd as night, and day serene as day!" 330
—But why this tedious record?—Age we know
Is garrulous; and solitude is apt
To anticipate the privilege of Age.
From far ye come; and surely with a hope
Of better entertainment—let us hence!" 335

   Loth to forsake the spot, and still more loth
To be diverted from our present theme,
I said, "My thoughts, agreeing, Sir, with yours,
Would push this censure farther;—for, if smiles
Of scornful pity be the just reward 340
Of Poesy, thus courteously employed
In framing models to improve the scheme
Of Man's existence, and recast the world,
Why should not grave Philosophy be stiled,
Herself, a Dreamer of a kindred stock, 345
A Dreamer yet more spiritless and dull?
Yes," said I, "shall the immunities to which
She doth lay claim, the precepts she bestows,
Establish sounder titles of esteem

For Her, who (all too timid and reserved   350
For onset, for resistance too inert,
Too weak for suffering, and for hope too tame)
Did place, in flowery Gardens curtained round
With world-excluding groves, the Brotherhood
Of soft Epicureans, taught—if they   355
The ends of being would secure, and win
The crown of wisdom—to yield up their souls
To a voluptuous unconcern, preferring
Tranquillity to all things. Or is She,"
I cried, "more worthy of regard, the Power,   360
Who, for the sake of sterner quiet, closed
The Stoic's heart against the vain approach
Of admiration, and all sense of joy?"

   His Countenance gave notice that my zeal
Accorded little with his present mind;   365
I ceased, and he resumed.—"Ah! gentle Sir,
Slight, if you will, the *means*; but spare to slight
The *end* of those, who did, by system, rank,
As the prime object of a wise Man's aim,
Security from shock of accident,   370
Release from fear; and cherished peaceful days
For their own sakes, as mortal life's chief good,
And only reasonable felicity.
What motive drew, what impulse, I would ask,
Through a long course of later ages, drove   375
The Hermit to his Cell in forest wide;
Or what detained him, till his closing eyes
Took their last farewell of the sun and stars,
Fast anchored in the desart?—Not alone
Dread of the persecuting sword—remorse,   380
Wrongs unredressed, or insults unavenged
And unavengeable, defeated pride,
Prosperity subverted, maddening want,
Friendship betrayed, affection unreturned,
Love with despair, or grief in agony:—   385

Not always from intolerable pangs
He fled; but, compassed round by pleasure, sighed
For independent happiness; craving peace,
The central feeling of all happiness,
Not as a refuge from distress or pain, 390
A breathing-time, vacation, or a truce,
But for its absolute self; a life of peace,
Stability without regret or fear;
That hath been, is, and shall be evermore!
Such the reward he sought; and wore out Life, 395
There, where on few external things his heart
Was set, and those his own; or, if not his,
Subsisting under Nature's steadfast law.

   What other yearning was the master tie
Of the monastic Brotherhood; upon Rock 400
Aerial, or in green secluded Vale,
One after one, collected from afar,
An undissolving Fellowship?—What but this,
The universal instinct of repose,
The longing for confirmed tranquillity, 405
Inward and outward; humble, yet sublime:—
The life where hope and memory are as one;
Earth quiet and unchanged; the human Soul
Consistent in self-rule; and heaven revealed
To meditation, in that quietness! 410
Such was their scheme:—thrice happy he who gained
The end proposed! And,—though the same were missed
By multitudes, perhaps obtained by none,—
They, for the attempt, and for the pains employed,
Do, in my present censure, stand redeemed 415
From the unqualified disdain, that once
Would have been cast upon them, by my Voice
Delivering its decisions from the seat
Of forward Youth:—that scruples not to solve
Doubts, and determine questions, by the rules 420
Of inexperienced judgment, ever prone

To overweening faith; and is inflamed,
By courage, to demand from real life
The test of act and suffering—to provoke
Hostility, how dreadful when it comes, 425
Whether affliction be the foe, or guilt!

   A Child of earth, I rested, in that stage
Of my past course to which these thoughts advert,
Upon earth's native energies; forgetting
That mine was a condition which required 430
Nor energy, nor fortitude—a calm
Without vicissitude; which, if the like
Had been presented to my view elsewhere,
I might have even been tempted to despise.
But that which was serene was also bright; 435
Enlivened happiness with joy o'erflowing,
With joy, and—oh! that memory should survive
To speak the word—with rapture! Nature's boon,
Life's genuine inspiration, happiness
Above what rules can teach, or fancy feign; 440
Abused, as all possessions are abused
That are not prized according to their worth.
And yet, what worth? what good is given to Men,
More solid than the gilded clouds of heaven,
What joy more lasting than a vernal flower? 445
None! 'tis the general plaint of human kind
In solitude, and mutually addressed
From each to all, for wisdom's sake:—This truth
The Priest announces from his holy seat;
And, crowned with garlands in the summer grove, 450
The Poet fits it to his pensive Lyre.
Yet, ere that final resting-place be gained,
Sharp contradictions hourly shall arise
To cross the way; and we, perchance, by doom
Of this same life, shall be compelled to grieve 455
That the prosperities of love and joy
Should be permitted, oft-times, to endure

So long, and be at once cast down for ever.
Oh! tremble Ye to whom hath been assigned
A course of days composing happy months, 460
And they as happy years; the present still
So like the past, and both, so firm a pledge
Of a congenial future, that the wheels
Of pleasure move without the aid of hope.
For Mutability is Nature's bane; 465
And slighted Hope will be avenged; and, when
Ye need her favours, Ye shall find her not;
But, in her stead—fear—doubt—and agony!"

   This was the bitter language of the heart;
But, while he spake, look, gesture, tone of voice, 470
Though discomposed and vehement, were such
As skill and graceful Nature might suggest
To a Proficient of the tragic scene,
Standing before the multitude, beset
With sorrowful events; and we, who heard 475
And saw, were moved. Desirous to divert,
Or stem, the current of the Speaker's thoughts,
We signified a wish to leave that Place
Of stillness and close privacy, which seemed
A nook for self-examination framed, 480
Or, for confession, in the sinner's need,
Hidden from all Men's view. To our attempt
He yielded not; but, pointing to a slope
Of mossy turf, defended from the sun;
And, on that couch inviting us to rest, 485
Towards that tender-hearted Man he turned
A serious eye, and thus his speech renewed.

   "You never saw, your eyes did never look
On the bright Form of Her whom once I loved.—
Her silver voice was heard upon the earth, 490
A sound unknown to you; else, honored Friend,
Your heart had borne a pitiable share

Of what I suffered, when I wept that loss,
And suffer now, not seldom, from the thought
That I remember, and can weep no more.— 495
Stripped as I am of all the golden fruit
Of self-esteem; and by the cutting blasts
Of self-reproach familiarly assailed;
I would not yet be of such wintry bareness,
But that some leaf of your regard should hang 500
Upon my naked branches:—lively thoughts
Give birth, full often, to unguarded words;
I grieve that, in your presence, from my tongue
Too much of frailty hath already dropped;
But that too much demands still more.
        You know, 505
Revered Compatriot;—and to you, kind Sir
(Not to be deemed a Stranger as you come
Following the guidance of these welcome feet
To our secluded Vale) it may be told,
That my demerits did not sue in vain 510
To One, on whose mild radiance many gazed
With hope, and all, with pleasure. This fair Bride—
In the devotedness of youthful Love
Preferring me to Parents, and the choir
Of gay companions, to the natal roof, 515
And all known places and familiar sights,
(Resigned with sadness gently weighing down
Her trembling expectations, but no more
Than did to her due honour, and to me
Yielded, that day, a confidence sublime 520
In what I had to build upon)—this Bride,
Young, modest, meek, and beautiful, I led
To a low Cottage in a sunny Bay,
Where the salt sea innocuously breaks,
And the sea breeze as innocently breathes, 525
On Devon's leafy shores;—a sheltered Hold,
In a soft clime encouraging the soil

To a luxuriant bounty!—As our steps
Approach the embowered Abode, our chosen Seat,
See, rooted in the earth, its kindly bed, 530
The unendangered Myrtle, decked with flowers,
Before the threshold stands to welcome us!
While, in the flowering Myrtle's neighbourhood,
Not overlooked but courting no regard
Those native plants, the Holly and the Yew, 535
Gave modest intimation to the mind
Of willingness with which they would unite
With the green Myrtle, to endear the hours
Of winter, and protect that pleasant place.
—Wild were the walks upon those lonely Downs, 540
Track leading into track, how marked, how worn
Into bright verdure, among fern and gorse
Winding away its never-ending line,
On their smooth surface, evidence was none:
But, there, lay open to our daily haunt, 545
A range of unappropriated earth,
Where youth's ambitious feet might move at large;
Whence, unmolested Wanderers, we beheld
The shining Giver of the Day diffuse
His brightness, o'er a tract of sea and land 550
Gay as our spirits, free as our desires,
As our enjoyments boundless.—From these Heights
We dropped, at pleasure, into sylvan Combs;
Where arbours of impenetrable shade,
And mossy seats detained us side by side, 555
With hearts at ease, and knowledge in our hearts
"That all the grove and all the day was ours."

   But in due season Nature interfered,
And called my Partner to resign her share
In the pure freedom of that wedded life, 560
Enjoyed by us in common.—To my hope,
To my heart's wish, my tender Mate became
The thankful captive of maternal bonds;

And those wild paths were left to me alone.
There, could I meditate on follies past; 565
And, like a weary Voyager escaped
From risk and hardship, inwardly retrace
A course of vain delights and thoughtless guilt,
And self-indulgence—without shame pursued.
There, undisturbed, could think of, and could thank 570
Her—whose submissive spirit was to me
Rule and restraint, my Guardian;—shall I say
That earthly Providence, whose guiding love
Within a port of rest had lodged me safe;
Safe from temptation, and from danger far? 575
Strains followed of acknowledgment addressed
To an Authority enthroned above
The reach of sight; from whom, as from their source,
Proceed all visible ministers of good
That walk the earth—Father of heaven and earth, 580
Father and king, and judge, adored and feared!
These acts of mind, and memory, and heart,
And spirit,—interrupted and relieved
By observations—transient as the glance
Of flying sunbeams, or to the outward form 585
Cleaving with power inherent and intense,
As the mute insect fixed upon the plant
On whose soft leaves it hangs, and from whose cup
Draws imperceptibly its nourishment,—
Endeared my wanderings; and the Mother's kiss, 590
And Infant's smile, awaited my return.

    In privacy we dwelt—a wedded pair
Companions daily, often all day long;
Not placed by fortune within easy reach
Of various intercourse, nor wishing aught 595
Beyond the allowance of our own fire-side,
The Twain within our happy cottage born,
Inmates, and heirs of our united love;
Graced mutually by difference of sex,

By the endearing names of nature bound, 600
And with no wider interval of time
Between their several births than served for One
To establish something of a leader's sway;
Yet left them joined by sympathy in age;
Equals in pleasure, fellows in pursuit. 605
On these two pillars rested as in air
Our solitude.
    It soothes me to perceive,
Your courtesy withholds not from my words
Attentive audience. But oh! gentle Friends,
As times of quiet and unbroken peace 610
Though for a Nation times of blessedness,
Give back faint echoes from the Historian's page;
So, in the imperfect sounds of this discourse,
Depressed I hear, how faithless is the voice
Which those most blissful days reverberate. 615
What special record can, or need be given
To rules and habits, whereby much was done
But all within the sphere of little things?
Of humble, though, to us, important cares,
And precious interests! Smoothly did our life 620
Advance, not swerving from the path prescribed;
Her annual, her diurnal round alike
Maintained with faithful care. And you divine
The worst effects which our condition saw
If you imagine changes slowly wrought, 625
And in their progress imperceptible,
Not wished for, sometimes noticed with a sigh,
(Whate'er of good or lovely they might bring)
Sighs of regret, for the familiar good,
And loveliness endeared—which they removed. 630

 Seven years of occupation undisturbed
Established seemingly a right to hold
That happiness; and use and habit gave
To what an alien spirit had acquired

A patrimonial sanctity. And thus, 635
With thoughts and wishes bounded to this world,
I lived and breathed; most grateful, if to enjoy
Without repining or desire for more,
For different lot, or change to higher sphere,
(Only except some impulses of pride 640
With no determined object, though upheld
By theories with suitable support)
Most grateful, if in such wise to enjoy
Be proof of gratitude for what we have;
Else, I allow, most thankless.—But at once 645
From some dark seat of fatal Power was urged
A claim that shattered all.—Our blooming Girl,
Caught in the gripe of Death, with such brief time
To struggle in as scarcely would allow
Her cheek to change its colour, was conveyed 650
From us, to regions inaccessible;
Where height, or depth, admits not the approach
Of living Man, though longing to pursue.
—With even as brief a warning—and how soon
With what short interval of time between 655
I tremble yet to think of—our last prop,
Our happy life's only remaining stay—
The Brother followed; and was seen no more!

    Calm as a frozen Lake when ruthless Winds
Blow fiercely, agitating earth and sky, 660
The Mother now remained; as if in her,
Who, to the lowest region of the soul,
Had been erewhile unsettled and disturbed,
This second visitation had no power
To shake; but only to bind up and seal; 665
And to establish thankfulness of heart
In Heaven's determinations, ever just.
The eminence on which her spirit stood,
Mine was unable to attain. Immense
The space that severed us! But, as the sight 670

Communicates with heaven's etherial orbs
Incalculably distant; so, I felt
That consolation may descend from far;
(And that is intercourse, and union, too,)
While, overcome with speechless gratitude, 675
And with a holier love inspired, I looked
On her—at once superior to my woes
And Partner of my loss.—O heavy change!
Dimness o'er this clear Luminary crept
Insensibly;—the immortal and divine 680
Yielded to mortal reflux; her pure Glory,
As from the pinnacle of worldly state
Wretched Ambition drops astounded, fell
Into a gulph obscure of silent grief,
And keen heart-anguish—of itself ashamed, 685
Yet obstinately cherishing itself:
And, so consumed, She melted from my arms;
And left me, on this earth, disconsolate.

   What followed cannot be reviewed in thought;
Much less, retraced in words. If She, of life 690
Blameless; so intimate with love and joy,
And all the tender motions of the Soul,
Had been supplanted, could I hope to stand?
Infirm, dependant, and now destitute!
I called on dreams and visions, to disclose 695
That which is veiled from waking thought; conjured
Eternity, as men constrain a Ghost
To appear and answer; to the Grave I spake
Imploringly;—looked up, and asked the Heavens
If Angels traversed their cerulean floors, 700
If fixed or wandering Star could tidings yield
Of the departed Spirit—what Abode
It occupies—what consciousness retains
Of former loves and interests. Then my Soul
Turned inward,—to examine of what stuff 705
Time's fetters are composed; and Life was put

To inquisition, long and profitless!
By pain of heart—now checked—and now impelled—
The intellectual Power, through words and things,
Went sounding on, a dim and perilous way! 710
And from those transports, and these toils abstruse,
Some trace am I enabled to retain
Of time, else lost;—existing unto me
Only by records in myself not found.

    From that abstraction I was rouzed,—and how? 715
Even as a thoughtful Shepherd by a flash
Of lightening startled in a gloomy cave
Of these wild hills. For, lo! the dread Bastile,
With all the chambers in its horrid Towers,
Fell to the ground:—by violence o'erthrown 720
Of indignation; and with shouts that drowned
The crash it made in falling! From the wreck
A golden Palace rose, or seemed to rise,
The appointed Seat of equitable Law
And mild paternal Sway. The potent shock 725
I felt; the transformation I perceived,
As marvellously seized as in that moment
When, from the blind mist issuing, I beheld
Glory—beyond all glory ever seen,
Confusion infinite of heaven and earth, 730
Dazzling the soul! Meanwhile, prophetic harps
In every grove were ringing, "War shall cease;
"Did ye not hear that conquest is abjured?
"Bring garlands, bring forth choicest flowers, to deck
"The Tree of Liberty."—My heart rebounded; 735
My melancholy Voice the chorus joined;
—"Be joyful all ye Nations, in all Lands,
"Ye that are capable of joy be glad!
"Henceforth, whate'er is wanting to yourselves
"In others ye shall promptly find;—and all 740
"Be rich by mutual and reflected wealth."

 Thus was I reconverted to the world;
Society became my glittering Bride,
And airy hopes my Children.—From the depths
Of natural passion, seemingly escaped,   745
My soul diffused itself in wide embrace
Of institutions, and the forms of things;
As they exist, in mutable array,
Upon life's surface. What, though in my veins
There flowed no Gallic blood, nor had I breathed   750
The air of France, not less than Gallic zeal
Kindled and burnt among the sapless twigs
Of my exhausted heart. If busy Men
In sober conclave met, to weave a web
Of amity, whose living threads should stretch   755
Beyond the seas, and to the farthest pole,
There did I sit, assisting. If, with noise
And acclamation, crowds in open air
Expressed the tumult of their minds, my voice
There mingled, heard or not. The powers of song   760
I left not uninvoked; and, in still groves,
Where mild Enthusiasts tuned a pensive lay
Of thanks and expectation, in accord
With their belief, I sang Saturnian Rule
Returned,—a progeny of golden years   765
Permitted to descend, and bless mankind.
—With promises the Hebrew Scriptures teem:
I felt the invitation; and resumed
A long-suspended office in the House
Of public worship, where, the glowing phrase   770
Of ancient Inspiration serving me,
I promised also,—with undaunted trust
Foretold; and added prayer to prophecy;
The admiration winning of the crowd,
The help desiring of the pure devout.   775

 Scorn and contempt forbid me to proceed!
But History, Time's slavish Scribe, will tell

How rapidly the Zealots of the cause
Disbanded—or in hostile ranks appeared;
Some, tired of honest service; these, outdone,   780
Disgusted, therefore, or appalled, by aims
Of fiercer Zealots—so Confusion reigned,
And the more faithful were compelled to exclaim,
As Brutus did to Virtue, "Liberty,
"I worshipped Thee, and find thee but a Shade!"   785

   Such recantation had for me no charm,
Nor would I bend to it; who should have grieved
At aught, however fair, which bore the mien
Of a conclusion, or catastrophe.
Why then conceal, that, when the simple good   790
In timid selfishness withdrew, I sought
Other support, not scrupulous whence it came,
And by what compromise it stood, not nice?
Enough if notions seemed to be high-pitched,
And qualities determined.—Ruling such,   795
And with such herding, I maintained a strife
Hopeless, and still more hopeless every hour;
But, in the process, I began to feel
That, if the emancipation of the world
Were missed, I should at least secure my own,   800
And be in part compensated. For rights,
Widely—inveterately usurped upon,
I spake with vehemence; and promptly seized
Whate'er Abstraction furnished for my needs
Or purposes; nor scrupled to proclaim,   805
And propagate, by liberty of life,
Those new persuasions. Not that I rejoiced,
Or even found pleasure, in such vagrant course,
For its own sake; but farthest from the walk
Which I had trod in happiness and peace,   810
Was most inviting to a troubled mind;
That, in a struggling and distempered world,
Beheld a cherished image of itself.

Yet, mark the contradictions of which Man
Is still the sport! Here Nature was my guide, 815
The Nature of the dissolute; but Thee,
O fostering Nature! I rejected, smiled
At others' tears in pity; and in scorn
At those, which thy soft influence sometimes drew
From my unguarded heart.—The tranquil shores 820
Of Britain circumscribed me; else, perhaps,
I might have been entangled among deeds,
Which, now, as infamous, I should abhor—
Despise, as senseless: for I strangely relished
The exasperated spirit of that Land, 825
Which turned an angry beak against the down
Of its own breast; as if it hoped, thereby,
To disencumber its impatient wings.
—But all was quieted by iron bonds
Of military sway. The shifting aims, 830
The moral interests, the creative might,
The varied functions and high attributes
Of civil Action, yielded to a Power
Formal, and odious, and contemptible.
—In Britain, ruled a panic dread of change; 835
The weak were praised, rewarded, and advanced;
And, from the impulse of a just disdain,
Once more did I retire into myself.
There feeling no contentment, I resolved
To fly, for safeguard, to some foreign shore, 840
Remote from Europe; from her blasted hopes;
Her fields of carnage, and polluted air.

   Fresh blew the wind, when o'er the Atlantic Main
The Ship went gliding with her thoughtless crew:
And who among them but an Exile, freed 845
From discontent, indifferent, pleased to sit
Among the busily-employed, not more
With obligation charged, with service taxed,
Than the loose pendant—to the idle wind

Upon the tall mast, streaming! But, ye Powers 850
Of soul and sense—mysteriously allied,
O, never let the Wretched, if a choice
Be left him, trust the freight of his distress
To a long voyage on the silent deep!
For, like a Plague, will Memory break out, 855
And, in the blank and solitude of things,
Upon his Spirit, with a fever's strength,
Will Conscience prey.—Feebly must They have felt
Who, in old time, attired with snakes and whips
The vengeful Furies. *Beautiful* regards 860
Were turned on me—the face of her I loved;
The Wife and Mother, pitifully fixing
Tender reproaches, insupportable!
Where now that boasted liberty? No welcome
From unknown Objects I received; and those, 865
Known and familiar, which the vaulted sky
Did, in the placid clearness of the night,
Disclose, had accusations to prefer
Against my peace. Within the cabin stood
That Volume—as a compass for the soul— 870
Revered among the Nations. I implored
Its guidance; but the infallible support
Of faith was wanting. Tell me, why refused
To One by storms annoyed and adverse winds,
Perplexed with currents, of his weakness sick, 875
Of vain endeavours tired, and by his own,
And by his Nature's ignorance, dismayed.

    Long-wished-for sight, the Western World appeared;
And, when the Ship was moored, I leapt ashore
Indignantly—resolved to be a Man, 880
Who, having o'er the past no power, would live
No longer in subjection to the past,
With abject mind—from a tyrannic Lord
Inviting penance, fruitlessly endured.
So like a Fugitive, whose feet have cleared 885

Some boundary, which his Followers may not cross
In prosecution of their deadly chace,
Respiring I looked round.—How bright the Sun,
How promising the Breeze! Can aught produced
In the old World compare, thought I, for power   890
And majesty with this gigantic Stream,
Sprung from the Desart? And behold, a City
Fresh, youthful, and aspiring! What are these
To me, or I to them? As much at least
As He desires that they should be, whom winds   895
And waves have wafted to this distant shore,
In the condition of a damaged seed,
Whose fibres cannot, if they would, take root.
Here may I roam at large;—my business is,
Roaming at large, to observe, and not to feel;   900
And, therefore, not to act—convinced that all
Which bears the name of action, howsoe'er
Beginning, ends in servitude—still painful,
And mostly profitless. And, sooth to say,
On nearer view, a motley spectacle   905
Appeared, of high pretensions—unreproved
But by the obstreperous voice of higher still;
Big Passions strutting on a petty stage;
Which a detached Spectator may regard
Not unamused.—But ridicule demands   910
Quick change of objects; and, to laugh alone,
In woods and wilds, or any lonely place,
At a composing distance from the haunts
Of strife and folly,—though it be a treat
As choice as musing Leisure can bestow;   915
Yet, in the very centre of the crowd
To keep the secret of a poignant scorn,
May suit an airy Demon; but, of all
Unsocial courses, 'tis the one least fit
For the gross spirit of Mankind,—the one   920
That soonest fails to please, and quickliest turns

Into vexation.—Let us, then, I said,
Leave this unknit Republic to the scourge
Of its own passions; and to Regions haste,
Whose shades have never felt the encroaching axe, 925
Or soil endured a transfer in the mart
Of dire rapacity. There, Man abides,
Primeval Nature's Child. A Creature weak
In combination (wherefore else driven back
So far, and of his old inheritance 930
So easily deprived?) but, for that cause,
More dignified, and stronger in himself,
Whether to act, judge, suffer, or enjoy.
True, the Intelligence of social Art
Hath overpowered his Forefathers, and soon 935
Will sweep the remnant of his line away;
But contemplations, worthier, nobler far
Than her destructive energies, attend
His Independence, when along the side
Of Mississippi, or that Northern Stream[1] 940
Which spreads into successive seas, he walks;
Pleased to perceive his own unshackled life,
And his innate capacities of soul,
There imaged: or, when having gained the top
Of some commanding Eminence, which yet 945
Intruder ne'er beheld, he thence surveys
Regions of wood and wide Savannah, vast
Expanse of unappropriated earth,
With mind that sheds a light on what he sees;
Free as the Sun, and lonely as the Sun, 950
Pouring above his head its radiance down
Upon a living, and rejoicing World!

    So, westward, tow'rd the unviolated Woods
I bent my way; and, roaming far and wide,
Failed not to greet the merry Mocking-bird; 955

---

1 See WW's note at the end of this volume.

And while the melancholy Muccawiss
(The sportive Bird's companion in the Grove)
Repeated, o'er and o'er, his plaintive cry,
I sympathized at leisure with the sound;
But that pure Archetype of human greatness, 960
I found him not. There, in his stead, appeared
A Creature, squalid, vengeful, and impure;
Remorseless, and submissive to no law
But superstitious fear, and abject sloth.
—Enough is told! Here am I—Ye have heard 965
What evidence I seek, and vainly seek;
What from my Fellow-beings I require,
And cannot find; what I myself have lost,
Nor can regain; how languidly I look
Upon this visible fabric of the World, 970
May be divined—perhaps it hath been said:—
But spare your pity, if there be in me
Aught that deserves respect: for I exist—
Within myself—not comfortless.—The tenor
Which my life holds, he readily may conceive 975
Whoe'er hath stood to watch a mountain Brook
In some still passage of its course, and seen,
Within the depths of its capacious breast,
Inverted trees, and rocks, and azure sky;
And, on its glassy surface, specks of foam, 980
And conglobated bubbles undissolved,
Numerous as stars; that, by their onward lapse,
Betray to sight the motion of the stream,
Else imperceptible; meanwhile, is heard
Perchance, a roar or murmur; and the sound 985
Though soothing, and the little floating isles
Though beautiful, are both by Nature charged
With the same pensive office; and make known
Through what perplexing labyrinths, abrupt
Precipitations, and untoward straits, 990
The earth-born wanderer hath passed; and quickly,

That respite o'er, like traverses and toils
Must be again encountered.—Such a stream
Is human Life; and so the Spirit fares
In the best quiet to its course allow'd: 995
And such is mine,—save only for a hope
That my particular current soon will reach
The unfathomable gulph, where all is still!"

END OF THE THIRD BOOK.

BOOK THE FOURTH

DESPONDENCY CORRECTED

Here closed the Tenant of that lonely Vale
His mournful Narrative—commenced in pain,
In pain commenced, and ended without peace:
Yet tempered, not unfrequently, with strains
Of native feeling, grateful to our minds;   5
And doubtless yielding some relief to his,
While we sate listening with compassion due.
Such pity yet surviving, with firm voice,
That did not falter though the heart was moved,
The Wanderer said—
     "One adequate support   10
For the calamities of mortal life
Exists, one only;—an assured belief
That the procession of our fate, howe'er
Sad or disturbed, is ordered by a Being
Of infinite benevolence and power,   15
Whose everlasting purposes embrace
All accidents, converting them to Good.
—The darts of anguish *fix* not where the seat
Of suffering hath been thoroughly fortified
By acquiescence in the Will Supreme   20
For Time and for Eternity; by faith,

Faith absolute in God, including hope,
And the defence that lies in boundless love
Of his perfections; with habitual dread
Of aught unworthily conceived, endured 25
Impatiently; ill-done, or left undone,
To the dishonour of his holy Name.
Soul of our souls, and safeguard of the world!
Sustain, Thou only canst, the sick of heart;
Restore their languid spirits, and recal 30
Their lost affections unto Thee, and thine!"

    Then, as we issued from that covert Nook,
He thus continued—lifting up his eyes
To Heaven.—"How beautiful this dome of sky,
And the vast hills, in fluctuation fixed 35
At thy command, how awful! Shall the Soul,
Human and rational, report of Thee
Even less than these?—Be mute who will, who can,
Yet I will praise thee with empassioned voice:
My lips, that may forget thee in the crowd, 40
Cannot forget thee here; where Thou hast built,
For thy own glory, in the wilderness!
Me didst thou constitute a Priest of thine,
In such a Temple as we now behold
Reared for thy presence: therefore, am I bound 45
To worship, here, and everywhere—as One
Not doomed to ignorance, though forced to tread,
From childhood up, the ways of poverty;
From unreflecting ignorance preserved,
And from debasement rescued.—By thy grace 50
The particle divine remained unquenched;
And, mid the wild weeds of a rugged soil,
Thy bounty caused to flourish deathless flowers,
From Paradise transplanted. Wintry age
Impends; the frost will gather round my heart; 55
And, if they wither, I am worse than dead!
—Come Labour, when the worn-out frame requires

Perpetual sabbath; come disease and want;
And sad exclusion through decay of sense;
But leave me unabated trust in Thee— 60
And let thy favour, to the end of life,
Inspire me with ability to seek
Repose and hope among eternal things—
Father of heaven and earth! and I am rich,
And will possess my portion in content! 65

   And what are things Eternal?—Powers depart,"
The grey-haired Wanderer steadfastly replied,
Answering the question which himself had asked,
"Possessions vanish, and Opinions change,
And Passions hold a fluctuating seat: 70
But, by the storms of circumstance unshaken,
And subject neither to eclipse or wane,
Duty exists;—immutably survive,
For our support, the measures and the forms,
Which an abstract Intelligence supplies; 75
Whose kingdom is, where Time and Space are not:
Of other converse, which mind, soul, and heart,
Do, with united urgency, require,
What more, that may not perish? Thou, dread Source,
Prime, self-existing Cause and End of all, 80
That, in the scale of Being, fill their place,
Above our human region, or below,
Set and sustained;—Thou—who didst wrap the cloud
Of Infancy around us, that Thyself,
Therein, with our simplicity awhile 85
Might'st hold, on earth, communion undisturbed—
Who from the anarchy of dreaming sleep,
Or from its death-like void, with punctual care,
And touch as gentle as the morning light,
Restor'st us, daily, to the powers of sense, 90
And reason's steadfast rule—thou, thou alone
Art everlasting, and the blessed Spirits,
Which thou includest, as the Sea her Waves:

For adoration thou endurest; endure
For consciousness the motions of thy will;   95
For apprehension those transcendent truths
Of the pure Intellect, that stand as laws,
(Submission constituting strength and power)
Even to thy Being's infinite majesty!
This Universe shall pass away—a frame   100
Glorious! because the shadow of thy might,
A step, or link, for intercourse with Thee.
Ah! if the time must come, in which my feet
No more shall stray where Meditation leads,
By flowing stream, through wood, or craggy wild,   105
Loved haunts like these, the unimprisoned Mind
May yet have scope to range among her own,
Her thoughts, her images, her high desires.
If the dear faculty of sight should fail,
Still, it may be allowed me to remember   110
What visionary powers of eye and soul
In youth were mine; when, stationed on the top
Of some huge hill—expectant, I beheld
The Sun rise up, from distant climes returned
Darkness to chase, and sleep, and bring the day   115
His bounteous gift! or saw him, tow'rds the Deep
Sink—with a retinue of flaming Clouds
Attended; then, my Spirit was entranced
With joy exalted to beatitude;
The measure of my soul was filled with bliss,   120
And holiest love; as earth, sea, air, with light,
With pomp, with glory, with magnificence!

    Those fervent raptures are for ever flown;
And, since their date, my Soul hath undergone
Change manifold, for better, or for worse: 125
Yet cease I not to struggle, and to aspire
Heavenward; and chide the part of me that flags,
Through sinful choice; or dread necessity,
On human Nature, from above, imposed.

'Tis, by comparison, an easy task 130
Earth to despise;[1] but to converse with Heaven,
This is not easy:—to relinquish all
We have, or hope, of happiness and joy,—
And stand in freedom loosened from this world;
I deem not arduous:—but must needs confess 135
That 'tis a thing impossible to frame
Conceptions equal to the Soul's desires;
And the most difficult of tasks to *keep*
Heights which the Soul is competent to gain.
—Man is of dust: etherial Hopes are his, 140
Which, when they should sustain themselves aloft,
Want due consistence; like a Pillar of smoke,
That with majestic energy from earth
Rises; but, having reached the thinner air,
Melts, and dissolves, and is no longer seen. 145
From this infirmity of mortal kind
Sorrow proceeds, which else were not;—at least,
If Grief be something hallowed and ordained,
If, in proportion, it be just and meet,
Through this, 'tis able to maintain its hold, 150
In that excess which Conscience disapproves.
For who could sink and settle to that point
Of selfishness; so senseless who could be
In framing estimates of loss and gain,
As long and perseveringly to mourn 155
For any Object of his love, removed
From this unstable world, if he could fix
A satisfying view upon that state
Of pure, imperishable blessedness,

---

[1] "''Tis, by comparison, an easy task
   Earth to despise, &c.'
   See, upon this subject, Baxter's most interesting review of his own opinions and sentiments in the decline of life. It may be found (lately reprinted) in Dr. Wordsworth's Ecclesiastical Biography." WW refers to Christopher Wordsworth's *Ecclesiastical Biography* (1810), which in turn quotes from Richard Baxter's *Narrative of the Most Memorable Passages of his Life and Times*.

Which Reason promises, and holy Writ   160
Ensures to all Believers?—Yet mistrust
Is of such incapacity, methinks,
No natural branch; despondency far less.
—And, if there be whose tender frames have drooped
Even to the dust; apparently, through weight   165
Of anguish unrelieved, and lack of power
An agonizing sorrow to transmute,
Infer not hence a hope from those withheld
When wanted most; a confidence impaired
So pitiably, that, having ceased to see   170
With bodily eyes, they are borne down by love
Of what is lost, and perish through regret.
Oh! no, full oft the innocent Sufferer sees
Too clearly; feels too vividly; and longs
To realize the Vision with intense   175
And overconstant yearning—there—there lies
The excess, by which the balance is destroyed.
Too, too contracted are these walls of flesh,
This vital warmth too cold, these visual orbs,
Though inconceivably endowed, too dim   180
For any passion of the soul that leads
To extacy; and, all the crooked paths
Of time and change disdaining, takes its course
Along the line of limitless desires.
I, speaking now from such disorder free,   185
Nor rapt, nor craving, but in settled peace,
I cannot doubt that They whom you deplore
Are glorified; or, if they sleep, shall wake
From sleep, and dwell with God in endless love.
Hope,—below this, consists not with belief   190
In mercy carried infinite degrees
Beyond the tenderness of human hearts:
Hope,—below this, consists not with belief
In perfect Wisdom, guiding mightiest Power,
That finds no limits but its own pure Will.   195

Here then we rest: not fearing to be left
In undisturbed possession of our creed
For aught that human reasoning can achieve,
To unsettle or perplex us: yet with pain
Acknowledging, and grievous self-reproach,   200
That, though immoveably convinced, we want
Zeal, and the virtue to exist by faith
As Soldiers live by courage; as, by strength
Of heart, the Sailor fights with roaring seas.
Alas! the endowment of immortal Power   205
Is matched unequally with custom, time,[1]
And domineering faculties of sense
In all; in most with superadded foes,
Idle temptations—open vanities
Of dissipation; countless, still-renewed,   210
Ephemeral offspring of the unblushing world;
And, in the private regions of the mind,
Ill-governed passions, ranklings of despite,
Immoderate wishes, pining discontent,
Distress and care. What then remains?—To seek   215
Those helps, for his occasions ever near,
Who lacks not will to use them; vows, renewed
On the first motion of a holy thought;
Vigils of contemplation; praise; and prayer,
A Stream, which, from the fountain of the heart,   220
Issuing however feebly, no where flows
Without access of unexpected strength.
But, above all, the victory is most sure
For Him, who, seeking faith by virtue, strives
To yield entire submission to the law   225
Of Conscience; Conscience reverenced and obeyed,
As God's most intimate Presence in the soul,

---

1   "'Alas! the endowment of immortal Power,
    Is matched unequally with custom, time, &c.'
      This subject is treated at length in the Ode at the conclusion of the second volume of Poems by the Author." WW refers to his "Intimations Ode" (see vol. 1 of this edition.

And his most perfect Image in the world.
—Endeavour thus to live; these rules regard,
These helps solicit; and a steadfast seat 230
Shall then be yours among the happy few
Who dwell on earth yet breathe empyreal air,
Sons of the morning. For your nobler Part,
Ere disencumbered of her mortal chains,
Doubt shall be quelled and trouble chased away; 235
With only such degree of sadness left
As may support longings of pure desire;
And strengthen love, rejoicing secretly
In the sublime attractions of the Grave."

   While, in this strain, the venerable Sage 240
Poured forth his aspirations, and announced
His judgments, near that lonely House we paced
A plot of green-sward, seemingly preserved
By Nature's care from wreck of scattered stones,
And from the encroachment of encircling heath: 245
Small space! but for reiterated steps
Smooth and commodious; as a stately deck
Which to and fro the Mariner is used
To tread for pastime; talking with his Mates,
Or haply thinking of far-distant Friends, 250
While the Ship glides before a steady breeze.
Stillness prevailed around us: and the Voice,
That spake, was capable to lift the soul
Tow'rds regions yet more tranquil. But, methought,
That He, whose fixed despondency had given 255
Impulse and motive to that strong discourse,
Was less upraised in spirit than abashed;
Shrinking from admonition, like a man
Who feels, that to exhort, is to reproach.
Yet not to be diverted from his aim, 260
The Sage continued.—"For that other loss,
The loss of confidence in social Man,
By the unexpected transports of our Age

Carried so high, that every thought—which looked
Beyond the temporal destiny of the Kind— 265
To many seemed superfluous; as, no cause
For such exalted confidence could e'er
Exist; so, none is now for such despair:
The two extremes are equally remote
From Truth and Reason;—do not, then, confound 270
One with the other, but reject them both;
And choose the middle point, whereon to build
Sound expectations. This doth he advise
Who shared at first the illusion; but was soon
Cast from the pedestal of pride by shocks 275
Which Nature gently gave, in woods and fields;
Nor unreproved by Providence, thus speaking
To the inattentive Children of the World,
"Vain-glorious Generation! what new powers
"On you have been conferred? what gifts, withheld 280
"From your Progenitors, have Ye received,
"Fit recompence of new desert? what claim
"Are ye prepared to urge, that my decrees
"For you should undergo a sudden change;
"And the weak functions of one busy day, 285
"Reclaiming and extirpating, perform
"What all the slowly-moving Years of Time,
"With their united force, have left undone?
"By Nature's gradual processes be taught,
"By Story be confounded. Ye aspire 290
"Rashly, to fall once more; and that false fruit,
"Which, to your over-weening spirits, yields
"Hope of a flight celestial, will produce
"Misery and shame. But Wisdom of her sons
"Shall not the less, though late, be justified." 295
Such timely warning," said the Wanderer, "gave
That visionary Voice; and, at this day,
When a Tartarian darkness overspreads
The groaning nations; when the Impious rule,

By will or by established ordinance, 300
Their own dire agents, and constrain the Good
To acts which they abhor; though I bewail
This triumph, yet the pity of my heart
Prevents me not from owning, that the law,
By which Mankind now suffers, is most just. 305
For by superior energies; more strict
Affiance in each other; faith more firm
In their unhallowed principles; the Bad
Have fairly earned a victory o'er the weak,
The vacillating, inconsistent Good. 310
Therefore, not unconsoled, I wait—in hope
To see the moment, when the righteous Cause
Shall gain Defenders zealous and devout
As They who have opposed her; in which Virtue
Will to her efforts tolerate no bounds 315
That are not lofty as her rights; aspiring
By impulse of her own etherial zeal.
That Spirit only can redeem Mankind;
And when that sacred Spirit shall appear
Then shall *our* triumph be complete as their's. 320
Yet, should this confidence prove vain, the Wise
Have still the keeping of their proper peace;
Are guardians of their own tranquillity.
They act, or they recede, observe, and feel;
"Knowing"—(to adopt the energetic words 325
Which a time-hallowed Poet hath employed)[1]
"Knowing the heart of Man is set to be
The centre of this World, about the which
Those revolutions of disturbances

---

[1] "The passage quoted from Daniel is taken from a poem addressed to the Lady Margaret, Countess of Cumberland, and the two last lines, printed in Italics, are by him translated from Seneca. The whole Poem is very beautiful. I will transcribe four stanzas from it, as they contain an admirable picture of the state of a wise Man's mind in a time of public commotion." WW's note attributes the lines in quotation marks to Samuel Daniel (1561–1619). They are quoted from Daniel's "To the Ladie Margaret, Countesse of Cumberland." The four stanzas WW quoted in his 1819 note are given in the notes at the end of this volume.

Still roll; where all the aspècts of misery 330
Predominate; whose strong effects are such
As he must bear, being powerless to redress;
And that unless above himself he can
Erect himself, how poor a thing is Man!"

   Happy is He who lives to understand! 335
Not human Nature only, but explores
All Natures,—to the end that he may find
The law that governs each; and where begins
The union, the partition where, that makes
Kind and degree, among all visible Beings; 340
The constitutions, powers, and faculties,
Which they inherit,—cannot step beyond,—
And cannot fall beneath; that do assign
To every Class its station and its office,
Through all the mighty Commonwealth of things; 345
Up from the creeping plant to sovereign Man.
Such Converse, if directed by a meek,
Sincere, and humble Spirit, teaches love;
For knowledge is delight; and such delight
Breeds love; yet, suited as it rather is 350
To thought and to the climbing intellect,
It teaches less to love, than to adore;
If that be not indeed the highest Love!"

   "Yet," said I, tempted here to interpose,
"The dignity of Life is not impaired 355
By aught that innocently satisfies
The humbler cravings of the heart; and He
Is a still happier Man, who, for those heights
Of speculation not unfit, descends;
And such benign affections cultivates 360
Among the inferior Kinds; not merely those
That he may call his own, and which depend,
As individual objects of regard,
Upon his care,—from whom he also looks

For signs and tokens of a mutual bond,— 365
But others, far beyond this narrow sphere,
Whom, for the very sake of love, he loves.
Nor is it a mean praise of rural life
And solitude, that they do favour most,
Most frequently call forth, and best sustain 370
These pure sensations; that can penetrate
The obstreperous City; on the barren Seas
Are not unfelt,—and much might recommend,
How much they might inspirit and endear,
The loneliness of this sublime Retreat!" 375

   "Yes," said the Sage, resuming the discourse
Again directed to his downcast Friend,
"If, with the froward will and groveling soul
Of Man offended, liberty is here,
And invitation every hour renewed, 380
To mark *their* placid state, who never heard
Of a command which they have power to break,
Or rule which they are tempted to transgress;
These, with a soothed or elevated heart,
May we behold, their knowledge register, 385
Observe their ways; and, free from envy, find
Complacence there:—but wherefore this to You?
I guess that, welcome to your lonely hearth,
The Redbreast feeds in winter from your hand;
A box perchance is from your casement hung 390
For the small Wren to build in;—not in vain,
The barriers disregarding that surround
This deep Abiding-place, before your sight
Mounts on the breeze the Butterfly—and soars,
Small Creature as she is, from earth's bright flowers 395
Into the dewy clouds. Ambition reigns
In the waste wilderness: the Soul ascends
Towards her native firmament of heaven,
When the fresh Eagle, in the month of May,
Upborne, at evening, on replenished wing, 400

This shady valley leaves,—and leaves the dark
Empurpled hills,—conspicuously renewing
A proud communication with the sun
Low sunk beneath the horizon!—List!—I heard,
From yon huge breast of rock, a solemn bleat;   405
Sent forth as if it were the Mountain's voice,
As if the visible Mountain made the cry.
Again!"—The effect upon the soul was such
As he expressed; for, from the mountain's heart
The solemn bleat appeared to come; there was   410
No other—and the region all around
Stood silent, empty of all shape of life.
—It was a Lamb—left somewhere to itself,
The plaintive Spirit of the Solitude!—
He paused, as if unwilling to proceed,   415
Through consciousness that silence in such place
Was best,—the most affecting eloquence.
But soon his thoughts returned upon themselves,
And, in soft tone of speech, he thus resumed.

"Ah! if the heart, too confidently raised,   420
Perchance too lightly occupied, or lulled
Too easily, despise or overlook
The vassalage that binds her to the earth,
Her sad dependance upon time, and all
The trepidations of mortality,   425
What place so destitute and void—but there
The little Flower her vanity shall check;
The trailing Worm reprove her thoughtless pride?

These craggy regions, these chaotic wilds,
Does that benignity pervade, that warms   430
The Mole contented with her darksome walk
In the cold ground; and to the Emmet gives
Her foresight; and the intelligence that makes
The tiny Creatures strong by social league;
Supports the generations, multiplies   435

Their tribes, till we behold a spacious plain
Or grassy bottom, all, with little hills—
Their labour—covered, as a Lake with waves;
Thousands of Cities, in the desert place
Built up of life, and food, and means of life! 440
Nor wanting here, to entertain the thought,
Creatures, that in communities exist,
Less, as might seem, for general guardianship
Or through dependance upon mutual aid,
Than by participation of delight 445
And a strict love of fellowship, combined.
What other spirit can it be, that prompts
The gilded summer Flies to mix and weave
Their sports together in the solar beam,
Or in the gloom of twilight hum their joy? 450
More obviously, the self-same influence rules
The feathered kinds; the Fieldfare's pensive flocks,
The cawing Rooks, and Sea-mews from afar,
Hovering above these inland Solitudes,
Unscattered by the wind, at whose loud call 455
Their voyage was begun: nor is its power
Unfelt among the sedentary Fowl
That seek yon Pool, and there prolong their stay
In silent congress; or together rouzed
Take flight; while with their clang the air resounds. 460
And, over all, in that etherial arch
Is the mute company of changeful clouds;
—Bright apparition suddenly put forth
The Rainbow, smiling on the faded storm;
The mild assemblage of the starry heavens; 465
And the great Sun, earth's universal Lord!

How bountiful is Nature! he shall find
Who seeks not; and to him, who hath not asked,
Large measure shall be dealt. Three sabbath-days
Are scarcely told, since, on a service bent 470
Of mere humanity, You clomb those Heights;

And what a marvellous and heavenly Shew
Was to your sight revealed! the Swains moved on,
And heeded not; you lingered, and perceived.
There is a luxury in self-dispraise; 475
And inward self-disparagement affords
To meditative Spleen a grateful feast.
Trust me, pronouncing on your own desert,
You judge unthankfully; distempered nerves
Infect the thoughts; the languor of the Frame 480
Depresses the Soul's vigour. Quit your Couch—
Cleave not so fondly to your moody Cell;
Nor let the hallowed Powers, that shed from heaven
Stillness and rest, with disapproving eye
Look down upon your taper, through a watch 485
Of midnight hours, unseasonably twinkling
In this deep Hollow; like a sullen star
Dimly reflected in a lonely pool.
Take courage, and withdraw yourself from ways
That run not parallel to Nature's course. 490
Rise with the Lark! your Matins shall obtain
Grace, be their composition what it may,
If but with her's performed; climb once again,
Climb every day, those ramparts; meet the breeze
Upon their tops,—adventurous as a Bee 495
That from your garden thither soars, to feed
On new-blown heath; let yon commanding rock
Be your frequented Watch-tower; roll the stone
In thunder down the mountains: with all your might
Chase the wild Goat; and, if the bold red Deer 500
Fly to these harbours, driven by hound and horn
Loud echoing, add your speed to the pursuit:
So, wearied to your Hut shall you return,
And sink at evening into sound repose."

   The Solitary lifted towards the hills 505
An animated eye; and thoughts were mine
Which this ejaculation clothed in words—

"Oh! what a joy it were, in vigorous health,
To have a Body (this our vital Frame
With shrinking sensibility endued, 510
And all the nice regards of flesh and blood)
And to the elements surrender it
As if it were a Spirit!—How divine,
The liberty, for frail, for mortal man
To roam at large among unpeopled glens 515
And mountainous retirements, only trod
By devious footsteps; regions consecrate
To oldest time! and, reckless of the storm
That keeps the raven quiet in her nest,
Be as a Presence or a Motion—one 520
Among the many there; and, while the Mists
Flying, and rainy Vapours, call out Shapes
And Phantoms from the crags and solid earth
As fast as a Musician scatters sounds
Out of an instrument; and, while the Streams— 525
(As at a first creation and in haste
To exercise their untried faculties)
Descending from the region of the clouds
And starting from the hollows of the earth
More multitudinous every moment—rend 530
Their way before them, what a joy to roam
An Equal among mightiest Energies;
And haply sometimes with articulate voice,
Amid the deafening tumult, scarcely heard
By him that utters it, exclaim aloud 535
Be this continued so from day to day,
Nor let it have an end from month to month!"

   "Yes," said the Wanderer, taking from my lips
The strain of transport, "whosoe'er in youth
Has, through ambition of his soul, given way 540
To such desires, and grasped at such delight,
Shall feel the stirrings of them late and long;
In spite of all the weakness that life brings,

Its cares and sorrows; he, though taught to own
The tranquillizing power of time, shall wake, 545
Wake sometimes to a noble restlessness—
Loving the spots which once he gloried in.

 Compatriot, Friend, remote are Garry's Hills,
The Streams far distant of your native Glen;
Yet is their form and Image here express'd 550
As by a duplicate, at least set forth
With brotherly resemblance. Turn your steps
Wherever fancy leads, by day by night
Are various engines working, not the same
As those by which your soul in youth was moved, 555
But by the great Artificer endued
With no inferior power. You dwell alone;
You walk, you live, you speculate alone;
Yet doth Remembrance, like a sovereign Prince,
For you a stately gallery maintain 560
Of gay or tragic pictures. You have seen,
Have acted, suffered, travelled far, observed
With no incurious eye; and books are your's,
Within whose silent chambers treasure lies
Preserved from age to age; more precious far 565
Than that accumulated store of gold
And orient gems, which for a day of need
The Sultan hides within ancestral tombs.
These hoards of truth you can unlock at will:
And music waits upon your skilful touch,— 570
Sounds which the wandering Shepherd from these Heights
Hears, and forgets his purpose;—furnished thus
How can you droop, if willing to be raised?

 A piteous lot it were to flee from Man—
Yet not rejoice in Nature. He—whose hours 575
Are by domestic Pleasures uncaressed
And unenlivened; who exists whole years
Apart from benefits received or done

'Mid the transactions of the bustling crowd;
Who neither hears, nor feels a wish to hear, 580
Of the world's interests—such a One hath need
Of a quick fancy and an active heart,
That for the day's consumption books may yield
A not unwholesome food, and earth and air
Supply his morbid humour with delight. 585
—Truth has her pleasure-grounds, her haunts of ease
And easy contemplation,—gay parterres,
And labyrinthine walks, her sunny glades
And shady groves, for recreation framed:
These may he range, if willing to partake 590
Their soft indulgences, and in due time
May issue thence, recruited for the tasks
And course of service Truth requires from those
Who tend her Altars, wait upon her Throne,
And guard her Fortresses. Who thinks, and feels, 595
And recognises ever and anon
The breeze of Nature stirring in his soul,
Why need such man go desperately astray,
And nurse "the dreadful appetite of death?"
If tired with Systems—each in its degree 600
Substantial—and all crumbling in their turn,
Let him build Systems of his own, and smile
At the fond work—demolished with a touch;
If unreligious, let him be at once,
Among ten thousand Innocents, enrolled 605
A Pupil in the many-chambered school,
Where Superstition weaves her airy dreams.

   Life's Autumn past, I stand on Winter's verge,
And daily lose what I desire to keep:
Yet rather would I instantly decline 610
To the traditionary sympathies
Of a most rustic ignorance, and take
A fearful apprehension from the owl
Or death-watch,—and as readily rejoice,

If two auspicious magpies crossed my way; 615
This rather would I do than see and hear
The repetitions wearisome of sense,
Where soul is dead, and feeling hath no place;
Where knowledge, ill begun in cold remark
On outward things, with formal inference ends: 620
Or if the Mind turn inward 'tis perplexed,
Lost in a gloom of uninspired research;
Meanwhile, the Heart within the Heart, the seat
Where Peace and happy Consciousness should dwell,
On its own axis restlessly revolves, 625
Yet nowhere finds the cheering light of truth.

   Upon the breast of new-created Earth
Man walked; and when and wheresoe'er he moved,
Alone or mated, Solitude was not.
He heard, upon the wind, the articulate Voice 630
Of God; and Angels to his sight appeared,
Crowning the glorious hills of Paradise;
Or through the groves gliding like morning mist
Enkindled by the sun. He sate—and talked
With winged Messengers; who daily brought 635
To his small Island in the etherial deep
Tidings of joy and love.—From these pure Heights
(Whether of actual vision, sensible
To sight and feeling, or that in this sort
Have condescendingly been shadowed forth 640
Communications spiritually maintained,
And Intuitions moral and divine)
Fell Human-kind—to banishment condemned
That flowing years repealed not: and distress
And grief spread wide; but Man escaped the doom 645
Of destitution;—Solitude was not.
—Jehovah—shapeless Power above all Powers,
Single and one, the omnipresent God,
By vocal utterance, or blaze of light,
Or cloud of darkness, localized in heaven, 650

On earth, enshrined within the wandering ark;
Or, out of Sion, thundering from his throne
Between the Cherubim—on the chosen Race
Showered miracles, and ceased not to dispense
Judgments, that filled the Land from age to age   655
With hope, and love, and gratitude, and fear;
And with amazement smote;—thereby to assert
His scorned, or unacknowledged Sovereignty.
And when the One, ineffable of name,
In nature indivisible, withdrew   660
From mortal adoration or regard,
Not then was Deity engulphed, nor Man,
The rational Creature, left, to feel the weight
Of his own reason, without sense or thought
Of higher reason and a purer will,   665
To benefit and bless, through mightier power:
—Whether the Persian—zealous to reject
Altar and Image and the inclusive walls
And roofs of Temples built by human hands,
The loftiest heights ascending, from their tops,   670
With myrtle-wreathed Tiara on his brows—
Presented sacrifice to Moon and Stars,
And to the winds and Mother Elements,
And the whole Circle of the Heavens, for him
A sensitive Existence, and a God,   675
With lifted hands invoked, and songs of praise:
Or, less reluctantly to bonds of Sense
Yielding his Soul, the Babylonian framed
For influence undefined a personal Shape;
And, from the Plain, with toil immense, upreared   680
Tower eight times planted on the top of Tower;
That Belus, nightly to his splendid Couch
Descending, there might rest; and, from that Height
Pure and serene, the Godhead overlook
Winding Euphrates, and the City vast   685
Of his devoted Worshippers, far-stretched;

With grove, and field, and garden, interspersed;
Their Town, and foodful Region for support
Against the pressure of beleaguring war.

    Chaldean Shepherds, ranging trackless fields,   690
Beneath the concave of unclouded skies
Spread like a sea, in boundless solitude,
Looked on the Polar Star, as on a Guide
And Guardian of their course, that never closed
His steadfast eye. The Planetary Five   695
With a submissive reverence they beheld;
Watched, from the centre of their sleeping flocks,
Those radiant Mercuries, that seemed to move
Carrying through Ether, in perpetual round,
Decrees and resolutions of the Gods;   700
And, by their aspects, signifying works
Of dim futurity, to Man revealed.
—The Imaginative Faculty was Lord
Of observations natural; and, thus
Led on, those Shepherds made report of Stars   705
In set rotation passing to and fro,
Between the orbs of our apparent sphere
And its invisible counterpart, adorned
With answering Constellations, under earth
Removed from all approach of living sight,   710
But present to the Dead; who, so they deemed,
Like those celestial Messengers, beheld
All accidents, and Judges were of all.

    The lively Grecian, in a Land of hills,
Rivers, and fertile plains, and sounding shores,   715
Under a cope of variegated sky,
Could find commodious place for every God,
Promptly received, as prodigally brought,
From the surrounding Countries—at the choice
Of all Adventurers. With unrivalled skill,   720
As nicest observation furnished hints

For studious fancy, did his hand bestow
On fluent Operations a fixed Shape;
Metal or Stone, idolatrously served.
And yet—triumphant o'er this pompous show   725
Of Art, this palpable array of Sense,
On every side encountered; in despite
Of the gross fictions, chaunted in the streets
By wandering Rhapsodists; and in contempt
Of doubt and bold denials hourly urged   730
Amid the wrangling Schools—a SPIRIT hung,
Beautiful Region! o'er thy Towns and Farms,
Statues and Temples, and memorial Tombs;
And emanations were perceived; and acts
Of immortality, in Nature's course,   735
Exemplified by mysteries, that were felt
As bonds, on grave Philosopher imposed
And armed Warrior; and in every grove
A gay or pensive tenderness prevailed
When piety more awful had relaxed.   740
—"Take, running River, take these Locks of mine"—
Thus would the Votary say—"this severed hair,
"My Vow fulfilling, do I here present,
"Thankful for my beloved Child's return.
"Thy banks, Cephisus, he again hath trod,   745
"Thy murmurs heard; and drunk the chrystal lymph
"With which thou dost refresh the thirsty lip,
"And moisten all day long these flowery fields."
And doubtless, sometimes, when the hair was shed
Upon the flowing stream, a thought arose   750
Of Life continuous, Being unimpaired;
That hath been, is, and where it was and is
There shall be,—seen, and heard, and felt, and known,
And recognized,—existence unexposed
To the blind walk of mortal accident;   755
From diminution safe and weakening age;
While Man grows old, and dwindles, and decays;

And countless generations of Mankind
Depart; and leave no vestige where they trod.

   We live by admiration, hope, and love; 760
And even as these are well and wisely fixed,
In dignity of being we ascend.
But what is error?—"Answer he who can!"
The Sceptic somewhat haughtily exclaimed,
"Love, Hope, and Admiration—are they not 765
Mad Fancy's favourite Vassals? Does not Life
Use them, full oft, as Pioneers to ruin,
Guides to destruction? Is it well to trust
Imagination's light when Reason's fails,
The unguarded taper where the guarded faints? 770
—Stoop from those heights, and soberly declare
What error is; and, of our errors, which
Doth most debase the mind; the genuine seats
Of power, where are they? Who shall regulate,
With truth, the scale of intellectual rank?" 775

   "Methinks," persuasively the Sage replied,
"That for this arduous office You possess
Some rare advantages. Your early days
A grateful recollection must supply
Of much exalted good that may attend 780
Upon the very humblest state.—Your voice
Hath in my hearing often testified
That poor Men's Children, they, and they alone,
By their condition taught, can understand
The wisdom of the prayer that daily asks 785
For daily bread. A consciousness is your's
How feelingly religion may be learned
In smoky Cabins, from a Mother's tongue—
Heard while the Dwelling vibrates to the din
Of the contiguous Torrent, gathering strength 790
At every moment—and, with strength, increase
Of fury; or while Snow is at the door,

Assaulting and defending, and the Wind,
A sightless Labourer, whistles at his work—
Fearful, but resignation tempers fear, 795
And piety is sweet to Infant minds.
—The Shepherd Lad, who in the sunshine carves,
On the green turf, a dial—to divide
The silent hours; and who to that report
Can portion out his pleasures, and adapt 800
His round of pastoral duties, is not left
With less intelligence for *moral* things
Of gravest import. Early he perceives,
Within himself, a measure and a rule,
Which to the Sun of Truth he can apply, 805
That shines for him, and shines for all Mankind.
Experience, daily fixing his regards
On Nature's wants, he knows how few they are,
And where they lie, how answered and appeased.
This knowledge ample recompence affords 810
For manifold privations; he refers
His notions to this standard; on this rock
Rests his desires; and hence, in after life,
Soul-strengthening patience, and sublime content.
Imagination—not permitted here 815
To waste her powers, as in the Worldling's mind,
On fickle pleasures, and superfluous cares,
And trivial ostentation—is left free
And puissant to range the solemn walks
Of time and nature, girded by a zone 820
That, while it binds, invigorates and supports.
Acknowledge, then, that whether by the side
Of his poor hut, or on the mountain top,
Or in the cultured field, a Man like this
(Take from him what you will upon the score 825
Of ignorance or illusion) lives and breathes
For noble purposes of mind: his heart
Beats to the heroic song of ancient days;

His eye distinguishes, his soul creates.
And those Illusions, which excite the scorn 830
Or move the pity of unthinking minds,
Are they not mainly outward Ministers
Of inward Conscience? with whose service charged
They come and go, appear and disappear;
Diverting evil purposes, remorse 835
Awakening, chastening an intemperate grief,
Or pride of heart abating: and, whene'er
For less important ends those Phantoms move,
Who would forbid them, if their presence serve,
Among wild mountains and unpeopled heaths, 840
Filling a space else vacant, to exalt
The forms of Nature, and enlarge her powers?

   Once more to distant Ages of the world
Let us revert, and place before our thoughts
The face which rural Solitude might wear 845
To the unenlightened Swains of pagan Greece.
—In that fair Clime, the lonely Herdsman, stretched
On the soft grass through half a summer's day,
With music lulled his indolent repose:
And, in some fit of weariness, if he, 850
When his own breath was silent, chanced to hear
A distant strain, far sweeter than the sounds
Which his poor skill could make, his Fancy fetched,
Even from the blazing Chariot of the Sun,
A beardless Youth, who touched a golden lute, 855
And filled the illumined groves with ravishment.
The nightly Hunter, lifting up his eyes
Towards the crescent Moon, with grateful heart
Called on the lovely wanderer who bestowed
That timely light, to share his joyous sport: 860
And hence, a beaming Goddess with her Nymphs,
Across the lawn and through the darksome grove,
(Not unaccompanied with tuneful notes
By echo multiplied from rock or cave)

Swept in the storm of chase, as Moon and Stars 865
Glance rapidly along the clouded heavens,
When winds are blowing strong. The Traveller slaked
His thirst from Rill or gushing Fount, and thanked
The Naiad.—Sunbeams, upon distant Hills
Gliding apace, with Shadows in their train, 870
Might, with small help from fancy, be transformed
Into fleet Oreads sporting visibly.
The Zephyrs, fanning as they passed, their wings,
Lacked not, for love, fair Objects, whom they wooed
With gentle whisper. Withered Boughs grotesque, 875
Stripped of their leaves and twigs by hoary age,
From depth of shaggy covert peeping forth
In the low vale, or on steep mountain side;
And, sometimes, intermixed with stirring horns
Of the live Deer, or Goat's depending beard; 880
These were the lurking Satyrs, a wild brood
Of gamesome Deities! or Pan himself,
The simple Shepherd's awe-inspiring God."

   No apter Strain could have been chosen: I marked
Its kindly influence, on the yielding brow 885
Of our Companion, gradually diffused;
While, listening, he had paced the noiseless turf,
Like one whose untired ear a murmuring stream
Detains; but tempted now to interpose
He with a smile exclaimed—
                "'Tis well you speak 890
At a safe distance from our native Land,
And from the Mansions where our youth was taught.
The true Descendants of those godly Men
Who swept from Scotland, in a flame of zeal,
Shrine, Altar, Image, and the massy Piles 895
That harboured them,—the Souls retaining yet
The churlish features of that after Race
Who fled to caves, and woods, and naked rocks,
In deadly scorn of superstitious rites,

Or what their scruples construed to be such, 900
How, think you, would they tolerate this scheme
Of fine propensities? that tends, if urged
Far as it might be urged, to sow afresh
The weeds of Romish Phantasy, in vain
Uprooted; would re-consecrate our Wells 905
To good Saint Fillan and to fair Saint Anne;
And from long banishment recal Saint Giles,
To watch again with tutelary love
O'er stately Edinborough throned on crags.
A blessed restoration to behold 910
The Patron, on the shoulders of his Priests,
Once more parading through her crowded streets;
Now simply guarded by the sober Powers
Of Science, and Philosophy, and Sense!"

 This answer followed.—"You have turned my thoughts 915
Upon our brave Progenitors, who rose
Against Idolatry with warlike mind,
And shrunk from vain observances to lurk
In caves, and woods, and under dismal rocks,
Deprived of shelter, covering, fire, and food; 920
Why?—for this very reason that they felt,
And did acknowledge, wheresoe'er they moved
A spiritual Presence, oft-times misconceived;
But still a high dependance, a divine
Bounty and government, that filled their hearts 925
With joy, and gratitude, and fear, and love;
And from their fervent lips drew hymns of praise
With which the desarts rang. Though favoured less,
Far less, than these, yet such, in their degree,
Were those bewildered Pagans of old time. 930
Beyond their own poor Natures and above
They looked; were humbly thankful for the good
Which the warm Sun solicited—and Earth
Bestowed; were gladsome,—and their moral sense
They fortified with reverence for the Gods; 935

And they had hopes that overstepped the Grave.

 Now, shall our great Discoverers," he exclaimed,
Raising his voice triumphantly, "obtain
From Sense and Reason less than These obtained,
Though far misled? Shall Men for whom our Age   940
Unbaffled powers of vision hath prepared,
To explore the world without and world within,
Be joyless as the blind? Ambitious Souls—
Whom Earth, at this late season, hath produced
To regulate the moving spheres, and weigh   945
The planets in the hollow of their hand;
And They who rather dive than soar, whose pains
Have solved the elements, or analysed
The thinking principle—shall They in fact
Prove a degraded Race? and what avails   950
Renown, if their presumption make them such?
Oh! there is laughter at their work in Heaven!
Enquire of ancient Wisdom; go, demand
Of mighty Nature, if 'twas ever meant
That we should pry far off yet be unraised;   955
That we should pore, and dwindle as we pore,
Viewing all objects unremittingly
In disconnection dead and spiritless;
And still dividing, and dividing still,
Break down all grandeur, still unsatisfied   960
With the perverse attempt, while littleness
May yet become more little; waging thus
An impious warfare with the very life
Of our own Souls!—And if indeed there be
An all-pervading Spirit, upon whom   965
Our dark foundations rest, could He design,
Or will his rites and services permit,
That this magnificent effect of Power,
The Earth we tread, the Sky which we behold
By day, and all the pomp which night reveals,   970
That these—and that superior Mystery

Our vital Frame, so fearfully devised,
And the dread Soul within it—should exist
Only to be examined, pondered, searched,
Probed, vexed, and criticised?—Accuse me not 975
Of arrogance, unknown Wanderer as I am,
If, having walked with Nature threescore years,
And offered, far as frailty would allow,
My heart a daily sacrifice to Truth,
I now affirm of Nature and of Truth, 980
Whom I have served, that their DIVINITY
Revolts, offended at the ways of Men
Swayed by such motives, to such end employed;
Philosophers, who, when the human Soul
Is of a thousand faculties composed, 985
And twice ten thousand interests, do yet prize
This Soul, and the transcendent Universe,
No more than as a Mirror that reflects
To proud Self-love her own intelligence;
That one, poor, finite Object, in the Abyss 990
Of infinite Being, twinkling restlessly!

   Nor higher place can be assigned to Him
And his Compeers—the laughing Sage of France.—
Crowned was He, if my Memory doth not err,
With laurel planted upon hoary hairs, 995
In sign of conquest by his Wit atchieved,
And benefits his Wisdom had conferred.
His tottering Body was oppressed with flowers;
Far less becoming ornaments than those
With which Spring often decks a mouldering Tree! 1000
Yet so it pleased a fond, a vain Old Man,
And a most frivolous People. Him I mean
Who framed, to ridicule confiding Faith,
This sorry Legend; which by chance we found
Piled in a nook, through malice, as might seem, 1005
Among more innocent rubbish."—Speaking thus,
With a brief notice when, and how, and where,

We had espied the Book, he drew it forth;
And courteously, as if the act removed,
At once, all traces from the good Man's heart   1010
Of unbenign aversion or contempt
Restored it to its owner. "Gentle Friend,"
Herewith he grasped the Solitary's hand,
"You have known better Lights and Guides than these—
Ah! let not aught amiss within dispose   1015
A noble Mind to practise on herself,
And tempt Opinion to support the wrongs
Of Passion: whatsoe'er is felt or feared,
From higher judgment-seats make no appeal
To lower: can you question that the Soul   1020
Inherits an allegiance, not by choice
To be cast off, upon an oath proposed
By each new upstart Notion? In the ports
Of levity no refuge can be found,
No shelter, for a spirit in distress.   1025
He, who by wilful disesteem of life
And proud insensibility to hope
Affronts the eye of Solitude, shall learn
That her mild nature can be terrible;
That neither she nor Silence lack the power   1030
To avenge their own insulted Majesty.
—O blest seclusion! when the Mind admits
The law of duty; and thereby can live,
Through each vicissitude of loss and gain,
Linked in entire complacence with her choice;   1035
When Youth's presumptuousness is mellowed down,
And Manhood's vain anxiety dismissed;
When Wisdom shews her seasonable fruit,
Upon the boughs of sheltering leisure hung
In sober plenty; when the spirit stoops   1040
To drink with gratitude the chrystal stream
Of unreproved enjoyment; and is pleased
To muse,—and be saluted by the air

Of meek repentance, wafting wall-flower scents
From out the crumbling ruins of fallen Pride   1045
And chambers of Transgression, now forlorn.
O, calm contented days, and peaceful nights!
Who, when such good can be obtained, would strive
To reconcile his Manhood to a couch,
Soft as may seem; but, under that disguise,   1050
Stuffed with the thorny substance of the past,
For fixed annoyance; and full oft beset
With floating dreams, disconsolate and black,
The vapoury phantoms of futurity?

   Within the soul a Faculty abides,   1055
That with interpositions, which would hide
And darken, so can deal, that they become
Contingences of pomp; and serve to exalt
Her native brightness. As the ample Moon,
In the deep stillness of a summer even   1060
Rising behind a thick and lofty Grove,
Burns like an unconsuming fire of light,
In the green trees; and, kindling on all sides
Their leafy umbrage, turns the dusky veil
Into a substance glorious as her own,   1065
Yea with her own incorporated, by power
Capacious and serene. Like power abides
In Man's celestial Spirit; Virtue thus
Sets forth and magnifies herself; thus feeds
A calm, a beautiful, and silent fire,   1070
From the incumbrances of mortal life,
From error, disappointment,—nay from guilt;
And sometimes, so relenting Justice wills,
From palpable oppressions of Despair."

   The Solitary by these words was touched   1075
With manifest emotion, and exclaimed,
"But how begin? and whence?—The Mind is free,
Resolve—the haughty Moralist would say,

This single act is all that we demand.
Alas! such wisdom bids a Creature fly   1080
Whose very sorrow is, that time hath shorn
His natural wings!—To Friendship let him turn
For succour; but perhaps he sits alone
On stormy waters, in a little Boat
That holds but him, and can contain no more!   1085
Religion tells of amity sublime
Which no condition can preclude; of One
Who sees all suffering, comprehends all wants,
All weakness fathoms, can supply all needs;
But is that bounty absolute?—His gifts,   1090
Are they not still, in some degree, rewards
For acts of service? Can his Love extend
To hearts that own not Him? Will showers of grace,
When in the sky no promise may be seen,
Fall to refresh a parched and withered land?   1095
Or shall the groaning Spirit cast her load
At the Redeemer's feet?"
     In rueful tone
With some impatience in his mien he spake;
And this reply was given.—
     "As Men from Men
Do in the constitution of their Souls   1100
Differ, by mystery not to be explained;
And as we fall by various ways, and sink
One deeper than another, self-condemned,
Through manifold degrees of guilt and shame,
So, manifold and various are the ways   1105
Of restoration, fashioned to the steps
Of all infirmity, and tending all
To the same point,—attainable by all;
Peace in ourselves, and union with our God.
—For Him, to whom I speak, an easy road   1110
Lies open: we have heard from You a voice
At every moment softened in its course

By tenderness of heart; have seen your Eye,
Even like an Altar lit by fire from Heaven,
Kindle before us.—Your discourse this day, 1115
That, like the fabled Lethe, wished to flow
In creeping sadness, through oblivious shades
Of death and night, has caught at every turn
The colours of the Sun. Access for you
Is yet preserved to principles of truth, 1120
Which the Imaginative Will upholds
In seats of wisdom, not to be approached
By the inferior Faculty that moulds,
With her minute and speculative pains,
Opinion, ever changing!—I have seen 1125
A curious Child, who dwelt upon a tract
Of inland ground, applying to his ear
The convolutions of a smooth-lipped Shell;
To which, in silence hushed, his very soul
Listened intensely; and his countenance soon 1130
Brightened with joy; for murmurings from within
Were heard,—sonorous cadences! whereby,
To his belief, the Monitor expressed
Mysterious union with its native Sea.
Even such a Shell the Universe itself 1135
Is to the ear of Faith; and there are times,
I doubt not, when to You it doth impart
Authentic tidings of invisible things;
Of ebb and flow, and ever-during power;
And central peace, subsisting at the heart 1140
Of endless agitation. Here you stand,
Adore, and worship, when you know it not;
Pious beyond the intention of your thought;
Devout above the meaning of your will.
—Yes, you have felt, and may not cease to feel. 1145
The estate of Man would be indeed forlorn
If false conclusions of the reasoning Power
Made the Eye blind, and closed the passages

Through which the Ear converses with the heart.
Has not the Soul, the Being of your Life   1150
Received a shock of awful consciousness,
In some calm season, when these lofty Rocks
At night's approach bring down the unclouded Sky,
To rest upon their circumambient walls;
A Temple framing of dimensions vast,   1155
And yet not too enormous for the sound
Of human anthems,—choral song, or burst
Sublime of instrumental harmony,
To glorify the Eternal! What if these
Did never break the stillness that prevails   1160
Here, if the solemn Nightingale be mute
And the soft Woodlark here did never chaunt
Her vespers, Nature fails not to provide
Impulse and utterance. The whispering Air
Sends inspiration from the shadowy heights,   1165
And blind recesses of the caverned rocks;
The little Rills, and Waters numberless,
Inaudible by day-light, blend their notes
With the loud Streams: and often, at the hour
When issue forth the first pale Stars, is heard,   1170
Within the circuit of this Fabric huge,
One Voice—the solitary Raven, flying
Athwart the concave of the dark-blue dome,
Unseen, perchance above the power of sight—
An iron knell! with echoes from afar,   1175
Faint—and still fainter—as the cry, with which
The wanderer accompanies her flight
Through the calm region, fades upon the ear,
Diminishing by distance till it seemed
To expire, yet from the Abyss is caught again,   1180
And yet again recovered!

               But descending
From these Imaginative Heights, that yield

Far-stretching views into Eternity,
Acknowledge that to Nature's humbler power
Your cherished sullenness is forced to bend   1185
Even here, where her amenities are sown
With sparing hand. Then trust yourself abroad
To range her blooming bowers, and spacious fields,
Where on the labours of the happy Throng
She smiles, including in her wide embrace   1190
City, and Town, and Tower,—and Sea with Ships
Sprinkled,—be our Companion while we track
Her rivers populous with gliding life;
While, free as air, o'er printless sands we march,
And pierce the gloom of her majestic woods;   1195
Roaming, or resting under grateful shade
In peace and meditative chearfulness;
Where living Things, and Things inanimate,
Do speak, at Heaven's command, to eye and ear,
And speak to social Reason's inner sense,   1200
With inarticulate language.
                              —For the Man,
Who, in this spirit, communes with the Forms
Of Nature, who with understanding heart,
Doth know and love, such Objects as excite
No morbid passions, no disquietude,   1205
No vengeance, and no hatred, needs must feel
The joy of that pure principle of love
So deeply, that, unsatisfied with aught
Less pure and exquisite, he cannot choose
But seek for objects of a kindred love   1210
In Fellow-natures, and a kindred joy.
Accordingly, he by degrees perceives
His feelings of aversion softened down;
A holy tenderness pervade his frame.
His sanity of reason not impaired,   1215
Say rather, all his thoughts now flowing clear,
From a clear Fountain flowing, he looks round

And seeks for good; and finds the good he seeks:
Until abhorrence and contempt are things
He only knows by name; and, if he hear   1220
From other mouths, the language which they speak,
He is compassionate; and has no thought,
No feeling, which can overcome his love.

   And further; by contemplating these Forms
In the relations which they bear to Man,   1225
He shall discern, how, through the various means
Which silently they yield, are multiplied
The spiritual Presences of absent Things,
Convoked by knowledge; and for his delight
Still ready to obey the gentle call.   1230
Trust me, that for the Instructed time will come
When they shall meet no object but may teach
Some acceptable lesson to their minds
Of human suffering, or of human joy.
For them shall all things speak of Man, they read   1235
Their duties in all forms; and general laws,
And local accidents, shall tend alike
To rouze, to urge; and with the will confer
The ability to spread the blessings wide
Of true philanthropy. The light of love   1240
Not failing, perseverance from their steps
Departing not, they shall at length obtain
The glorious habit by which Sense is made
Subservient still to moral purposes,
Auxiliar to divine. That change shall clothe   1245
The naked Spirit, ceasing to deplore
The burthen of existence. Science then
Shall be a precious Visitant; and then,
And only then, be worthy of her name.
For then her Heart shall kindle; her dull Eye,   1250
Dull and inanimate, no more shall hang
Chained to its object in brute slavery;
But taught with patient interest to watch

The processes of things, and serve the cause
Of order and distinctness, not for this 1255
Shall it forget that its most noble use,
Its most illustrious province, must be found
In furnishing clear guidance, a support
Not treacherous, to the Mind's *excursive* Power.
—So build we up the Being that we are; 1260
Thus deeply drinking-in the Soul of Things
We shall be wise perforce; and while inspired
By choice, and conscious that the Will is free,
Unswerving shall we move, as if impelled
By strict necessity, along the path 1265
Of order and of good. Whate'er we see,
Whate'er we feel, by agency direct
Or indirect shall tend to feed and nurse
Our faculties, shall fix in calmer seats
Of moral strength, and raise to loftier heights 1270
Of love divine, our intellectual Soul."

 Here closed the Sage that eloquent harangue,
Poured forth with fervour in continuous stream;
Such as, remote 'mid savage wilderness,
An Indian Chief discharges from his breast 1275
Into the hearing of the assembled Tribes,
In open circle seated round, and hushed
As the unbreathing air, when not a leaf
Stirs in the mighty woods.—So did he speak:
The words he uttered shall not pass away; 1280
For they sank into me—the bounteous gift
Of One whom time and nature had made wise,
Gracing his language with authority
Which hostile spirits silently allow;
Of One accustomed to desires that feed 1285
On fruitage gathered from the Tree of Life,
To hopes on knowledge and experience built;
Of One in whom persuasion and belief
Had ripened into faith, and faith become

A passionate intuition; whence the Soul, 1290
Though bound to Earth by ties of pity and love,
From all injurious servitude was free.

   The Sun, before his place of rest were reached,
Had yet to travel far, but unto us,
To us who stood low in that hollow Dell 1295
He had become invisible,—a pomp
Leaving behind of yellow radiance spread
Upon the mountain sides, in contrast bold
With ample shadows, seemingly no less
Than those resplendent lights his rich bequest, 1300
A dispensation of his evening power.
—Adown the path which from the Glen had led
The funeral Train, the Shepherd and his Mate
Were seen descending;—forth in transport ran
Our little Page; the rustic Pair approach; 1305
And in the Matron's aspect may be read
A plain assurance that the words which told
How that neglected Pensioner was sent,
Before his time, into a quiet grave,
Had done to her humanity no wrong. 1310
But we are kindly welcomed; promptly served
With ostentatious zeal.—Along the floor
Of the small Cottage in the lonely Dell
A grateful Couch was spread for our repose;
Where, in the guise of Mountaineers, we slept, 1315
Stretched upon fragrant heath, and lulled by sound
Of far-off Torrents charming the still night,
And to tired limbs and over-busy thoughts
Inviting sleep and soft forgetfulness.

END OF THE FOURTH BOOK.

BOOK THE FIFTH.

THE PASTOR.

Farewell deep Valley, with thy one rude House,
And its small lot of life-supporting fields,
And guardian rocks!—With unreverted eyes
I cannot pass thy bounds, attractive Seat!
To the still influx of the morning light 5
Open, and day's pure chearfulness, but veiled
From human observation, as if yet
Primæval Forests wrapped thee round with dark
Impenetrable shade; once more farewell
Majestic Circuit, beautiful Abyss, 10
By Nature destined from the birth of things
For quietness profound!
                    Upon the side
Of that green Slope, the outlet of the Vale,
Lingering behind my Comrades, thus I breathed
A parting tribute to a spot that seemed 15
Like the fixed centre of a troubled World.
And now, pursuing leisurely my way,
How vain, thought I, it is by change of place
To seek that comfort which the mind denies;
Yet trial and temptation oft are shunned 20
Wisely; and by such tenor do we hold
Frail Life's possessions, that even they whose fate
Yields no peculiar reason of complaint
Might, by the promise that is here, be won
To steal from active duties, and embrace 25
Obscurity, and calm forgetfulness.
—Knowledge, methinks, in these disordered times,
Should be allowed a privilege to have
Her Anchorites, like Piety of old;
Men, who, from faction sacred, and unstained 30
By war, might, if so minded, turn aside
Uncensured, and subsist, a scattered few

Living to God and Nature, and content
With that communion. Consecrated be
The Spots where such abide! But happier still 35
The Man, whom, furthermore, a hope attends
That meditation and research may guide
His privacy to principles and powers
Discovered, or invented; or set forth
Through his acquaintance with the ways of truth, 40
In lucid order; so that, when his course
Is run, some faithful Eulogist may say,
He sought not praise, and praise did overlook
His inobtrusive merit; but his life,
Sweet to himself, was exercised in good 45
That shall survive his name and memory.

   Acknowledgments of gratitude sincere
Accompanied these musings;—fervent thanks
For my own peaceful lot and happy choice;
A choice that from the passions of the world 50
Withdrew, and fixed me in a still retreat,
Sheltered, but not to social duties lost,
Secluded, but not buried; and with song
Cheering my days, and with industrious thought,
With the ever-welcome company of books 55
By virtuous friendship's soul-sustaining aid,
And with the blessings of domestic love.

   Thus occupied in mind I paced along,
Following the rugged road, by sledge or wheel
Worn in the moorland, till I overtook 60
My two Associates, in the morning sunshine
Halting together on a rocky knoll,
From which the road descended rapidly
To the green meadows of another Vale.

   Here did our pensive Host put forth his hand 65
In sign of farewell. "Nay," the Old Man said,

"The fragrant Air its coolness still retains;
The Herds and Flocks are yet abroad to crop
The dewy grass; you cannot leave us now,
We must not part at this inviting hour."　　　　　　　　70
To that injunction, earnestly expressed,
He yielded, though reluctant; for his Mind
Instinctively disposed him to retire
To his own Covert; as a billow, heaved
Upon the beach, rolls back into the Sea.　　　　　　　　75
—So we descend; and winding round a rock
Attain a point that shewed the Valley—stretched
In length before us; and, not distant far,
Upon a rising ground a grey Church-tower,
Whose battlements were screened by tufted trees.　　　　80
And, tow'rds a chrystal Mere, that lay beyond
Among steep hills and woods embosomed, flowed
A copious Stream with boldly-winding course;
Here traceable, there hidden—there again
To sight restored, and glittering in the Sun.　　　　　　85
On the Stream's bank, and every where, appeared
Fair Dwellings, single or in social knots;
Some scattered o'er the level, others perched
On the hill sides, a cheerful quiet scene,
Now in its morning purity arrayed.　　　　　　　　　　90

　"As, 'mid some happy Valley of the Alps,"
Said I, "once happy, ere tyrannic Power
Wantonly breaking in upon the Swiss,
Destroyed their unoffending Commonwealth,
A popular equality doth seem　　　　　　　　　　　　95
Here to prevail; and yet a House of State
Stands yonder, one beneath whose roof, methinks,
A rural Lord might dwell." "No feudal pomp,"
Replied our Friend, a Chronicler who stood
Where'er he moved upon familiar ground,　　　　　　　100
"Nor feudal power is there; but there abides,
 In his allotted Home, a genuine Priest,

The Shepherd of his Flock; or, as a King
Is stiled, when most affectionately praised,
The Father of his People. Such is he, 105
And rich and poor, and young and old, rejoice
Under his spiritual sway, collected round him
In this sequestered Realm. He hath vouchsafed
To me some portion of his kind regard;
And something also of his inner mind 110
Hath he imparted—but I speak of him
As he is known to all. The calm delights
Of unambitious piety he chose,
And learning's solid dignity; though born
Of knightly race, nor wanting powerful friends. 115
This good to reap, these pleasures to secure,
Hither, in prime of manhood, he withdrew
From academic bowers. He loved the spot,
Who does not love his native soil? he prized
The ancient rural character, composed 120
Of simple manners, feelings unsuppressed
And undisguised, and strong and serious thought;
A character reflected in himself,
With such embellishment as well beseems
His rank and sacred function. This deep vale 125
Is lengthened out by many a winding reach,
Not visible to us; and one of these
A turretted manorial Hall adorns;
In which the good Man's Ancestors have dwelt
From age to age, the Patrons of this Cure. 130
To them, and to his decorating hand,
The Vicar's Dwelling, and the whole Domain,
Owes that presiding aspect which might well
Attract your notice; statelier than could else
Have been bestowed, in course of common chance, 135
On an unwealthy mountain Benefice."

   This said, oft halting we pursued our way;
Nor reached the Village Church-yard till the sun,

Travelling at steadier pace than ours, had risen
Above the summits of the highest hills,　　　　　　　140
And round our path darted oppressive beams.

    As chanced, the portals of the sacred Pile
Stood open, and we entered. On my frame,
At such transition from the fervid air,
A grateful coolness fell, that seemed to strike　　　145
The heart, in concert with that temperate awe
And natural reverence, which the Place inspired.
Not framed to nice proportions was the Pile,
But large and massy; for duration built.
With pillars crowded, and the roof upheld　　　　　150
By naked rafters intricately crossed,
Like leafless underboughs, in some thick grove,
All withered by the depth of shade above.
Admonitory Texts inscribed the walls,
Each, in its ornamental scroll, enclosed,—　　　　　155
Each also crowned with winged heads—a pair
Of rudely-painted Cherubim. The floor
Of nave and aisle, in unpretending guise,
Was occupied by oaken benches, ranged
In seemly rows; the chancel only shewed　　　　　　160
Some inoffensive marks of earthly state
And vain distinction. A capacious pew
Of sculptured oak stood here, with drapery lined;
And marble Monuments were here displayed
Upon the walls; and on the floor beneath　　　　　　165
Sepulchral stones appeared, with emblems graven,
And foot-worn epitaphs, and some with small
And shining effigies of brass inlaid.
—The tribute by these various records claimed,
Without reluctance did we pay; and read　　　　　　170
The ordinary chronicle of birth,
Office, alliance, and promotion—all
Ending in dust; of upright Magistrates,
Grave Doctors strenuous for the Mother Church,

And uncorrupted Senators—alike 175
To King and People true. A brazen plate,
Not easily decyphered, told of One
Whose course of earthly honour was begun
In quality of page among the Train
Of the eighth Henry, when he crossed the seas 180
His royal state to shew, and prove his strength
In tournament, upon the fields of France.
Another Tablet registered the death,
And praised the gallant bearing of a Knight
Tried in the sea-fights of the second Charles. 185
Near this brave Knight his Father lay entombed;
And, to the silent language giving voice,
I read,—how in his manhood's earlier day
He, 'mid the afflictions of intestine War
And rightful Government subverted, found 190
One only solace, that he had espoused
A virtuous Lady tenderly beloved
For her benign perfections: and for this
Yet more endeared to him, that in her state
Of wedlock richly crowned with heaven's regard, 195
She with a numerous Issue filled his House,
Who throve, like Plants, uninjured by the Storm
That laid their Country waste. No need to speak
Of less particular notices assigned
To Youth or Maiden gone before their time, 200
And Matrons and unwedded Sisters old;
Whose charity and goodness were rehearsed
In modest panegyric. "These dim lines,
What would they tell?" said I,—but, from the task
Of puzzling out that faded Narrative, 205
With whisper soft my venerable Friend
Called me; and looking down the darksome aisle
I saw the Tenant of the lonely Vale
Standing apart; with curved arm reclined
On the baptismal Font; his pallid face 210

Upturned, as if his mind were rapt, or lost
In some abstraction;—gracefully he stood,
The semblance bearing of a sculptured Form
That leans upon a monumental Urn
In peace, from morn to night, from year to year.   215

   Him from that posture did the Sexton rouze;
Who entered, humming carelessly a tune,
Continuation haply of the notes
That had beguiled the work from which he came
With spade and mattock o'er his shoulder hung;   220
To be deposited, for future need,
In their appointed place. The pale Recluse
Withdrew; and straight we followed,—to a spot
Where sun and shade were intermixed; for there
A broad Oak, stretching forth its leafy arms   225
From an adjoining pasture, overhung
Small space of that green church-yard with a light
And pleasant awning. On the moss-grown wall
My ancient Friend and I together took
Our seats; and thus the Solitary spake,   230
Standing before us. "Did you note the mien
Of that self-solaced, easy-hearted churl,
Death's Hireling, who scoops out his Neighbour's grave,
Or wraps an old Acquaintance up in clay,
As unconcerned as when he plants a tree?   235
I was abruptly summoned by his voice
From some affecting images and thoughts
And from the company of serious words.
Much, yesterday, was said in glowing phrase
Of our sublime dependencies, and hopes   240
For future states of Being; and the wings
Of speculation, joyfully outspread,
Hovered above our destiny on earth;
But stoop, and place the prospect of the soul
In sober contrast with reality   245
And Man's substantial life. If this mute earth

Of what it holds could speak, and every grave
Were as a volume, shut, yet capable
Of yielding its contents to eye and ear,
We should recoil, stricken with sorrow and shame,   250
To see disclosed, by such dread proof, how ill
That which is done accords with what is known
To reason, and by conscience is enjoined;
How idly, how perversely, Life's whole course,
To this conclusion, deviates from the line,   255
Or of the end stops short, proposed to all
At its aspiring outset. Mark the Babe
Not long accustomed to this breathing world;
One that hath barely learned to shape a smile,
Though yet irrational of Soul to grasp   260
With tiny fingers, to let fall a tear,
And, as the heavy cloud of sleep dissolves,
To stretch his limbs, bemocking, as might seem,
The outward functions of intelligent Man;
A grave Proficient in amusive feats   265
Of puppetry, that from the lap declare
His expectations, and announce his claims
To that inheritance which millions rue
That they were ever born to! In due time
A day of solemn ceremonial comes;   270
When they, who for this Minor hold in trust
Rights that transcend the unblest heritage
Of mere Humanity, present their Charge,
For this occasion daintily adorned,
At the baptismal Font. And when the pure   275
And consecrating element hath cleansed
The original stain, the Child is there received
Into the second Ark, Christ's Church, with trust
That he, from wrath redeemed, therein shall float
Over the billows of this troublesome world   280
To the fair land of everlasting Life.
Corrupt affections, covetous desires,

Are all renounced; high as the thought of man
Can carry virtue, virtue is professed;
A dedication made, a promise given 285
For due provision to controul and guide,
And unremitting progress to ensure
In holiness and truth."
                    "You cannot blame,"
Here interposing fervently I said,
"Rites which attest that Man by nature lies 290
Bedded for good and evil in a gulph
Fearfully low; nor will your judgment scorn
Those services, whereby attempt is made
To lift the Creature tow'rds that eminence
On which, now fallen, erewhile in majesty 295
He stood; or if not so, whose top serene
At least he feels 'tis given him to descry;
Not without aspirations, evermore
Returning, and injunctions from within
Doubt to cast off and weariness; in trust 300
That what the Soul perceives, if glory lost,
May be through pains and persevering hope
Recovered; or, if hitherto unknown,
Lies within reach, and one day shall be gained."

    "I blame them not," he calmly answered—"no; 305
The outward ritual and established forms
With which Communities of Men invest
These inward feelings, and the aspiring vows
To which the lips give public utterance
Are both a natural process; and by me 310
Shall pass uncensured; though the issue prove,
Bringing from age to age its own reproach,
Incongruous, impotent, and blank.—But oh!
If to be weak is to be wretched—miserable,
As the lost Angel by a human voice 315
Hath mournfully pronounced, then, in my mind,
Far better not to move at all than move

By impulse sent from such illusive Power,
That finds and cannot fasten down; that grasps
And is rejoiced, and loses while it grasps;   320
That tempts, emboldens—doth a while sustain,
And then betrays; accuses and inflicts
Remorseless punishment; and so retreads
The inevitable circle: better far
Than this, to graze the herb in thoughtless peace,   325
By foresight or remembrance, undisturbed!

   Philosophy! and thou more vaunted name
Religion! with thy statelier retinue,
Faith, Hope, and Charity—from the visible world
Choose for your Emblems whatsoe'er ye find   330
Of safest guidance and of firmest trust,—
The Torch, the Star, the Anchor; nor except
The Cross itself, at whose unconscious feet
The Generations of Mankind have knelt
Ruefully seized, and shedding bitter tears,   335
And through that conflict seeking rest—of you,
High-titled Powers, am I constrained to ask,
Here standing, with the unvoyageable sky
In faint reflection of infinitude
Stretched overhead, and at my pensive feet   340
A subterraneous magazine of bones
In whose dark vaults my own shall soon be laid,
Where are your triumphs? your dominion where?
And in what age admitted and confirmed?
—Not for a happy Land do I enquire,   345
Island or Grove, that hides a blessed few
Who, with obedience willing and sincere,
To your serene authorities conform;
But whom I ask, of individual Souls,
Have ye withdrawn from Passion's crooked ways,   350
Inspired, and thoroughly fortified?—If the Heart
Could be inspected to its inmost folds
By sight undazzled with the glare of praise,

Who shall be named—in the resplendent line
Of Sages, Martyrs, Confessors—the Man 355
Whom the best might of Conscience, Truth, and Hope,
For one day's little compass, has preserved
From painful and discreditable shocks
Of contradiction, from some vague desire
Culpably cherished, or corrupt relapse 360
To some unsanctioned fear?"
                         "If this be so,
And Man," said I, "be in his noblest shape
Thus pitiably infirm; then, He who made,
And who shall judge the Creature, will forgive.
—Yet, in its general tenor, your complaint 365
Is all too true; and surely not misplaced.
For, from this pregnant spot of ground, such thoughts
Rise to the notice of a serious Mind
By natural exhalation. With the Dead
In their repose, the Living in their mirth, 370
Who can reflect, unmoved, upon the round
Of smooth and solemnized complacencies,
By which, on Christian Lands from age to age
Profession mocks Performance. Earth is sick,
And heaven is weary, of the hollow words 375
Which States and Kingdoms utter when they talk
Of truth and justice. Turn to private life
And social neighbourhood; look we to ourselves;
A light of duty shines on every day
For all; and yet how few are warmed or cheered! 380
How few who mingle with their fellow-men
And still remain self-governed, and apart,
Like this our honoured friend; and thence acquire
Right to expect his vigorous decline,
That promises to the end a blest old age!" 385

  "Yet," with a smile of triumph thus exclaimed
The Solitary, "In the life of Man,
If to the poetry of common speech

Faith may be given, we see as in a glass
A true reflection of the circling year, 390
With all its seasons. Grant that Spring is there,
In spite of many a rough untoward blast,
Hopeful and promising with buds and flowers;
Yet where is glowing Summer's long rich day,
That *ought* to follow, faithfully expressed? 395
And mellow Autumn, charged with bounteous fruit,
Where is she imaged? in what favoured clime
Her lavish pomp, and ripe magnificence?
—Yet, while the better part is missed, the worse
In Man's autumnal season is set forth 400
With a resemblance not to be denied,
And that contents him; bowers that hear no more
The voice of gladness, less and less supply
Of outward sunshine and internal warmth;
And, with this change, sharp air and falling leaves, 405
Foretelling total Winter, blank and cold.

   How gay the Habitations that adorn
This fertile Valley! Not a House but seems
To give assurance of content within;
Embosomed happiness, and placid love; 410
As if the sunshine of the day were met
With answering brightness in the hearts of all
Who walk this favoured ground. But chance-regards,
And notice forced upon incurious ears;
These, if these only, acting in despite 415
Of the encomiums by my Friend pronounced
On humble life, forbid the judging mind
To trust the smiling aspect of this fair
And noiseless Commonwealth. The simple race
Of Mountaineers, by Nature's self removed 420
From foul temptations, and by constant care
Of a good Shepherd tended, as themselves
Do tend their flocks, These share Man's general lot
With little mitigation. They escape,

Perchance, guilt's heavier woes; and do not feel 425
The tedium of fantastic idleness;
Yet life, as with the multitude, with them,
Is fashioned like an ill constructed tale;
That on the outset wastes its gay desires,
Its fair adventures, its enlivening hopes, 430
And pleasant interests—for the sequel leaving
Old things repeated with diminished grace;
And all the laboured novelties, at best
Imperfect substitutes, whose use and power
Evince the want and weakness whence they spring." 435

   While in this serious mood we held discourse,
The reverend Pastor tow'rds the Church-yard gate
Approached; and, with a mild respectful air
Of native cordiality, our Friend
Advanced to greet him. With a gracious mien 440
Was he received, and mutual joy prevailed.
Awhile they stood in conference, and I guess
That He, who now upon the mossy wall
Sate by my side, had vanished, if a wish
Could have transferred him to his lonely House 445
Within the circuit of those guardian rocks.
—For me, I looked upon the pair, well pleased:
Nature had framed them both, and both were marked
By circumstance with intermixture fine
Of contrast and resemblance. To an Oak 450
Hardy and grand, a weather-beaten Oak,
Fresh in the strength and majesty of age,
One might be likened: flourishing appeared,
Though somewhat past the fulness of his prime,
The Other—like a stately Sycamore, 455
That spreads, in gentler pomp, its honied shade.

   A general greeting was exchanged; and soon
The Pastor learned that his approach had given
A welcome interruption to discourse

Grave, and in truth full often sad.—"Is Man 460
A Child of hope? Do generations press
On generations, without progress made?
Halts the Individual, ere his hairs be grey,
Perforce? Are we a Creature in whom good
Preponderates, or evil? Doth the Will 465
Acknowledge Reason's law? A living Power
Is Virtue, or no better than a name?
Fleeting as health or beauty, and unsound!
So that the only substance which remains,
(For thus the tenor of complaint hath run) 470
Among so many shadows, are the pains
And penalties of miserable life,
Doomed to decay, and then expire in dust!
—Our cogitations this way have been drawn,
These are the points," the Wanderer said, "on which 475
Our Inquest turns.—Accord, good Sir! the light
Of your experience, to dispel this gloom.
By your persuasive wisdom shall the Heart
That frets, or languishes, be stilled and cheered."

  "Our Nature," said the Priest, in mild reply, 480
"Angels may weigh and fathom: they perceive,
With undistempered and unclouded spirit,
The object as it is; but, for ourselves,
That speculative height we may not reach.
The good and evil are our own; and we 485
Are that which we would contemplate from far.
Knowledge, for us, is difficult to gain—
Is difficult to gain and hard to keep—
As Virtue's self; like Virtue is beset
With snares; tried, tempted, subject to decay. 490
Love, admiration, fear, desire, and hate,
Blind were we without these; through these alone
Are capable to notice or discern
Or to record; we judge, but cannot be
Indifferent judges. 'Spite of proudest boast 495

Reason, best Reason, is to imperfect Man
An effort only, and a noble aim;
A crown, an attribute of sovereign power,
Still to be courted—never to be won!
—Look forth, or each man dive into himself, 500
What sees he but a Creature too perturbed,
That is transported to excess; that yearns,
Regrets, or trembles, wrongly, or too much;
Hopes rashly, in disgust as rash recoils;
Battens on spleen, or moulders in despair. 505
Thus truth is missed, and comprehension fails;
And darkness and delusion round our path
Spread, from disease, whose subtile injury lurks
Within the very faculty of sight.

Yet for the general purposes of faith 510
In Providence, for solace and support,
We may not doubt that who can best subject
The will to Reason's law, and strictliest live
And act in that obedience, he shall gain
The clearest apprehension of those truths, 515
Which unassisted reason's utmost power
Is too infirm to reach. But—waiving this,
And our regards confining within bounds
Of less exalted consciousness—through which
The very multitude are free to range— 520
We safely may affirm that human life
Is either fair or tempting, a soft scene
Grateful to sight, refreshing to the soul,
Or a forbidding tract of cheerless view;
Even as the same is looked at, or approached. 525
Permit me," said the Priest continuing, "here
To use an illustration of my thought,
Drawn from the very spot on which we stand.
—In changeful April, when, as he is wont,
Winter has reassumed a short lived sway 530
And whitened all the surface of the fields,

If—from the sullen region of the North
Towards the circuit of this holy ground
Your walk conducts you, ere the vigorous sun,
High climbing, hath attained his noon-tide height— 535
These Mounds, transversely lying side by side
From east to west, before you will appear
A dreary plain of unillumined snow,
With more than wintry cheerlessness and gloom
Saddening the heart. Go forward, and look back; 540
On the same circuit of this church-yard ground
Look, from the quarter whence the Lord of light,
Of life, of love, and gladness, doth dispense
His beams; which, unexcluded in their fall,
Upon the southern side of every grave 545
Have gently exercised a melting power,
Then will a vernal prospect greet your eye,
All fresh and beautiful, and green and bright,
Hopeful and cheerful:—vanished is the snow,
Vanished or hidden; and the whole Domain, 550
To some, too lightly minded, might appear
A meadow carpet for the dancing hours.
—This Contrast, not unsuitable to Life,
Is to that other state more apposite,
Death, and its twofold aspect; wintry—one, 555
Cold, sullen, blank, from hope and joy shut out;
The other, which the ray divine hath touched,
Replete with vivid promise, bright as spring."

"We see, then, as we feel," the Wanderer thus
With a complacent animation spake, 560
"And, in your judgment, Sir! the Mind's repose
On evidence is not to be ensured
By act of naked Reason. Moral truth
Is no mechanic structure, built by rule;
And which, once built, retains a steadfast shape 565
And undisturbed proportions; but a thing
Subject, you deem, to vital accidents;

And, like the water-lilly, lives and thrives;
Whose root is fixed in stable earth, whose head
Floats on the tossing waves. With joy sincere   570
I re-salute these sentiments, confirmed
By your authority. But how acquire
The inward principle, that gives effect
To outward argument; the passive will
Meek to admit; the active energy,   575
Strong and unbounded to embrace, and firm
To keep and cherish? How shall Man unite
A self-forgetting tenderness of heart
And earth-despising dignity of soul?
Wise in that union, and without it blind!"   580

   "The way," said I, "to court, if not obtain
The ingenuous Mind, apt to be set aright;
This, in the lonely Dell discoursing, you
Declared at large; and by what exercise
From visible nature or the inner self   585
Power may be trained, and renovation brought
To those who need the gift. But, after all,
Is aught so certain as that Man is doomed
To breathe beneath a vault of ignorance?
The natural roof of that dark house in which   590
His soul is pent! How little can be known,
This is the wise man's sigh; how far we err,
This is the good man's not unfrequent pang.
And they perhaps err least, the lowly Class
Whom a benign necessity compels   595
To follow Reason's least ambitious course;
Such do I mean who, unperplexed by doubt
And unincited by a wish to look
Into high objects farther than they may,
Pace to and fro, from morn till even-tide,   600
The narrow avenue of daily toil
For daily bread."

"Yes," buoyantly exclaimed
The pale Recluse—"praise to the sturdy plough,
And patient spade, and shepherd's simple crook,
And ponderous loom—resounding while it holds 605
Body and mind in one captivity;
And let the light mechanic tool be hailed
With honour; which, encasing, by the power
Of long companionship, the Artist's hand,
Cuts off that hand, with all its world of nerves, 610
From a too busy commerce with the heart!
—Inglorious implements of craft and toil,
Both ye that shape and build, and ye that force,
By slow solicitation, Earth to yield
Her annual bounty, sparingly dealt forth 615
With wise reluctance, you would I extol
Not for gross good alone which ye produce,
But for the impertinent and ceaseless strife
Of proofs and reasons ye preclude—in those
Who to your dull society are born, 620
And with their humble birth-right rest content.
—Would I had ne'er renounced it!"
       A slight flush
Of moral anger previously had tinged
The Old Man's cheek; but, at this closing turn
Of self-reproach, it passed away. Said he, 625
"That which we feel we utter; as we think
So have we argued; reaping for our pains
No visible recompense. For our relief
You," to the Pastor turning thus he spake,
"Have kindly interposed. May I entreat 630
Your further help? The mine of real life
Dig for us; and present us, in the shape
Of virgin ore, that gold which we by pains
Fruitless as those of aery Alchemists
Seek from the torturing crucible. There lies 635
Around us a Domain where You have long

Held spiritual sway, have guided and consoled,
And watched the outward course and inner heart.
Give us, for our abstractions, solid facts;
For our disputes, plain pictures. Say what Man   640
He is who cultivates yon hanging field;
What qualities of mind She bears, who comes,
For morn and evening service, with her pail,
To that green pasture; place before our sight
The Family who dwell within yon House   645
Fenced round with glittering laurel; or in that
Below, from which the curling smoke ascends.
Or rather, as we stand on holy earth
And have the Dead around us,[1] take from them
Your instances; for they are both best known,   650
And by frail Man most equitably judged.
Epitomize the life; pronounce, You can,
Authentic epitaphs on some of these
Who, from their lowly mansions hither brought,
Beneath this turf lie mouldering at our feet.   655
So, by your records, may our doubts be solved;
And so, not searching higher, we may learn
To prize the breath we share with human kind;
And look upon the dust of Man with awe."

    The Priest replied.—"An office you impose   660
For which peculiar requisites are mine;
Yet much, I feel, is wanting—else the task
Would be most grateful. True indeed it is

---

1 "*Leo.*   You, Sir, would help me to the History
          Of half these Graves?
   Priest.   For eight-Score winters past,
          With what I've witnessed, and with what I've heard,
          Perhaps I might; . . . .
          By turning o'er these hillocks one by one
          We two could travel, Sir, through a strange round,
          Yet all in the broad high-way of the world.
              Author's Poem of the Brothers,
              Published in the Lyrical Ballads in the year 1800." WW.
   See *The Brothers*, ll. 185–191, in vol. 2 of this edition.

That They whom Death has hidden from our sight
Are worthiest of the Mind's regard; with these 665
The future cannot contradict the past:
Mortality's last exercise and proof
Is undergone; the transit made that shews
The very soul, revealed as it departs.
Yet, on your first suggestion, will I give, 670
Ere we descend into these silent vaults,
One Picture from the living.—
                                    You behold,
High on the breast of yon dark mountain—dark
With stony barrenness, a shining speck
Bright as a sun-beam sleeping till a shower 675
Brush it away, or cloud pass over it;
And such it might be deemed—a sleeping sun-beam;
But 'tis a plot of cultivated ground,
Cut off, an island in the dusky waste;
And that attractive brightness is its own. 680
The lofty Site, by nature framed to tempt
Amid a wilderness of rocks and stones
The Tiller's hand, a Hermit might have chosen,
For opportunity presented, thence
Far forth to send his wandering eye o'er land 685
And ocean, and look down upon the works,
The habitations, and the ways of men,
Himself unseen! But no tradition tells
That ever Hermit dipped his maple dish
In the sweet spring that lurks mid yon green fields; 690
And no such visionary views belong
To those who occupy and till the ground,
And on the bosom of the mountain dwell—
A wedded Pair, in childless solitude.
—A House of stones collected on the spot, 695
By rude hands built, with rocky knolls in front,
Backed also by a ledge of rock, whose crest
Of birch-trees waves above the chimney top;

In shape, in size, and colour, an abode
Such as in unsafe times of Border war 700
Might have been wished for and contrived—to elude
The eye of roving Plunderer, for their need
Suffices; and unshaken bears the assault
Of their most dreaded foe, the strong South-west,
In anger blowing from the distant sea. 705
—Alone within her solitary Hut;
There, or within the compass of her fields,
At any moment may the Dame be found,
True as the Stock-dove to her shallow nest
And to the grove that holds it. She beguiles 710
By intermingled work of house and field
The summer's day, and winter's; with success
Not equal, but sufficient to maintain,
Even at the worst, a smooth stream of content,
Until the expected hour at which her Mate 715
From the far-distant Quarry's vault returns;
And by his converse crowns a silent day
With evening cheerfulness. In powers of mind,
In scale of culture, few among my Flock
Hold lower rank than this sequestered Pair. 720
But humbleness of heart descends from heaven;
And that best gift of heaven hath fallen on them;
Abundant recompence for every want.
—Stoop from your height, ye proud, and copy these!
Who, in their noiseless dwelling-place, can hear 725
The voice of wisdom whispering scripture texts
For the mind's government, or temper's peace;
And recommending, for their mutual need,
Forgiveness, patience, hope, and charity!"

"Much was I pleased," the grey-haired Wanderer said, 730
"When to those shining fields our notice first
You turned; and yet more pleased have from your lips
Gathered this fair report of those who dwell
In that Retirement; whither, by such course

Of evil hap and good as oft awaits 735
A lone way-faring Man, I once was brought.
Dark on my road the autumnal evening fell
While I was traversing yon mountain-pass,
And night succeeded with unusual gloom;
So that my feet and hands at length became 740
Guides better than mine eyes—until a light
High in the gloom appeared, too high, methought,
For human habitation; but I longed
To reach it, destitute of other hope.
I looked with steadiness as Sailors look 745
On the north star, or watch-tower's distant lamp,
And saw the light—now fixed—and shifting now—
Not like a dancing meteor, but in line
Of never-varying motion, to and fro.
It is no night-fire of the naked hills, 750
Said I, some friendly covert must be near.
With this persuasion thitherward my steps
I turn, and reach at last the guiding Light;
Joy to myself! but to the heart of Her
Who there was standing on the open hill, 755
(The same kind Matron whom your tongue hath praised)
Alarm and disappointment! The alarm
Ceased, when she learned through what mishap I came,
And by what help had gained those distant fields.
Drawn from her Cottage, on that open height 760
Bearing a lantern in her hand she stood,
Or paced the ground—to guide her Husband home,
By that unwearied signal, kenned afar;
An anxious duty! which the lofty Site,
Far from all public road or beaten way 765
And traversed only by a few faint paths,
Imposes, whensoe'er untoward chance
(Such chance is rare) detains him till the night
Falls black upon the hills. "But come," she said,
"Come let me lead you to our poor Abode. 770

Behind those rocks it stands, as if it shunned,
In churlishness, the eye of all mankind;
But the few Guests who seek the door receive
Most hearty welcome."—Entering I beheld
A blazing fire—beside a cleanly hearth 775
Sate down; and to her office, with leave asked,
The Dame returned.—Before that glowing pile
Of mountain turf required the Builder's hand
Its wasted splendour to repair, the door
Opened, and she re-entered with glad looks, 780
Her Helpmate following. Hospitable fare,
Frank conversation, made the evening's treat.
Need a bewildered Traveller wish for more?
But more was given; the eye, the mind, the heart,
Found exercise in noting, as we sate 785
By the bright fire, the good Man's face—composed
Of features elegant; an open brow
Of undisturbed humanity; a cheek
Suffused with something of a feminine hue;
Eyes beaming courtesy and mild regard; 790
But, in the quicker turns of the discourse,
Expression slowly varying, that evinced
A tardy apprehension. From a fount
Lost, thought I, in the obscurities of time,
But honoured once, these features and that mien 795
May have descended, though I see them here.
In such a Man, so gentle and subdued,
Withal so graceful in his gentleness,
A race illustrious for heroic deeds,
Humbled, but not degraded, may expire. 800
This pleasing fancy (cherished and upheld
By sundry recollections of such fall
From high to low, ascent from low to high,
As books record, and even the careless mind
Cannot but notice among men and things) 805
Went with me to the place of my repose.

    Rouzed by the crowing cock at dawn of day,
I yet had risen too late to interchange
A morning salutation with my Host,
Gone forth already to the far-off seat   810
Of his day's work. "Three dark mid-winter months
"Pass," said the Matron, "and I never see,
"Save when the Sabbath brings its kind release,
"My Help-mate's face by light of day. He quits
"His door in darkness, nor till dusk returns.   815
"And, through heaven's blessing, thus we gain the bread
"For which we pray; and for the wants provide
"Of sickness, accident, and helpless age.
"Companions have I many; many Friends,
"Dependants, Comforters—my Wheel, my Fire,   820
"All day the House-clock ticking in mine ear,
"The cackling Hen, the tender Chicken brood,
"And the wild Birds that gather round my porch.
"This honest Sheep-dog's countenance I read;
"With him can talk; nor seldom waste a word   825
"On Creatures less intelligent and shrewd.
"And if the blustering Wind that drives the clouds
"Care not for me, he lingers round my door,
"And makes me pastime when our tempers suit;
"—But, above all, my Thoughts are my support."   830
The Matron ended—nor could I forbear
To exclaim—"O happy! yielding to the law
Of these privations, richer in the main!
While thankless thousands are oppressed and clogged
By ease and leisure—by the very wealth   835
And pride of opportunity made poor;
While tens of thousands falter in their path,
And sink, through utter want of cheering light,
For you the hours of labour do not flag;
For you each Evening hath its shining Star,   840
And every Sabbath-day its golden Sun."

    "Yes!" said the Solitary, with a smile

That seemed to break from an expanding heart,
"The untutored Bird may found, and so construct,
And with such soft materials line her nest, 845
Fixed in the centre of a prickly brake,
That the thorns wound her not; they only guard.
Powers, not unjustly likened to those gifts
Of happy instinct which the woodland Bird
Shares with her species, Nature's grace sometimes 850
Upon the Individual doth confer,
Among the higher creatures born and trained
To use of reason. And, I own, that tired
Of the ostentatious world—a swelling stage
With empty actions and vain passions stuffed, 855
And from the private struggles of mankind
Hoping for less than I could wish to hope,
Far less than once I trusted and believed—
I love to hear of Those, who, not contending
Nor summoned to contend for Virtue's prize, 860
Miss not the humbler good at which they aim;
Blest with a kindly faculty to blunt
The edge of adverse circumstance, and turn
Into their contraries the petty plagues
And hindrances with which they stand beset. 865
—In early youth among my native hills
I knew a Scottish Peasant who possessed
A few small Crofts of stone-encumbered ground;
Masses of every shape and size, that lay
Scattered about beneath the mouldering walls 870
Of a rough precipice; and some, apart,
In quarters unobnoxious to such chance,
As if the moon had showered them down in spite,
But he repined not. Though the plough was scared
By these obstructions, "round the shady stones 875
A fertilizing moisture," said the Swain,
"Gathers, and is preserved; and feeding dews
"And damps, through all the droughty Summer day,

"From out their substance issuing, maintain
"Herbage that never fails; no grass springs up 880
"So green, so fresh, so plentiful, as mine!"
See, in this well conditioned Soul, a Third
To match with your good Couple that put forth
Their homely graces on the mountain side.
But thinly sown these Natures; rare at least 885
The mutual aptitude of seed and soil
That yields such kindly product. He—whose bed
Perhaps yon loose sods cover, the poor Pensioner
Brought yesterday from our sequestered dell
Here to lie down in lasting quiet—he, 890
If living now, could otherwise report
Of rustic loneliness: that grey-haired Orphan—
So call him, for humanity to him
No parent was—could feelingly have told,
In life, in death, what Solitude can breed 895
Of selfishness, and cruelty, and vice;
Or, if it breed not, hath not power to cure.
—But your compliance, Sir! with our request
My words too long have hindered."
       Undeterred,
Perhaps incited rather, by these shocks, 900
In no ungracious opposition, given
To the confiding spirit of his own
Experienced faith, the reverend Pastor said,
Around him looking, "Where shall I begin?
Who shall be first selected from my Flock 905
Gathered together in their peaceful fold?"
He paused—and having lifted up his eyes
To the pure Heaven, he cast them down again
Upon the earth beneath his feet; and spake.
—"To a mysteriously-consorted Pair 910
This place is consecrate; to Death and Life,
And to the best Affections that proceed
From their conjunction. Consecrate to faith

In Him who bled for man upon the Cross;
Hallowed to Revelation; and no less 915
To Reason's mandates; and the hopes divine
Of pure Imagination;—above all,
To Charity, and Love; that have provided,
Within these precincts, a capacious bed
And receptacle, open to the good 920
And evil, to the just and the unjust;
In which they find an equal resting-place:
Even as the multitude of kindred brooks
And streams, whose murmur fills this hollow vale,
Whether their course be turbulent or smooth, 925
Their waters clear or sullied, all are lost
Within the bosom of yon chrystal Lake,
And end their journey in the same repose!

   And blest are they who sleep; and we that know,
While in a spot like this we breathe and walk, 930
That All beneath us by the wings are covered
Of motherly Humanity, outspread
And gathering all within their tender shade,
Though loth and slow to come! A battle-field,
In stillness left when slaughter is no more, 935
With this compared, is a strange spectacle!
A rueful sight the wild shore strewn with wrecks
And trod by people in afflicted quest
Of friends and kindred, whom the angry Sea
Restores not to their prayer! Ah! who would think 940
That all the scattered subjects which compose
Earth's melancholy vision through the space
Of all her climes; these wretched—these depraved,
To virtue lost, insensible of peace,
From the delights of charity cut off, 945
To pity dead—the Oppressor and the Oppressed;
Tyrants who utter the destroying word,
And Slaves who will consent to be destroyed;
Were of one species with the sheltered few,

Who with a dutiful and tender hand 950
Did lodge, in an appropriated spot,
This file of Infants; some that never breathed
The vital air; and others, who, allowed
That privilege, did yet expire too soon,
Or with too brief a warning, to admit 955
Administration of the holy rite
That lovingly consigns the Babe to the arms
Of Jesus, and his everlasting care.
These that in trembling hope are laid apart;
And the besprinkled Nursling, unrequired 960
Till he begins to smile upon the breast
That feeds him; and the tottering Little-one
Taken from air and sunshine when the rose
Of Infancy first blooms upon his cheek;
The thinking, thoughtless School-boy; the bold Youth 965
Of soul impetuous, and the bashful Maid
Smitten while all the promises of life
Are opening round her; those of middle age,
Cast down while confident in strength they stand,
Like pillars fixed more firmly, as might seem, 970
And more secure, by very weight of all
That, for support, rests on them; the decayed
And burthensome; and, lastly, that poor few
Whose light of reason is with age extinct;
The hopeful and the hopeless, first and last, 975
The earliest summoned and the longest spared,
Are here deposited, with tribute paid
Various; but unto each some tribute paid;
As if, amid these peaceful hills and groves,
Society were touched with kind concern, 980
And gentle "Nature grieved that One should die;"[1]
Or, if the change demanded no regret,

---

1 "*'And suffering Nature grieved that one should die.'*
 Southey's Retrospect."
 WW quotes l. 140 of Robert Southey's *The Retrospect*.

Observed the liberating stroke—and blessed.
—And whence that tribute? wherefore these regards?[1]
Not from the naked *Heart* alone of Man 985
(Though framed to high distinction upon earth
As the sole spring and fountain-head of tears,
His own peculiar utterance for distress
Or gladness) No," the philosophic Priest
Continued, "'tis not in the vital seat 990
Of feeling to produce them, without aid
From the pure Soul, the Soul sublime and pure;
With her two faculties of Eye and Ear,
The one by which a Creature, whom his sins
Have rendered prone, can upward look to heaven; 995
The other that empowers him to perceive
The voice of Deity, on height and plain
Whispering those truths in stillness, which the Word,
To the four quarters of the winds, proclaims.
Not without such assistance could the use 1000
Of these benign observances prevail.
Thus are they born, thus fostered, and maintained;
And by the care prospective of our wise
Forefathers, who, to guard against the shocks,
The fluctuation and decay of things, 1005
Embodied and established these high Truths
In solemn Institutions:—Men convinced
That Life is Love and Immortality,
The Being one, and one the Element.
There lies the channel, and original bed, 1010
From the beginning, hollowed out and scooped
For Man's Affections—else betrayed and lost,
And swallowed up mid desarts infinite!

---

1 "The sentiments and opinions here uttered are in unison with those expressed in the following Essay upon Epitaphs, which was furnished by the author for Mr. Coleridge's periodical work, the Friend; and as they are dictated by a spirit congenial to that which pervades this and the two succeeding books, the sympathizing reader will not be displeased to see the Essay here annexed." WW's essay is reproduced in the notes at the end of this volume.

—This is the genuine course, the aim, and end,
Of prescient Reason; all conclusions else   1015
Are abject, vain, presumptuous, and perverse.
The faith partaking of those holy times,
Life, I repeat, is energy of Love
Divine or human; exercised in pain,
In strife, and tribulation; and ordained,   1020
If so approved and sanctified, to pass,
Through shades and silent rest, to endless joy."

END OF THE FIFTH BOOK.

BOOK THE SIXTH

THE CHURCH-YARD AMONG THE MOUNTAINS

Hail to the Crown by Freedom shaped—to gird
An English Sovereign's brow! and to the Throne
Whereon he sits! Whose deep foundations lie
In veneration and the People's love,
Whose steps are equity, whose seat is law.   5
—Hail to the State of England! And conjoin
With this a salutation as devout,
Made to the spiritual Fabric of her Church;
Founded in truth; by blood of Martyrdom
Cemented; by the hands of Wisdom reared   10
In beauty of Holiness, with order'd pomp,
Decent, and unreproved. The voice, that greets
The majesty of both, shall pray for both;
That, mutually protected and sustained,
They may endure as long as sea surrounds   15
This favoured Land, or sunshine warms her soil.
—And, O, ye swelling hills, and spacious plains!
Besprent from shore to shore with steeple-towers,
And spires whose "silent finger points to Heaven;"[1]

---

1 "An instinctive taste teaches men to build their churches in flat countries with

Nor wanting, at wide intervals, the bulk 20
Of ancient Minster, lifted above the cloud
Of the dense air, which town or city breeds
To intercept the sun's glad beams—may ne'er
That true succession fail of English Hearts,
That can perceive, not less than heretofore 25
Our Ancestors did feelingly perceive,
What in those holy Structures ye possess
Of ornamental interest, and the charm
Of pious sentiment diffused afar,
And human charity, and social love. 30
—Thus never shall the indignities of Time
Approach their reverend graces, unopposed;
Nor shall the Elements be free to hurt
Their fair proportions; nor the blinder rage
Of bigot zeal madly to overturn; 35
And, if the desolating hand of war
Spare them, they shall continue to bestow—
Upon the thronged abodes of busy Men
(Depraved, and ever prone to fill their minds
Exclusively with transitory things) 40
An air and mien of dignified pursuit;
Of sweet civility—on rustic wilds.
—The Poet, fostering for his native land
Such hope, entreats that Servants may abound
Of those pure Altars worthy; Ministers 45
Detached from pleasure, to the love of gain
Superior, insusceptible of pride,
And by ambition's longings undisturbed;
Men, whose delight is where their duty leads
Or fixes them; whose least distinguished day 50
Shines with some portion of that heavenly lustre

---

spire-steeples, which as they cannot be referred to any other object, point as with silent finger to the sky and stars, and sometimes when they reflect the brazen light of a rich though rainy sunset, appear like a pyramid of flame burning heaven-ward. See 'The Friend,' by S. T. Coleridge, No. 14. p. 223." WW quotes from an essay by Coleridge.

Which makes the Sabbath lovely in the sight
Of blessed Angels, pitying human cares.
—And, as on earth it is the doom of Truth
To be perpetually attacked by foes 55
Open or covert, be that Priesthood still,
For her defence, replenished with a Band
Of strenuous Champions, in scholastic arts
Thoroughly disciplined; nor (if in course
Of the revolving World's disturbances 60
Cause should recur, which righteous Heaven avert!
To meet such trial) from their spiritual Sires
Degenerate; who, constrained to wield the sword
Of disputation, shrunk not, though assailed
With hostile din, and combating in sight 65
Of angry umpires, partial and unjust.
And did, thereafter, bathe their hands in fire,
So to declare the conscience satisfied:
Nor for their bodies would accept release,
But, blessing God and praising him, bequeathed, 70
With their last breath, from out the smouldering flame,
The faith which they by diligence had earned,
And through illuminating grace received,
For their dear Country-men, and all mankind.
O high example, constancy divine! 75

   Even such a Man (inheriting the zeal
And from the sanctity of elder times
Not deviating,—a Priest, the like of whom,
If multiplied, and in their stations set,
Would o'er the bosom of a joyful Land 80
Spread true Religion, and her genuine fruits)
Before me stood that day; on holy ground
Fraught with the relics of mortality,
Exalting tender themes, by just degrees
To lofty raised; and to the highest, last; 85
The head and mighty paramount of truths;
Immortal life, in never-fading worlds,

For mortal Creatures, conquered and secured.

   That basis laid, those principles of faith
Announced, as a preparatory act   90
Of reverence to the spirit of the place;
The Pastor cast his eyes upon the ground,
Not, as before, like one oppressed with awe,
But with a mild and social chearfulness;
Then to the Solitary turned, and spake.   95

   "At morn or eve, in your retired Domain,
Perchance you not unfrequently have marked
A Visitor—intent upon the task
Of prying, low and high, for herbs and flowers:
Too delicate employ, as would appear,   100
For One, who, though of drooping mien, had yet,
From Nature's kindliness, received a frame
Robust as ever rural labour bred."

   The Solitary answered. "Such a Form
Full well I recollect. We often crossed   105
Each other's path; but, as the Intruder seemed
Fondly to prize the silence which he kept,
And I as willingly did cherish mine,
We met, and passed, like shadows. I have heard,
From my good Host, that he was crazed in brain   110
By unrequited love; and scaled the rocks,
Dived into caves, and pierced the matted woods,
In hope to find some virtuous herb, of power
To cure his malady!"
                          The Vicar smiled,
"Alas! before to-morrow's sun goes down   115
His habitation will be here: for him
That open grave is destined."
                                    "Died he then
Of pain and grief," the Solitary asked,
"Believe it not—oh! never could that be!"

"He loved," the vicar answered, "deeply loved, 120
Loved fondly, truly, fervently; and pined
When he had told his love, and sued in vain,
—Rejected—yea repelled—and, if with scorn
Upon the haughty maiden's brow, 'tis but
A high-prized plume which female Beauty wears. 125
That he could brook, and glory in;—but when
The tidings came that she whom he had wooed
Was wedded to another, and his heart
Was forced to rend away its only hope,
Then, Pity could have scarcely found on earth 130
An Object worthier of regard than he,
In the transition of that bitter hour!
Lost was she, lost; nor could the sufferer say
That in the act of preference he had been
Unjustly dealt with; but the Maid was gone! 135
She, whose dear name with unregarded sighs
He long had blessed, whose Image was preserved—
Shrined in his breast with fond idolatry,
Had vanished from his prospects and desires;
Not by translation to the heavenly Choir 140
Who have put off their mortal spoils—ah no!
She lives another's wishes to complete,
"Joy be their lot, and happiness," he cried,
"His lot and hers, as misery is mine!"

   Such was that strong concussion; but the Man 145
Who trembled, trunk and limbs, like some huge Oak
By a fierce tempest shaken, soon resumed
The stedfast quiet natural to a Mind
Of composition gentle and sedate,
And in its movements circumspect and slow. 150
Of rustic Parents bred, He had been trained,
(So prompted their aspiring wish) to skill
In numbers and the sedentary art
Of penmanship,—with pride professed, and taught
By his endeavours in the mountain dales. 155

Now, those sad tidings weighing on his heart,
To books, and papers, and the studious desk,
He stoutly readdressed himself—resolved
To quell his pain, and enter on the path
Of old pursuits with keener appetite   160
And closer industry. Of what ensued,
Within his soul, no outward sign appeared
Till a betraying sickliness was seen
To tinge his cheek; and through his frame it crept
With slow mutation unconcealable;   165
Such universal change as autumn makes
In the fair body of a leafy grove
Discoloured, then divested. 'Tis affirmed
By Poets skilled in nature's secret ways
That Love will not submit to be controlled   170
By mastery:—and the good Man lacked not Friends
Who strove to instil this truth into his mind,
A mind in all heart-mysteries unversed.
"Go to the hills," said one, "remit awhile
"This baneful diligence:—at early morn   175
"Court the fresh air, explore the heaths and woods;
"And, leaving it to others to foretell,
"By calculations sage, the ebb and flow
"Of tides, and when the moon will be eclipsed,
"Do you, for your own benefit, construct   180
"A calendar of flowers, plucked as they blow
"Where health abides, and chearfulness, and peace."
The attempt was made;—'tis needless to report
How hopelessly:—but Innocence is strong,
And an entire simplicity of mind   185
A thing most sacred in the eye of Heaven,
That opens, for such Sufferers, relief
Within their souls, a fount of grace divine;
And doth commend their weakness and disease
To Nature's care, assisted in her office   190
By all the Elements that round her wait

To generate, to preserve, and to restore;
And by her beautiful array of Forms
Shedding sweet influence from above, or pure
Delight exhaling from the ground they tread." 195

  "Impute it not to impatience, if," exclaimed
The Wanderer, "I infer that he was healed
By perseverance in the course prescribed."

  "You do not err: the powers, which had been lost
By slow degrees, were gradually regained; 200
The fluttering nerves composed; the beating heart
In rest established; and the jarring thoughts
To harmony restored.—But yon dark mold
Will cover him; in height of strength—to earth
Hastily smitten, by a fever's force. 205
Yet not with stroke so sudden as refused
Time to look back with tenderness on her
Whom he had loved in passion,—and to send
Some farewell words; and, with those words, a prayer
That, from his dying hand, she would accept, 210
Of his possessions, that which most he prized;
A Book, upon the surface of whose leaves
Some chosen plants, disposed with nicest care,
In undecaying beauty were preserved.
Mute register, to him, of time and place, 215
And various fluctuations in the breast;
To her, a monument of faithful Love
Conquered, and in tranquillity retained!

  Close to his destined habitation, lies
One whose Endeavours did at length achieve 220
A victory less worthy of regard,
Though marvellous in its kind. A Place exists
High in these mountains, that allured a Band
Of keen Adventurers to unite their pains,
In search of treasure there by Nature formed, 225

And there concealed: but they who tried were foiled,
And all desisted, all, save he alone;
Who taking counsel of his own clear thoughts,
And trusting only to his own weak hands,
Urged unremittingly the stubborn work,   230
Unseconded, uncountenanc'd; then, as time
Passed on, while still his lonely efforts found
No recompence, derided; and, at length,
By many pitied, as insane of mind;
By others dreaded as the luckless Thrall   235
Of subterraneous Spirits, feeding hope
By various mockery of sight and sound;
Hope, after hope, encouraged and destroyed.
—But when the Lord of seasons had matured
The fruits of earth through space of twice ten years,   240
The mountain's entrails offered to the view
Of the Old Man, and to his trembling grasp,
His bright, his long-deferred, his dear reward.
Not with more transport did Columbus greet
A world, his rich discovery! But our Swain,   245
A very Hero till his point was gained,
Proved all unable to support the weight
Of prosperous fortune. On the fields he looked
With an unsettled liberty of thought,
Of schemes and wishes; in the day-light walked   250
Giddy and restless; ever and anon
Quaffed in his gratitude immoderate cups;
And truly might be said to die of joy!
—He vanish'd; but conspicuous to this day
The Path remains that linked his Cottage-door   255
To the Mine's mouth; a long, and slanting track,
Upon the rugged mountain's stony side,
Worn by his daily visits to and from
The darksome centre of a constant hope.
This Vestige, neither force of beating rain,   260
Nor the vicissitudes of frost and thaw

Shall cause to fade, 'till ages pass away;
And it is named, in memory of the event,
THE PATH OF PERSEVERANCE."
                    "Thou, from whom
Man has his strength," exclaimed the Wanderer, "oh! 265
Do Thou direct it!—to the Virtuous grant
The penetrative eye which can perceive
In this blind world the guiding vein of hope,
That, like this Labourer, such may dig their way,
"Unshaken, unseduced, unterrified;" 270
Grant to the Wise his firmness of resolve!"

    "That prayer were not superfluous," said the Priest,
"Amid the noblest relics, proudest Dust,
That Westminster, for Britain's glory, holds,
Within the bosom of her awful Pile, 275
Ambitiously collected. Yet the sigh,
Which wafts that prayer to Heaven, is due to all,
Wherever laid, who living fell below
Their virtue's humbler mark; a sigh of pain
If to the opposite extreme they sank. 280
How would you pity Her who yonder rests;
Him, farther off; the Pair, who here are laid;
But, above all, that mixture of Earth's Mold
Whom sight of this green Hillock to my mind
Recalls.—*He* lived not till his locks were nipped 285
By seasonable frost of age; nor died
Before his temples, prematurely forced
To mix the manly brown with silver grey,
Gave obvious instance of the sad effect
Produced, when thoughtless Folly hath usurped 290
The natural crown which sage Experience wears.
—Gay, volatile, ingenious, quick to learn,
And prompt to exhibit all that he possessed
Or could perform; a zealous actor—hired
Into the troop of mirth, a soldier—sworn 295
Into the lists of giddy enterprize

Such was he; yet, as if within his frame
Two several Souls alternately had lodged,
Two sets of manners, could the youth put on;
And, fraught with antics as the Indian bird   300
That writhes and chatters in her wiry cage,
Was graceful, when it pleased him, smooth and still
As the mute Swan that floats adown the stream,
Or, on the waters of the unruffled lake,
Anchors her placid beauty. Not a Leaf,   305
That flutters on the bough, more light than He;
And not a Flower, that droops in the green shade,
More winningly reserved! If Ye inquire
How such consummate elegance was bred
Amid these wilds; a Composition framed   310
Of qualities so adverse—to diffuse,
Where'er he moved, diversified delight;
A simple answer may suffice, even this,
'Twas Nature's will; who sometimes undertakes,
For the reproof of human vanity,   315
Art to outstrip in her peculiar walk.
Hence, for this Favourite, lavishly endowed
With personal gifts, and bright instinctive wit,
While both, embellishing each other, stood
Yet farther recommended by the charm   320
Of fine demeanor, and by dance and song,
And skill in letters, every fancy shaped
Fair expectations; nor, when to the World's
Capacious field forth went the Adventurer, there
Were he and his attainments overlooked,   325
Or scantily rewarded; but all hopes,
Cherished for him, he suffered to depart,
Like blighted buds; or clouds that mimicked Land
Before the Sailor's eye; or diamond drops
That sparkling decked the morning grass; or aught   330
That was attractive—and hath ceased to be!
—Yet, when this Prodigal returned, the rites

Of joyful greeting were on him bestowed,
Who, by humiliation undeterred,
Sought for his weariness a place of rest   335
Within his Father's gates.—Whence came He?—clothed
In tattered garb, from hovels where abides
Necessity, the stationary Host
Of vagrant Poverty; from rifted barns
Where no one dwells but the wide-staring Owl   340
And the Owl's Prey; none permanently house
But many harbour; from these Haunts, to which
He had descended from the proud Saloon,
He came, the Ghost of beauty and of health,
The Wreck of gaiety! But soon revived   345
In strength, in power refitted, he renewed
His suit to Fortune; and she smiled again
Upon a fickle Ingrate. Thrice he rose,
Thrice sunk as willingly. For He, whose nerves
Were used to thrill with pleasure, while his voice   350
Softly accompanied the tuneful harp,
By the nice finger of fair Ladies, touched
In glittering Halls, was able to derive
Not less enjoyment from an abject choice.
Who happier for the moment?—Who more blithe   355
Than this fallen Spirit; in those dreary Holds
His Talents lending to exalt the freaks
Of merry-making Beggars,—now, provoked
To laughter multiplied in louder peals
By his malicious wit; then, all enchained   360
With mute astonishment, themselves to see
In their own arts outdone, their fame eclipsed,
As by the very presence of the Fiend
Who dictates and inspires illusive feats,
For knavish purposes! The City, too,   365
(With shame I speak it) to her guilty bowers
Allured him, sunk so low in self-respect
As there to linger, there to eat his bread,

Hired Minstrel of voluptuous blandishment;
Charming the air with skill of hand or voice, 370
Listen who would, be wrought upon who might,
Sincerely wretched Hearts, or falsely gay.
—Truths I record to many known, for such
The not unfrequent tenor of his boast
In ears that relished the report;—but all 375
Was from his Parents happily concealed;
Who saw enough for blame and pitying love.
They also were permitted to receive
His last, repentant breath; and closed his eyes,
No more to open on that irksome world 380
Where he had long existed in the state
Of a young Fowl beneath one Mother hatched,
Though from another sprung—of different kind:
Where he had lived, and could not cease to live,
Distracted in propensity; content 385
With neither element of good or ill;
And yet in both rejoicing; man unblest;
Of contradictions infinite the slave,
Till his deliverance, when Mercy made him
One with Himself, and one with those who sleep." 390

  "'Tis strange," observed the Solitary, "strange
It seems, and scarcely less than pitiful
That in a Land where Charity provides
For all who can no longer feed themselves,
A Man like this should choose to bring his shame 395
To the parental door; and with his sighs
Infect the air which he had freely breathed
In happy infancy. He could not pine,
Whencee'er rejected howsoe'er forlorn,
Through lack of converse, no, he must have found 400
Abundant exercise for thought and speech
In his dividual Being, self-reviewed,
Self-catechized, self-punished.—Some there are
Who, drawing near their final Home, and much

And daily longing that the same were reached,   405
Would rather shun than seek the fellowship
Of kindred mold.—Such haply here are laid?"

  "Yes," said the Priest, "the Genius of our Hills
Who seems, by these stupendous barriers cast
Round his Domain, desirous not alone   410
To keep his own, but also to exclude
All other progeny, doth sometimes lure,
Even by this studied depth of privacy,
The unhappy Alien hoping to obtain
Concealment, or seduced by wish to find,   415
In place from outward molestation free,
Helps to internal ease. Of many such
Could I discourse; but as their stay was brief
So their departure only left behind
Fancies, and loose conjectures. Other trace   420
Survives, for worthy mention, of a Pair
Who, from the pressure of their several fates,
Meeting as Strangers, in a petty Town
Whose blue roofs ornament a distant reach
Of this far-winding Vale, remained as Friends   425
True to their choice; and gave their bones in trust
To this loved Cemetery, here to lodge
With unescutcheoned privacy interred
Far from the Family-vault.—A Chieftain One
By right of birth; within whose spotless breast   430
The fire of ancient Caledonia burned.
He, with the foremost whose impatience hailed
The Stuart, landing to resume, by force
Of arms, the crown which Bigotry had lost,
Arouzed his clan; and, fighting at their head,   435
With his brave sword endeavoured to prevent
Culloden's fatal overthrow.—Escaped
From that disastrous rout, to foreign shores
He fled; and when the lenient hand of Time
Those troubles had appeased, he sought and gained,   440

For his obscured condition, an obscure
Retreat, within this nook of English ground.
—The Other, born in Britain's southern tract,
Had fixed his milder loyalty, and placed
His gentler sentiments of love and hate, 445
There, where they placed them who in conscience prized
The new succession, as a line of Kings
Whose oath had virtue to protect the Land
Against the dire assaults of Papacy
And arbitrary Rule. But launch thy Bark 450
On the distempered flood of public life,
And cause for most rare triumph will be thine
If, spite of keenest eye and steadiest hand,
The Stream, that bears thee forward, prove not, soon
Or late, a perilous Master. He, who oft, 455
Under the battlements and stately trees
That round his Mansion cast a sober gloom,
Had moralized on this, and other truths
Of kindred import, pleased and satisfied,
Was forced to vent his wisdom with a sigh 460
Heaved from the heart in fortune's bitterness
When he had crushed a plentiful estate
By ruinous Contest, to obtain a Seat
In Britain's Senate. Fruitless was the attempt:
And while the uproar of that desperate strife 465
Continued yet to vibrate on his ear,
The vanquished Whig, beneath a *borrowed* name,
(For the mere sound and echo of his own
Haunted him with sensations of disgust
Which he was glad to lose) slunk from the World 470
To the deep shade of these untravelled Wilds;
In which the Scottish Laird had long possessed
An undisturbed Abode.—Here, then, they met,
Two doughty Champions; flaming Jacobite
And sullen Hanoverian! You might think 475
That losses and vexations, less severe

Than those which they had severally sustained,
Would have inclined each to abate his zeal
For his ungrateful cause; no,—I have heard
My reverend Father tell that, mid the calm   480
Of that small Town encountering thus, they filled,
Daily, its Bowling-green with harmless strife;
Plagued with uncharitable thoughts the Church;
And vexed the Market-place. But in the breasts
Of these Opponents gradually was wrought,   485
With little change of general sentiment,
Such change towards each other, that their days
By choice were spent in constant fellowship;
And if, at times, they fretted with the yoke,
Those very bickerings made them love it more.   490

   A favourite boundary to their lengthened walks
This Church-yard was. And, whether they had come
Treading their path in sympathy and linked
In social converse, or by some short space
Discreetly parted to preserve the peace,   495
One Spirit seldom failed to extend its sway
Over both minds, when they awhile had marked
The visible quiet of this holy ground
And breathed its soothing air;—the Spirit of hope
And saintly magnanimity; that, spurning   500
The field of selfish difference and dispute,
And every care which transitory things,
Earth, and the kingdoms of the earth, create,
Doth, by a rapture of forgetfulness,
Preclude forgiveness, from the praise debarred,   505
Which else the Christian Virtue might have claimed.
—There live who yet remember here to have seen
Their courtly Figures,—seated on the stump
Of an old Yew, their favourite resting-place.
But, as the Remnant of the long-lived Tree   510
Was disappearing by a swift decay,
They, with joint care, determined to erect,

Upon its site, a Dial, which should stand
For public use; and also might survive							515
As their own private monument; for this
Was the particular spot, in which they wished,
(And Heaven was pleased to accomplish the desire)
That, undivided, their Remains should lie.
So, where the mouldered Tree had stood, was raised
Yon Structure, framing, with the ascent of steps				520
That to the decorated Pillar lead,
A work of art, more sumptuous, as might seem,
Than suits this Place; yet built in no proud scorn
Of rustic homeliness; they only aimed
To ensure for it respectful guardianship.						525
Around the margin of the Plate, whereon
The Shadow falls, to note the stealthy hours
Winds an inscriptive Legend"—At these words
Thither we turned; and, gathered, as we read,
The appropriate sense, in Latin numbers couched.			530
"Time flies; it is his melancholy task
"To bring, and bear away, delusive hopes,
"And re-produce the troubles he destroys.
"But, while his blindness thus is occupied,
"Discerning Mortal! do thou serve the will					535
"Of Time's eternal Master, and that peace,
"Which the World wants, shall be for Thee confirmed."

   "Smooth verse, inspired by no unlettered Muse,"
Exclaimed the Sceptic, "and the strain of thought
Accords with Nature's language;—the soft voice				540
Of yon white torrent falling down the rocks
Speaks, less distinctly, to the same effect.
If, then, their blended influence be not lost
Upon our hearts, not wholly lost, I grant,
Even upon mine, the more are we required					545
To feel for those, among our fellow men,
Who, offering no obeisance to the world,
Are yet made desperate by "too quick a sense

Of constant infelicity"—cut off
From peace like Exiles on some barren rock, 550
Their life's appointed prison; not more free
Than Centinels, between two armies, set,
With nothing better, in the chill night air,
Than their own thoughts to comfort them.—Say why
That ancient story of Prometheus chained? 555
The Vulture—the inexhaustible repast
Drawn from his vitals! Say what meant the woes
By Tantalus entailed upon his race,
And the dark sorrows of the line of Thebes?
Fictions in form, but in their substance truths, 560
Tremendous truths! familiar to the men
Of long-past times; nor obsolete in ours.
—Exchange the Shepherd's frock of native grey
For robes with regal purple tinged; convert
The crook into a sceptre;—give the pomp 565
Of circumstance, and here the tragic Muse
Shall find apt subjects for her highest art.
—Amid the groves, beneath the shadowy hills
The generations are prepared; the pangs,
The internal pangs are ready; the dread strife 570
Of poor humanity's afflicted will
Struggling in vain with ruthless destiny."

   "Though," said the Priest in answer, "these be terms
Which a divine philosophy rejects,
We, whose established and unfailing trust 575
Is in controuling Providence, admit
That through all stations human life abounds
With mysteries,—for if Faith were left untried
How could the might—that lurks within her—then
Be shewn? her glorious excellence—that ranks 580
Among the first of Powers and Virtues—proved?
Our system is not fashioned to preclude
That sympathy which you for others ask;
And I could tell, not travelling for my theme

Beyond the limits of these humble graves, 585
Of strange disasters; but I pass them by,
Loth to disturb what heaven hath hushed in peace."
—Still less, far less am I inclined to treat
Of Man degraded in his Maker's sight
By the deformities of brutish vice: 590
For, though from these materials might be framed
Harsh portraiture, in which a vulgar face
And a coarse outside of repulsive life
And unaffecting manners may at once
Be recognized by all"—"Ah! do not think," 595
The Wanderer somewhat eagerly exclaimed,
"Wish could be ours that you, for such poor gain,
(Gain shall I call it?—gain of what?—for whom?)
Should breathe a word tending to violate
Your own pure spirit. Not a step we look for 600
In slight of that forbearance and reserve
Which common human-heartedness inspire,
And mortal ignorance and frailty claim,
Upon this sacred ground, if no where else."

   "True," said the Solitary, "be it far 605
From us to infringe the laws of charity.
Let judgment here in mercy be pronounced;
This, self-respecting Nature prompts, and this
Wisdom enjoins; but, if the thing we seek
Be genuine knowledge, bear we then in mind 610
How, from his lofty throne, the Sun can fling
Colours as bright on exhalations bred
By weedy pool or pestilential swamp,
As by the rivulet sparkling where it runs,
Or the pellucid Lake."
                      "Small risk," said I, 615
"Of such illusion do we here incur;
Temptation here is none to exceed the truth;
No evidence appears that they, who rest
Within this ground, were covetous of praise,

Or of remembrance even, deserved or not. 620
Green is the Church-yard, beautiful and green;
Ridge rising gently by the side of ridge:
A heaving surface—almost wholly free
From interruption of sepulchral stones,
And mantled o'er with aboriginal turf 625
And everlasting flowers. These Dalesmen trust
The lingering gleam of their departed Lives
To oral records and the silent heart;
Depository faithful, and more kind
Than fondest Epitaphs: for, if it fail, 630
What boots the sculptured Tomb? And who can blame,
Who rather would not envy, men that feel
This mutual confidence; if from such source
The practice flow,—if thence, or from a deep
And general humility in death? 635
Nor should I much condemn it, if it spring
From disregard of Time's destructive power,
As only capable to prey on things
Of earth, and human nature's mortal part.
Yet—in less simple districts, where we see 640
Stone lift its forehead emulous of stone
In courting notice, and the ground all paved
With commendations of departed worth,
Reading, where'er we turn, of innocent lives,
Of each domestic charity fulfilled 645
And sufferings meekly borne—I, for my part,
Though with the silence pleased which here prevails,
Among those fair recitals also range
Soothed by the natural spirit which they breathe.
And, in the centre of a world whose soil 650
Is rank with all unkindness, compassed round
With such Memorials, I have sometimes felt
That 'twas no momentary happiness
To have *one* enclosure where the voice that speaks
In envy or detraction is not heard; 655

Which malice may not enter; where the traces
Of evil inclinations are unknown;
Where love and pity tenderly unite
With resignation; and no jarring tone
Intrudes, the peaceful concert to disturb 660
Of amity and gratitude."
                    "Thus sanctioned,"
The Pastor said, "I willingly confine
My narratives to subjects that excite
Feelings with these accordant; love, esteem
And admiration; lifting up a veil, 665
A sun-beam introducing among hearts
Retired and covert; so that ye shall have
Clear Images before your gladdened eyes
Of Nature's unambitious underwood,
And flowers that prosper in the shade. And when 670
I speak of such among my flock as swerved
Or fell, those only will I single out
Upon whose lapse, or error, something more
Than brotherly forgiveness may attend:
To such will we restrict our notice, else 675
Better my tongue were mute. And yet there are,
I feel, good reasons why we should not leave
Wholly untraced a more forbidding way.
For strength to persevere and to support,
And energy to conquer and repel, 680
These elements of virtue, that declare
The native grandeur of the human Soul,
Are oft-times not unprofitably shewn
In the perverseness of a selfish course:
Truth every day exemplified, no less 685
In the grey cottage by the murmuring stream
Than the fantastic Conqueror's roving camp,
Or in the factious Senate, unappalled
While merciless proscription ebbs and flows.
—There," said the Vicar pointing as he spake, 690

"A woman rests in peace; surpassed by few
In power of mind, and eloquent discourse.
Tall was her stature; her complexion dark
And saturnine; her port erect, her head
Not absolutely raised, as if to hold 695
Converse with heaven, nor yet depressed tow'rds earth,
But in projection carried, as she walked
For ever musing. Sunken were her eyes;
Wrinkled and furrowed with habitual thought
Was her broad forehead; like the brow of One 700
Whose visual nerve shrinks from a painful glare
Of overpowering light.—While yet a Child,
She, mid the humble Flowerets of the vale,
Towered like the imperial Thistle, not unfurnished
With its appropriate grace, yet rather framed 705
To be admired, than coveted and loved.
Even at that age, she ruled as sovereign Queen
Among her Play-mates; else their simple sports
Had wanted power to occupy a mind
Held in subjection by a strong controul 710
Of studious application, self-imposed.
Books were her creditors; to them she paid,
With pleasing, anxious eagerness, the hours
Which they exacted; were it time allowed,
Or seized upon by stealth, or fairly won, 715
By stretch of industry, from other tasks.
—Oh! pang of sorrowful regret for them
Whom, in their youth, sweet study has enthralled,
That they have lived for harsher servitude,
Whether in soul, in body, or estate! 720
Such doom was hers; yet nothing could subdue
Her keen desire of knowledge; or efface
Those brighter images—by books impressed
Upon her memory; faithfully as stars
That occupy their places,—and, though oft 725
Hidden by clouds, and oft bedimmed by haze,

Are not to be extinguished, or impaired.

    Two passions, both degenerate, for they both
Began in honour, gradually obtained
Rule over her, and vexed her daily life;   730
An unrelenting, avaricious thrift;
And a strange thraldom of maternal love,
That held her spirit, in its own despite,
Bound by vexation, and regret, and scorn.
Constrained forgiveness, and relenting vows,   735
And tears, in pride suppressed, in shame concealed,
To a poor dissolute Son, her only Child.
—Her wedded days had opened with mishap,
Whence dire dependance.—What could she perform
To shake the burthen off? Ah! there she felt,   740
Indignantly, the weakness of her sex,
The injustice of her low estate.—She mused;
Resolved, adhered to her resolve; her heart
Closed by degrees to charity; and, thence
Expecting not Heaven's blessing, placed her trust   745
In ceaseless pains and parsimonious care,
Which got, and sternly hoarded each day's gain.

    Thus all was re-established, and a pile
Constructed, that sufficed for every end,
Save the contentment of the Builder's mind;   750
A mind by nature indisposed to aught
So placid, so inactive, as content;
A Mind intolerant of lasting peace,
And cherishing the pang which it deplored.
Dread life of conflict! which I oft compared   755
To the agitation of a brook that runs
Down rocky mountains—buried now and lost
In silent pools, unfathomably deep;—
Now, in a moment, starting forth again
With violence, and proud of its escape;—   760
Until it sink once more, by slow degrees,

Or instantly, into as dark repose.

    A sudden illness seized her in the strength
Of life's autumnal season.—Shall I tell
How on her bed of death the Matron lay,   765
To Providence submissive, so she thought;
But fretted, vexed, and wrought upon—almost
To anger, by the malady, that griped
Her prostrate frame with unrelaxing power,
As the fierce Eagle fastens on the Lamb.   770
She prayed, she moaned—her Husband's Sister watched
Her dreary pillow, waited on her needs;
And yet the very sound of that kind foot
Was anguish to her ears!—"And must she rule,"
This was the dying Woman heard to say   775
In bitterness, "and must she rule and reign,
"Sole Mistress of this house, when I am gone?
"Sit by my fire—possess what I possessed—
"Tend what I tended—calling it her own!"
Enough;—I fear, too much.—Of nobler feeling   780
Take this example.—One autumnal evening,
While she was yet in prime of health and strength,
I well remember, while I passed her door,
Musing with loitering step, and upward eye
Turned tow'rds the planet Jupiter, that hung   785
Above the centre of the Vale, a voice
Roused me, her voice; it said, "That glorious Star
"In its untroubled element will shine
"As now it shines, when we are laid in earth
"And safe from all our sorrows."—She is safe,   790
And her uncharitable acts, I trust,
And harsh unkindnesses, are all forgiven;
Though, in this Vale, remembered with deep awe!"

The Vicar paused; and tow'rds a seat advanced,
A long stone-seat, framed in the Church-yard wall;   795

Part under shady sycamore, and part
Offering a place of rest in pleasant sunshine,
Even as may suit the comers old or young
Who seek the House of worship, while the Bells
Yet ring with all their voices, or before   800
The last hath ceased its solitary knoll.
To this commodious resting-place he led;
Where, by his side, we all sate down; and there
His office, uninvited, he resumed.

   "As, on a sunny bank, a tender Lamb   805
Lurks in safe shelter from the winds of March,
Screened by its Parent, so that little mound
Lies guarded by its neighbour; the small heap
Speaks for itself;—an Infant there doth rest,
The sheltering Hillock is the Mother's grave.   810
If mild discourse, and manners that conferred
A natural dignity on humblest rank;
If gladsome spirits, and benignant looks,
That for a face not beautiful did more
Than beauty for the fairest face can do;   815
And if religious tenderness of heart,
Grieving for sin, and penitential tears
Shed when the clouds had gathered and distained
The spotless ether of a maiden life;
If these may make a hallowed spot of earth   820
More holy in the sight of God or Man;
Then, on that mold, a sanctity shall brood,
Till the stars sicken at the day of doom.

   Ah! what a warning for a thoughtless Man,
Could field or grove, or any spot of earth,   825
Shew to his eye an image of the pangs
Which it hath witnessed, render back an echo
Of the sad steps by which it hath been trod!
There, by her innocent Baby's precious grave,
Yea, doubtless, on the turf that roofs her own, 830

The Mother oft was seen to stand, or kneel
In the broad day, a weeping Magdalene.
Now she is not; the swelling turf reports
Of the fresh shower, but of poor Ellen's tears
Is silent; nor is any vestige left   835
Upon the pathway, of her mournful tread;
Nor of that pace with which she once had moved
In virgin fearlessness, a step that seemed
Caught from the pressure of elastic turf
Upon the mountains wet with morning dew,   840
In the prime hour of sweetest scents and airs.
—Serious and thoughtful was her mind; and yet,
By reconcilement exquisite and rare,
The form, port, motions of this Cottage-girl
Were such as might have quickened and inspired   845
A Titian's hand, addressed to picture forth
Oread or Dryad glancing through the shade
When first the Hunter's startling horn is heard
Upon the golden hills. A spreading Elm
Stands in our Valley, called THE JOYFUL TREE;   850
An Elm distinguished by that festive name,
From dateless usage which our Peasants hold
Of giving welcome to the first of May
By dances round its trunk.—And if the sky
Permit, like honours, dance and song, are paid   855
To the Twelfth Night; beneath the frosty Stars
Or the clear Moon. The Queen of these gay sports,
If not in beauty yet in sprightly air,
Was hapless Ellen.—No one touched the ground
So deftly, and the nicest Maiden's locks   860
Less gracefully were braided;—but this praise,
Methinks, would better suit another place.

    She loved,—and fondly deemed herself beloved.
The road is dim, the current unperceived,
The weakness painful and most pitiful,   865
By which a virtuous Woman, in pure youth,

May be delivered to distress and shame.
Such fate was hers.—The last time Ellen danced,
Among her Equals, round *The Joyful Tree*,
She bore a secret burthen; and full soon 870
Was left to tremble for a breaking vow,—
Then, to bewail a sternly-broken vow,
Alone, within her widowed Mother's house.
It was the season sweet, of budding leaves,
Of days advancing tow'rds their utmost length, 875
And small birds singing to their happy mates.
Wild is the music of the autumnal wind
Among the faded woods; but these blithe notes
Strike the deserted to the heart;—I speak
Of what I know, and what we feel within. 880
—Beside the Cottage in which Ellen dwelt
Stands a tall ash-tree; to whose topmost twig
A Thrush resorts, and annually chaunts,
At morn and evening, from that naked perch,
While all the undergrove is thick with leaves, 885
A time-beguiling ditty, for delight
Of his fond partner, silent in the nest.
—"Ah why," said Ellen, sighing to herself,
"Why do not words, and kiss, and solemn pledge;
"And nature that is kind in Woman's breast, 890
"And reason that in Man is wise and good,
"And fear of him who is a righteous Judge,
"Why do not these prevail for human life,
"To keep two Hearts together, that began
"Their spring-time with one love, and that have need 895
"Of mutual pity and forgiveness, sweet
"To grant, or be received, while that poor Bird,
"—O come and hear him! Thou who hast to me
"Been faithless, hear him, though a lowly Creature,
"One of God's simple children that yet know not 900
"The universal Parent, how he sings
"As if he wished, the firmament of Heaven

"Should listen, and give back to him the voice
"Of his triumphant constancy and love;
"The proclamation that he makes, how far 905
"His darkness doth transcend our fickle light!"

   Such was the tender passage, not by me
Repeated without loss of simple phrase,
Which I perused, even as the words had been
Committed by forsaken Ellen's hand 910
To the blank margin of a Valentine,
Bedropped with tears. 'Twill please you to be told
That, studiously withdrawing from the eye
Of all companionship, the Sufferer yet
In lonely reading found a meek resource. 915
How thankful for the warmth of summer days,
And their long twilight!—friendly to that stealth
With which she slipped into the Cottage-barn,
And found a secret oratory there;
Or, in the garden, pored upon her book 920
By the last lingering help of open sky,
Till the dark night dismissed her to her bed.
Thus did a waking Fancy sometimes lose
The unconquerable pang of despised love.

   A kindlier passion opened on her soul 925
When that poor Child was born. Upon its face
She looked as on a pure and spotless gift
Of unexpected promise, where a grief
Or dread was all that had been thought of—joy
Far sweeter than bewildered Traveller feels 930
Upon a perilous waste, where all night long
Through darkness he hath toiled and fearful storm,
When he beholds the first pale speck serene
Of day-spring—in the gloomy east revealed,
And greets it with thanksgiving. "Till this hour," 935
Thus in her Mother's hearing Ellen spake,
"There was a stony region in my heart;

"But he, at whose command the parched rock
"Was smitten, and poured forth a quenching stream,
"Hath softened that obduracy, and made 940
"Unlooked-for gladness in the desert place,
"To save the perishing; and, henceforth, I look
"Upon the light with cheerfulness, for thee
"My Infant; and for that good Mother dear,
"Who bore me,—and hath prayed for me in vain;— 945
"Yet not in vain, it shall not be in vain."
She spake, nor was the assurance unfulfilled,
And if heart-rending thoughts would oft return
They stayed not long.—The blameless Infant grew;
The Child whom Ellen and her Mother loved 950
They soon were proud of; tended it and nursed,
A soothing comforter, although forlorn;
Like a poor singing-bird from distant lands;
Or a choice shrub, which he, who passes by
With vacant mind, not seldom may observe 955
Fair-flowering in a thinly-peopled house,
Whose window, somewhat sadly, it adorns.
—Through four months' space the Infant drew its food
From the maternal breast; then scruples rose;
Thoughts, which the rich are free from, came and crossed 960
The sweet affection. She no more could bear
By her offence to lay a twofold weight
On a kind parent willing to forget
Their slender means, so, to that parent's care
Trusting her child, she left their common home, 965
And with contented spirit undertook
A Foster-Mother's office.
                    'Tis, perchance,
Unknown to you that in these simple Vales
The natural feeling of equality
Is by domestic service unimpaired; 970
Yet, though such service be, with us, removed
From sense of degradation, not the less

The ungentle mind can easily find means
To impose severe restraints and laws unjust:
Which hapless Ellen now was doomed to feel. 975

   In selfish blindness, for I will not say
In naked and deliberate cruelty,
The Pair, whose Infant she was bound to nurse,
Forbad her all communion with her own.
They argued that such meeting would disturb 980
The Mother's mind, distract her thoughts, and thus
Unfit her for her duty—in which dread,
Week after week, the mandate was enforced.
—So near!—yet not allowed, upon that sight
To fix her eyes—alas! 'twas hard to bear! 985
But worse affliction must be borne—far worse;
For 'tis Heaven's will—that, after a disease
Begun and ended within three days' space,
Her Child should die; as Ellen now exclaimed,
Her own—deserted Child!—Once, only once, 990
She saw it in that mortal malady:
And, on the burial day, could scarcely gain
Permission to attend its obsequies.
She reached the house—last of the funeral train;
And some One, as she entered, having chanced 995
To urge unthinkingly their prompt departure,
"Nay," said she, with commanding look, a spirit
Of anger never seen in her before,
"Nay ye must wait my time!" and down she sate,
And by the unclosed coffin kept her seat 1000
Weeping and looking, looking on and weeping
Upon the last sweet slumber of her Child,
Until at length her soul was satisfied.

   You see the Infant's Grave;—and to this Spot,
The Mother, oft as she was sent abroad 1005
And whatsoe'er the errand, urged her steps:
Hither she came; and here she stood, or knelt

In the broad day—a rueful Magdalene!
So call her; for not only she bewailed
A Mother's loss, but mourned in bitterness 1010
Her own transgression; Penitent sincere
As ever raised to Heaven a streaming eye.
—At length the Parents of the Foster-child
Noting that in despite of their commands
She still renewed, and could not but renew, 1015
Those visitations, ceased to send her forth;
Or, to the garden's narrow bounds, confined.
I failed not to remind them that they erred:
For holy Nature might not thus be crossed,
Thus wronged in woman's breast: in vain I pleaded: 1020
But the green stalk of Ellen's life was snapped
And the flower drooped; as every eye could see,
It hung its head in mortal languishment.
—Aided by this appearance I at length
Prevailed; and, from those bonds released, she went 1025
Home to her mother's house. The Youth was fled;
The rash Betrayer could not face the shame
Or sorrow which his senseless guilt had caused;
And little would his presence, or proof given
Of a relenting soul, have now availed; 1030
For, like a shadow, he was passed away
From Ellen's thoughts; had perished to her mind
For all concerns of fear, or hope, or love,
Save only those which to their common shame,
And to his moral being appertained: 1035
Hope from that quarter would, I know, have brought
A heavenly comfort; there she recognised
An unrelaxing bond, a mutual need;
There, and, as seemed, there only.—She had raised,
Her fond maternal Heart had built a Nest 1040
In blindness all too near the river's edge;
That Work a summer flood with hasty swell
Had swept away; and now her Spirit longed

For its last flight to Heaven's security.
—The bodily frame was wasted day by day; 1045
Meanwhile, relinquishing all other cares,
Her mind she strictly tutored to find peace
And pleasure in endurance. Much she thought,
And much she read; and brooded feelingly
Upon her own unworthiness.—To me, 1050
As to a spiritual comforter and friend,
Her heart she opened; and no pains were spared
To mitigate, as gently as I could,
The sting of self-reproach, with healing words.
—Meek Saint! through patience glorified on earth! 1055
In whom, as by her lonely hearth she sate,
The ghastly face of cold decay put on
A sun-like beauty, and appeared divine!
May I not mention—that, within these walls,
In due observance of her pious wish, 1060
The Congregation joined with me in prayer
For her Soul's good? Nor was that office vain.
—Much did she suffer: but, if any Friend,
Beholding her condition, at the sight
Gave way to words of pity or complaint, 1065
She stilled them with a prompt reproof, and said,
"He who afflicts me knows what I can bear;
"And, when I fail, and can endure no more,
"Will mercifully take me to himself."
So, through the cloud of death, her Spirit passed 1070
Into that pure and unknown world of love,
Where injury cannot come:—and here is laid
The mortal Body by her Infant's side."

   The Vicar ceased; and downcast looks made known
That Each had listened with his inmost heart. 1075
For me, the emotion scarcely was less strong
Or less benign than that which I had felt
When, seated near my venerable Friend,
Beneath those shady elms, from him I heard

The story that retraced the slow decline 1080
Of Margaret sinking on the lonely Heath,
With the neglected House in which she dwelt.
—I noted that the Solitary's cheek
Confessed the power of nature.—Pleased though sad,
More pleased than sad, the grey-haired Wanderer sate; 1085
Thanks to his pure imaginative soul
Capacious and serene, his blameless life,
His knowledge, wisdom, love of truth, and love
Of human kind! He was it who first broke
The pensive silence, saying, "Blest are they 1090
Whose sorrow rather is to suffer wrong
Than to do wrong, although themselves have erred.
This Tale gives proof that Heaven most gently deals
With such, in their affliction.—Ellen's fate,
Her tender spirit, and her contrite heart, 1095
Call to my mind dark hints which I have heard
Of One who died within this Vale, by doom
Heavier, as his offence was heavier far.
Where, Sir, I pray you, where are laid the bones
Of Wilfred Armathwaite?"—The Vicar answered, 1100
"In that green nook, close by the Church-yard wall,
Beneath yon hawthorn, planted by myself
In memory and for warning, and in sign
Of sweetness where dire anguish had been known,
Of reconcilement after deep offence, 1105
There doth he lie.—In this his native Vale
He owned and tilled a little plot of land;
Here, with his Consort and his Children, saw
Days—that were seldom crossed by petty strife,
Years—safe from large misfortune; and maintained 1110
That course which minds, of insight not too keen,
Might look on with entire complacency.
Yet, in himself and near him, there were faults
At work to undermine his happy state
By sure, though tardy progress. Active, prompt, 1115

And lively was the Housewife; in the Vale
None more industrious; but her industry,
Ill-judged, full oft, and specious, tended more
To splendid neatness; to a shewy, trim,
And overlaboured purity of house;   1120
Than to substantial thrift. He, on his part,
Generous and easy-minded, was not free
From carelessness; and thus, in lapse of time,
These joint infirmities induced decay
Of worldly substance; and distress of mind,   1125
That to a thoughtful Man was hard to shun,
And which he could not cure. A blooming Girl
Served in the house, a Favourite that had grown
Beneath his eye, encouraged by his care.
Poor now in tranquil pleasure he gave way   1130
To thoughts of troubled pleasure; he became
A lawless Suitor to the Maid; and she
Yielded unworthily.—Unhappy Man!
That which he had been weak enough to do
Was misery in remembrance; he was stung,   1135
Stung by his inward thoughts, and by the smiles
Of Wife and Children stung to agony.
Wretched at home he gained no peace abroad;
Ranged though the mountains, slept upon the earth,
Asked comfort of the open air, and found   1140
No quiet in the darkness of the night,
No pleasure in the beauty of the day.
His flock he slighted: his paternal fields
Became a clog to him, whose spirit wished
To fly, but whither? And this gracious Church,   1145
That wears a look so full of peace, and hope,
And love, benignant Mother of the Vale,
How fair amid her brood of Cottages!
She was to him a sickness and reproach.
Much to the last remained unknown; but this   1150
Is sure, that through remorse and grief he died;

Though pited among Men, absolved by God,
He could not find forgiveness in himself;
Nor could endure the weight of his own shame.

    Here rests a Mother. But from her I turn   1155
And from her Grave.—Behold—upon that Ridge,
Which, stretching boldly from the mountain side,
Carries into the centre of the Vale
Its rocks and woods—the Cottage where she dwelt;
And where yet dwells her faithful Partner, left   1160
(Full eight years past) the solitary prop
Of many helpless Children. I begin
With words which might be prelude to a Tale
Of sorrow and dejection; but I feel
No sadness, when I think of what mine eyes   1165
See daily in that happy Family.
—Bright Garland form they for the pensive brow
Of their undrooping Father's widowhood,
Those six fair Daughters, budding yet—not one,
Not one of all the band, a full blown Flower!   1170
Depressed, and desolate of soul, as once
That Father was, and filled with anxious fear,
Now by experience taught, he stands assured,
That God, who takes away, yet takes not half
Of what he seems to take; or gives it back,   1175
Not to our prayer, but far beyond our prayer;
He gives it—the boon produce of a soil
Which our endeavours have refused to till,
And Hope hath never watered. The Abode,
Whose grateful Owner can attest these truths,   1180
Even were the object nearer to our sight
Would seem in no distinction to surpass
The rudest habitations. Ye might think
That it had sprung self-raised from earth, or grown
Out of the living rock, to be adorned   1185
By Nature only; but, if thither led,
Ye would discover, then, a studious work

Of many fancies, prompting many hands.
—Brought from the woods the honeysuckle twines
Around the porch, and seems, in that trim place,   1190
A Plant no longer wild; the cultured rose
There blossoms, strong in health, and will be soon
Roof-high; the wild pink crowns the garden wall,
And with the flowers are intermingled stones
Sparry and bright, the scatterings of the hills.   1195
These ornaments, that fade not with the year,
A hardy Girl continues to provide;
Who, mounting fearlessly the rocky heights,
Her Father's prompt Attendant, does for him
All that a Boy could do; but with delight   1200
More keen and prouder daring: yet hath she,
Within the garden, like the rest, a bed
For her own flowers and favourite herbs—a space,
By sacred charter, holden for her use.
—These, and whatever else the garden bears   1205
Of fruit or flower, permission asked or not,
I freely gather; and my leisure draws
A not unfrequent pastime from the sight
Of the Bees murmuring round their sheltered hives
In that Enclosure; while the mountain rill,   1210
That sparkling thrids the rocks, attunes his voice
To the pure course of human life, which there
Flows on in solitude from year to year.
—But at the closing-in of night, then most
This Dwelling charms me. Covered by the gloom,   1215
Then, in my walks, I oftentimes stop short,
(Who could refrain?) and feed by stealth my sight
With prospect of the Company within,
Laid open through the blazing window:—there
I see the eldest Daughter at her wheel   1220
Spinning amain, as if to overtake
The never-halting time; or, in her turn,
Teaching some Novice of the Sisterhood

That skill in this, or other household work;
Which, from her Father's honoured hand, herself 1225
While she was yet a little One, had learned.
—Mild Man! he is not gay, but they are gay;
And the whole House seems filled with gaiety.
—Thrice happy, then, the Mother may be deemed,
The Wife, who rests beneath that turf, from which 1230
I turned, that ye in mind might witness where,
And how her Spirit yet survives on Earth.

   The next three Ridges—those upon the left—
By close connexion with our present thoughts
Tempt me to add, in praise of humble worth, 1235
Their brief and unobtrusive history.
—One Hillock, ye may note, is small and low,
Sunk almost to a level with the plain
By weight of time; the Others, undepressed,
Are bold and swelling. There a Husband sleeps, 1240
Deposited, in pious confidence
Of glorious resurrection with the just,
Near the loved Partner of his early days;
And, in the bosom of that family mold,
A second Wife is gathered to his side; 1245
The approved Assistant of an arduous course
From his mid noon of manhood to old age!
He also of his Mate deprived, was left
Alone—'mid many Children; One a Babe
Orphaned as soon as born. Alas! 'tis not 1250
In course of nature that a Father's wing
Should warm these Little-ones; and can he *feed?*
That was a thought of agony more keen.
For, hand in hand with Death, by strange mishap
And chance-encounter on their diverse road, 1255
The ghastlier shape of Poverty had entered
Into that House, unfeared and unforeseen.
He had stepped forth, in time of urgent need,
The generous Surety of a Friend: and now

The widowed Father found that all his rights   1260
In his paternal fields were undermined.
Landless he was and pennyless.—The dews
Of night and morn that wet the mountain sides,
The bright stars twinkling on their dusky tops,
Were conscious of the pain that drove him forth   1265
From his own door, he knew not when—to range
He knew not where; distracted was his brain,
His heart was cloven; and full oft he prayed,
In blind despair, that God would take them all.
—But suddenly, as if in one kind moment   1270
To encourage and reprove, a gleam of light
Broke from the very bosom of that cloud
Which darkened the whole prospect of his days.
For He, who now possessed the joyless right
To force the Bondsman from his house and lands,   1275
In pity, and by admiration urged
Of his unmurmuring and considerate mind
Meekly submissive to the law's decree,
Lightened the penalty with liberal hand.
—The desolate Father raised his head, and looked   1280
On the wide world in hope. Within these walls,
In course of time was solemnized the vow
Whereby a virtuous Woman, of grave years
And of prudential habits, undertook
The sacred office of a wife to him,   1285
Of Mother to his helpless family.
—Nor did she fail, in nothing did she fail,
Through various exercise of twice ten years,
Save in some partial fondness for that Child
Which at the birth she had received, the Babe   1290
Whose heart had known no Mother but herself.
—By mutual efforts; by united hopes;
By daily-growing help of boy and girl,
Trained early to participate that zeal
Of industry, which runs before the day   1295

And lingers after it; by strong restraint
Of an economy which did not check
The heart's more generous motions tow'rds themselves
Or to their neighbours; and by trust in God;
This Pair insensibly subdued the fears   1300
And troubles that beset their life: and thus
Did the good Father and his second Mate
Redeem at length their plot of smiling fields.
These, at this day, the eldest Son retains:
The younger Offspring, through the busy world,   1305
Have all been scattered wide, by various fates;
But each departed from the native Vale,
In beauty flourishing, and moral worth."

END OF THE SIXTH BOOK.

BOOK THE SEVENTH

THE CHURCH-YARD AMONG THE MOUNTAINS

CONTINUED

While thus from theme to theme the Historian passed,
The words he uttered, and the scene that lay
Before our eyes, awakened in my mind
Vivid remembrance of those long-past hours;
When, in the hollow of some shadowy Vale,   5
(What time the splendour of the setting sun
Lay beautiful on Snowdon's craggy top,
On Cader Idris, or huge Penmanmaur)
A wandering Youth, I listened with delight
To pastoral melody or warlike air,   10
Drawn from the chords of the ancient British harp
By some accomplished Master; while he sate
Amid the quiet of the green recess,
And there did inexhaustibly dispense

An interchange of soft or solemn tunes   15
Tender or blithe; now, as the varying mood
Of his own spirit urged,—now, as a voice
From Youth or Maiden, or some honoured Chief
Of his compatriot villagers (that hung
Around him, drinking in the empassioned notes   20
Of the time-hallowed minstrelsy) required
For their heart's ease or pleasure. Strains of power
Were they, to seize and occupy the sense;
But to a higher mark than song can reach
Rose this pure eloquence. And, when the stream   25
Which overflowed the soul was passed away,
A consciousness remained that it had left,
Deposited upon the silent shore
Of memory, images and precious thoughts;
That shall not die, and cannot be destroyed.   30

  "These grassy heaps lie amicably close,"
Said I, "like surges heaving in the wind
Upon the surface of a mountain pool;
—Whence comes it, then, that yonder we behold
Five graves, and only five, that lie apart,   35
Unsociable company and sad;
And, furthermore, appearing to encroach
On the smooth play-ground of the Village-school?"

  The Vicar answered. "No disdainful pride
In them who rest beneath, nor any course   40
Of strange or tragic accident, hath helped
To place those Hillocks in that lonely guise.
—Once more look forth, and follow with your eyes
The length of road which from yon mountain's base
Through bare enclosures stretches, 'till its line   45
Is lost among a little tuft of trees,—
Then, reappearing in a moment, quits
The cultured fields,—and up the heathy waste
Mounts, as you see, in mazes serpentine,

Towards an easy outlet of the Vale. 50
—That little shady spot, that sylvan tuft,
By which the road is hidden, also hides
A Cottage from our view,—though I discern,
(Ye scarcely can) amid its sheltering trees,
The smokeless chimney-top.—All unembowered 55
And naked stood that lowly Parsonage
(For such in truth it is, and appertains
To a small Chapel in the Vale beyond)
When hither came its last Inhabitant.

    Rough and forbidding were the choicest roads 60
By which our Northern wilds could then be crossed;
And into most of these secluded Vales
Was no access for wain, heavy or light.
So, at his Dwelling-place the Priest arrived
With store of household goods, in panniers slung 65
On sturdy horses graced with jingling bells,
And on the back of more ignoble beast;
That, with like burthen of effects most prized
Or easiest carried, closed the motley train.
Young was I then, a school-boy of eight years; 70
But still, methinks, I see them as they passed
In order, drawing tow'rds their wished-for home.
—Rocked by the motion of a trusty Ass
Two ruddy Children hung, a well-poised freight,
Each in his basket nodding drowsily; 75
Their bonnets, I remember, wreathed with flowers
Which told that 'twas the pleasant month of June;
And, close behind, the comely Matron rode,
A Woman of soft speech and gracious smile,
And with a Lady's mien.—From far they came, 80
Even from Northumbrian hills; yet theirs had been
A merry journey—rich in pastime—cheered
By music, prank, and laughter-stirring jest;
And freak put on, and arch word dropped—to swell
The cloud of fancy and uncouth surmise 85

That gathered round the slowly-moving train.
—"Whence do they come? and with what errand charged?
"Belong they to the fortune-telling Tribe
"Who pitch their Tents beneath the green-wood Tree?
"Or are they Strollers, furnished to enact 90
"Fair Rosamond, and the Children of the Wood,
"And, by that whiskered Tabby's aid, set forth
"The lucky venture of sage Whittington,
"When the next Village hears the Show announced
"By blast of trumpet?" Plenteous was the growth 95
Of such conjectures, overheard; or seen
On many a staring countenance pourtrayed
Of Boor or Burgher, as they marched along.
And more than once their steadiness of face
Was put to proof, and exercise supplied 100
To their inventive humour, by stern looks,
And questions in authoritative tone,
From some staid Guardian of the public peace,
Checking the sober steed on which he rode,
In his suspicious wisdom: oftener still, 105
By notice indirect or blunt demand
From Traveller halting in his own despite,
A simple curiosity to ease.
Of which adventures, that beguiled and cheered
Their grave migration, the good Pair would tell, 110
With undiminished glee, in hoary age.

  A Priest he was by function; but his course
From his youth up, and high as manhood's noon,
(The hour of life to which he then was brought)
Had been irregular; I might say, wild: 115
By books unsteadied, by his pastoral care
Too little checked. An active, ardent mind;
A fancy pregnant with resource and scheme
To cheat the sadness of a rainy day:
Hands apt for all ingenious arts and games; 120
A generous spirit, and a body strong

To cope with stoutest Champions of the bowl;
Had earned for him sure welcome, and the rights
Of a prized Visitant, in the jolly hall
Of country Squire; or at the statelier board   125
Of Duke or Earl, from scenes of courtly pomp
Withdrawn,—to while away the summer hours
In condescension among rural guests.

With these high Comrades he had revelled long,
Had frolicked many a year; a simple Clerk   130
By hopes of coming patronage beguiled
And vexed, until the weary heart grew sick.
And so, abandoning each higher aim
And all his shewy Friends, at length he turned
For a life's stay, though slender yet assured,   135
To this remote and humble Chapelry;
Which had been offered to his doubtful choice
By an unthought of Patron. Bleak and bare
They found the Cottage, their allotted home:
Naked without and rude within; a spot   140
With which the scantily-provided Cure
Not long had been endowed: and far remote
The Chapel stood, divided from that House
By an unpeopled tract of mountain waste.
—Yet cause was none, whate'er regret might hang   145
On his own mind, to quarrel with the choice
Or the necessity that fixed him here;
Apart from old temptations, and constrained
To punctual labour in his sacred charge.
See him a constant Preacher to the Poor!   150
And visiting, though not with saintly zeal
Yet when need was with no reluctant will,
The sick in body, or distressed in mind;
And, by as salutary change, compelled,
Month after month, in that obscure Abode   155
To rise from timely sleep, and meet the day
With no engagement, in his thoughts, more proud

Or splendid than his garden could afford,
His fields,—or mountains by the heath-cock ranged,
Or these wild brooks; from which he now returned   160
Contentedly, to take a temperate meal
At his own board, where sate his gentle Mate
And three fair Children, plentifully fed
Though simply, from their little household farm;
With acceptable treat of fish or fowl   165
By nature yielded to his practised hand,
To help the small but certain comings-in
Of that spare Benefice. Yet not the less
Their's was a hospitable board, and their's
A charitable door.—So days and years   170
Passed on;—the inside of that rugged House
Was trimmed and brightened by the Matron's care,
And gradually enriched with things of price,
Which might be lacked for use or ornament.
What, though no soft and costly sofa there   175
Insidiously stretched out its lazy length,
And no vain mirror glittered on the walls,
Yet were the windows of the low Abode
By shutters weather-fended, which at once
Repelled the storm and deadened its loud roar.   180
There, snow-white curtains hung in decent folds;
Tough moss, and long-enduring mountain-plants,
That creep along the ground with sinuous trail,
Were nicely braided, and composed a work
Like Indian mats, that with appropriate grace   185
Lay at the threshold and the inner doors.
And a fair carpet, woven of home-spun wool,
But tinctured daintily with florid hues,
For seemliness and warmth, on festive days,
Covered the smooth blue slabs of mountain stone   190
With which the parlour-floor, in simplest guise
Of pastoral home-steads, had been long inlaid.
—These pleasing works the Housewife's skill produced:

Meanwhile, the unsedentary Master's hand
Was busier with his task, to rid, to plant, 195
To rear for food, for shelter, and delight;
A thriving covert! And when wishes, formed
In youth, and sanctioned by the riper mind,
Restored me to my native Valley, here
To end my days; well pleased was I to see 200
The once-bare Cottage, on the mountain-side,
Screened from assault of every bitter blast;
While the dark shadows of the summer leaves
Danced in the breeze, upon its mossy roof.
Time, which had thus afforded willing help 205
To beautify with Nature's fairest growth
This rustic Tenement, had gently shed,
Upon its Master's frame, a wintry grace;
The comeliness of unenfeebled age.
But how could I say, gently? for he still 210
Retained a flashing eye, a burning palm,
A stirring foot, and head which beat at nights
Upon its pillow with a thousand schemes.
Few likings had he dropped, few pleasures lost;
Generous and charitable, prompt to serve; 215
And still his harsher passions kept their hold,
Anger and indignation; still he loved
The sound of titled names, and talked in glee
Of long-past banquetings with high-born Friends:
Then, from those lulling fits of vain delight 220
Uproused by recollected injury, railed
At their false ways disdainfully,—and oft
In bitterness, and with a threatening eye
Of fire, incensed beneath its hoary brow.
—These transports, with staid looks of pure good will 225
And with soft smile, his Consort would reprove.
She, far behind him in the race of years,
Yet keeping her first mildness, was advanced
Far nearer, in the habit of her soul,

To that still region whither all are bound. 230
—Him might we liken to the setting Sun
As I have seen it, on some gusty day,
Struggling and bold, and shining from the west
With an inconstant and unmellowed light.
—She was a soft attendant Cloud, that hung 235
As if with wish to veil the restless orb;
From which it did itself imbibe a ray
Of pleasing lustre.—But no more of this;
I better love to sprinkle on the sod
Which now divides the Pair, or rather say 240
Which still unites them, praises, like heaven's dew,
Without distinction falling upon both.
—Yoke-fellows were they long and well approved
To endure and to perform.
      With frugal pains,
Yet in a course of generous discipline, 245
Did this poor Churchman and his Consort rear
Their progeny.—Of three—sent forth to try
The paths of fortune in the open world,
One, not endowed with firmness to resist
The suit of pleasure, to his native Vale 250
Returned, and humbly tilled his Father's glebe.
—The youngest Daughter, too, in duty stayed
To lighten her declining Mother's care.
But, ere the bloom was passed away which health
Preserved to adorn a cheek no longer young, 255
Her heart, in course of nature, finding place
For new affections, to the holy state
Of wedlock they conducted her; but still
The Bride adhering to those filial cares
Dwelt with her Mate beneath her Father's roof. 260

 Our very first in eminence of years
This old Man stood, the Patriarch of the Vale!
And, to his unmolested mansion, Death
Had never come, through space of forty years;

Sparing both old and young in that Abode.   265
Suddenly then they disappeared:—not twice
Had summer scorched the fields,—not twice had fallen,
On those high Peaks, the first autumnal snow,—
Before the greedy visiting was closed
And the long-privileged House left empty—swept   270
As by a plague: yet no rapacious plague
Had been among them; all was gentle death,
One after one, with intervals of peace.
  —A happy consummation! an accord
Sweet, perfect,—to be wished for! save that here   275
Was something which to mortal sense might sound
Like harshness,—that the old grey-headed Sire,
The oldest, he was taken last,—survived
When the meek Partner of his age, his Son,
His Daughter, and that late and high-prized gift,   280
His little smiling Grandchild, were no more.

  "All gone, all vanished! he deprived and bare,
"How will he face the remnant of his life?
"What will become of him?" we said, and mused
In sad conjectures, "Shall we meet him now   285
"Haunting with rod and line the craggy brooks?
"Or shall we overhear him, as we pass,
"Striving to entertain the lonely hours
"With music?" (for he had not ceased to touch
The harp or viol which himself had framed,   290
For their sweet purposes, with perfect skill.)
"What titles will he keep? will he remain
"Musician, Gardener, Builder, Mechanist,
"A Planter, and a rearer from the Seed?
"A Man of hope and forward-looking mind   295
"Even to the last!"—Such was he, unsubdued.
But Heaven was gracious; yet a little while,
And this Survivor, with his cheerful throng
Of open schemes, and all his inward hoard
Of unsunned griefs, too many and too keen,   300

Was overcome by unexpected sleep,
In one blest moment. Like a shadow thrown
Softly and lightly from a passing cloud,
Death fell upon him, while reclined he lay
For noon-tide solace on the summer grass, 305
The warm lap of his Mother Earth: and so,
Their lenient term of separation past,
That Family (whose graves you there behold)
By yet a higher privilege, once more
Were gathered to each other."
                      Calm of mind 310
And silence waited on these closing words;
Until the Wanderer (whether moved by fear
Lest in these passages of life were some
That might have touched the sick heart of his Friend
Too nearly, or intent to reinforce 315
His own firm spirit in degree depressed
By tender sorrow for our mortal state)
Thus silence broke; "Behold a thoughtless Man
From vice and premature decay preserved
By useful habits, to a fitter soil 320
Transplanted, ere too late.—The Hermit, lodged
In the untrodden desert, tells his beads,
With each repeating its allotted prayer,
And thus divides and thus relieves the time;
Smooth task, with his compared! whose mind could string, 325
Not scantily, bright minutes on the thread
Of keen domestic anguish,—and beguile
A solitude, unchosen, unprofessed;
Till gentlest death released him.—Far from us
Be the desire—too curiously to ask 330
How much of this is but the blind result
Of cordial spirits and vital temperament,
And what to higher powers is justly due.
But you, Sir, know that in a neighbouring Vale
A Priest abides before whose life such doubts 335

Fall to the ground; whose gifts of nature lie
Retired from notice, lost in attributes
Of Reason,—honourably effaced by debts
Which her poor treasure-house is content to owe,
And conquests over her dominion gained, 340
To which her frowardness must needs submit.
In this one Man is shown a temperance—proof
Against all trials; industry severe
And constant as the motion of the day;
Stern self-denial round him spread, with shade 345
That might be deemed forbidding, did not there
All generous feelings flourish and rejoice;
Forbearance, charity in deed and thought,
And resolution competent to take
Out of the bosom of simplicity 350
All that her holy customs recommend,
And the best ages of the world prescribe.
—Preaching, administering, in every work
Of his sublime vocation, in the walks
Of worldly intercourse 'twixt man and man, 355
And in his humble Dwelling he appears
A Labourer, with moral virtue girt,
With spiritual graces, like a glory, crowned."

"Doubt can be none," the Pastor said, "for whom
"This Portraiture is sketched.—The Great, the Good, 360
The Well-beloved, the Fortunate, the Wise,
These Titles Emperors and Chiefs have borne,
Honour assumed or given: and Him, the Wonderful,
Our simple Shepherds, speaking from the heart,
Deservedly have styled.—From his Abode 365
In a dependant Chapelry, that lies
Behind yon hill, a poor and rugged wild,
Which in his soul he lovingly embraced,—
And, having once espoused, would never quit;
Hither, ere long, that lowly, great, good Man 370
Will be conveyed. An unelaborate Stone

May cover him; and by its help, perchance,
A century shall hear his name pronounced,
With images attendant on the sound;
Then, shall the slowly-gathering twilight close 375
In utter night; and of his course remain
No cognizable vestiges, no more
Than of this breath, which frames itself in words
To speak of him, and instantly dissolves.
—Noise is there not enough in doleful war— 380
But that the heaven-born Poet must stand forth
And lend the echoes of his sacred shell,
To multiply and aggravate the din?
Pangs are there not enough in hopeless love—
And, in requited passion, all too much 385
Of turbulence, anxiety, and fear—
But that the Minstrel of the rural shade
Must tune his pipe, insidiously to nurse
The perturbation in the suffering breast,
And propagate its kind, where'er he may? 390
—Ah who (and with such rapture as befits
The hallowed theme) will rise and celebrate
The good Man's deeds and purposes; retrace
His struggles, his discomfiture deplore,
His triumphs hail, and glorify his end? 395
That Virtue, like the fumes and vapoury clouds
Through fancy's heat redounding in the brain,
And like the soft infections of the heart,
By charm of measured words may spread through fields
And cottages, and Piety survive 400
Upon the lips of Men in hall or bower;
Not for reproof, but high and warm delight,
And grave encouragement, by song inspired.
—Vain thought! but wherefore murmur or repine?
The memory of the just survives in heaven: 405
And, without sorrow, will this ground receive
That venerable clay. Meanwhile the best

Of what it holds confines us to degrees
In excellence less difficult to reach,
And milder worth: nor need we travel far 410
From those to whom our last regards were paid
For such example.
               Almost at the root
Of that tall Pine, the shadow of whose bare
And slender stem, while here I sit at eve,
Oft stretches tow'rds me, like a long straight path 415
Traced faintly in the green sward; there, beneath
A plain blue Stone, a gentle Dalesman lies,
From whom, in early childhood, was withdrawn
The precious gift of hearing. He grew up
From year to year in loneliness of soul; 420
And this deep mountain Valley was to him
Soundless, with all its streams. The bird of dawn
Did never rouse this Cottager from sleep
With startling summons; not for his delight
The vernal cuckoo shouted; not for him 425
Murmured the labouring bee. When stormy winds
Were working the broad bosom of the lake
Into a thousand thousand sparkling waves,
Rocking the trees, or driving cloud on cloud
Along the sharp edge of yon lofty crags, 430
The agitated scene before his eye
Was silent as a picture: evermore
Were all things silent, wheresoe'er he moved.
Yet, by the solace of his own pure thoughts
Upheld, he duteously pursued the round 435
Of rural labours; the steep mountain-side
Ascended with his staff and faithful dog;
The plough he guided, and the scythe he swayed;
And the ripe corn before his sickle fell
Among the jocund reapers. For himself, 440
All watchful and industrious as he was,
He wrought not; neither field nor flock he owned:

No wish for wealth had place within his mind;
Nor husband's love, nor father's hope or care.
Though born a younger Brother, need was none   445
That from the floor of his paternal home
He should depart, to plant himself anew.
And when, mature in manhood, he beheld
His Parents laid in earth, no loss ensued
Of rights to him; but he remained well pleased,   450
By the pure bond of independent love
An inmate of a second family,
The fellow-labourer and friend of him
To whom the small inheritance had fallen.
—Nor deem that his mild presence was a weight   455
That pressed upon his Brother's house, for books
Were ready comrades whom he could not tire,—
Of whose society the blameless Man
Was never satiate. Their familiar voice,
Even to old age, with unabated charm   460
Beguiled his leisure hours; refreshed his thoughts;
Beyond its natural elevation raised
His introverted spirit; and bestowed
Upon his life an outward dignity
Which all acknowledged. The dark winter night,   465
The stormy day, had each its own resource;
Song of the muses, sage historic tale,
Science severe, or word of holy Writ
Announcing immortality and joy
To the assembled spirits of the just,   470
From imperfection and decay secure.
—Thus soothed at home, thus busy in the field,
To no perverse suspicion he gave way,
No languor, peevishness, nor vain complaint:
And they, who were about him, did not fail   475
In reverence, or in courtesy; they prized
His gentle manners:—and his peaceful smiles,
The gleams of his slow-varying countenance,

Were met with answering sympathy and love.

   At length, when sixty years and five were told,   480
A slow disease insensibly consumed
The powers of nature; and a few short steps
Of friends and kindred bore him from his home
(Yon Cottage shaded by the woody crags)
To the profounder stillness of the grave.   485
—Nor was his funeral denied the grace
Of many tears, virtuous and thoughtful grief;
Heart-sorrow rendered sweet by gratitude.
And now that monumental Stone preserves
His name, and unambitiously relates   490
How long, and by what kindly outward aids,
And in what pure contentedness of mind,
The sad privation was by him endured.
—And yon tall Pine-tree, whose composing sound
Was wasted on the good Man's living ear,   495
Hath now its own peculiar sanctity;
And, at the touch of every wandering breeze,
Murmurs, not idly, o'er his peaceful grave.

   Soul-cheering Light, most bountiful of Things!
Guide of our way, mysterious Comforter!   500
Whose sacred influence, spread through earth and heaven,
We all too thanklessly participate,
Thy gifts were utterly withheld from Him
Whose place of rest is near yon ivied Porch.
Yet, of the wild brooks ask if he complained;   505
Ask of the channelled rivers if they held
A safer, easier, more determined course.
What terror doth it strike into the mind
To think of One, who cannot see, advancing
Towards some precipice's airy brink!   510
But, timely warned, *He* would have stayed his steps;
Protected, say enlightened, by his ear,
And on the very brink of vacancy

Not more endangered than a Man whose eye
Beholds the gulph beneath.—No floweret blooms 515
Throughout the lofty range of these rough hills,
Or in the woods, that could from him conceal
Its birth-place; none whose figure did not live
Upon his touch. The bowels of the earth
Enriched with knowledge his industrious mind; 520
The ocean paid him tribute from the stores
Lodged in her bosom; and, by science led,
His genius mounted to the plains of Heaven.
—Methinks I see him—how his eye-balls rolled,
Beneath his ample brow, in darkness paired,— 525
But each instinct with spirit; and the frame
Of the whole countenance alive with thought,
Fancy, and understanding; while the voice
Discoursed of natural and moral truth
With eloquence, and such authentic power, 530
That, in his presence, humbler knowledge stood
Abashed, and tender pity overawed."

  "A noble—and, to unreflecting minds,
A marvellous spectacle," the Wanderer said,
"Beings like these present! But proof abounds 535
Upon the earth that faculties, which seem
Extinguished, do not, *therefore*, cease to be.
And to the mind among her powers of sense
This transfer is permitted,—not alone
That the bereft may win their recompence; 540
But for remoter purposes of love
And charity; nor last nor least for this,
That to the imagination may be given
A type and shadow of an awful truth,
How, likewise, under sufferance divine, 545
Darkness is banished from the realms of Death,
By man's imperishable spirit, quelled.
Unto the men who see not as we see
Futurity was thought, in ancient times,

To be laid open, and they prophesied. 550
And know we not that from the blind have flowed
The highest, holiest raptures of the lyre;
And wisdom married to immortal verse?"

   Among the humbler Worthies, at our feet
Lying insensible to human praise, 555
Love, or regret,—*whose* lineaments would next
Have been pourtrayed, I guess not; but it chanced
That near the quiet church-yard where we sate
A Team of horses, with a ponderous freight
Pressing behind, adown a rugged slope, 560
Whose sharp descent confounded their array,
Came at that moment, ringing noisily.

   "Here," said the Pastor, "do we muse, and mourn
The waste of death; and lo! the giant Oak
Stretched on his bier!—-that massy timber wain; 565
Nor fail to note the Man who guides the team."

   He was a Peasant of the lowest class:
Grey locks profusely round his temples hung
In clustering curls, like ivy, which the bite
Of Winter cannot thin; the fresh air lodged 570
Within his cheek, as light within a cloud;
And he returned our greeting with a smile.
When he had passed, the Solitary spake,
—"A Man he seems of cheerful yesterdays
And confident to-morrows,—with a face 575
Not worldly-minded; for it bears too much
Of Nature's impress,—gaiety and health,
Freedom and hope; but keen, withal, and shrewd.
His gestures note,—and hark! his tones of voice
Are all vivacious as his mien and looks." 580

   The Pastor answered. "You have read him well.
Year after year is added to his store
With *silent* increase: summers, winters—past,

Past or to come; yea, boldly might I say,
Ten summers and ten winters of the space 585
That lies beyond life's ordinary bounds,
Upon his sprightly vigor, cannot fix
The obligation of an anxious mind,
A pride in having, or a fear to lose;
Possessed like outskirts of some large Domain, 590
By any one more thought of than by him
Who holds the land in fee, its careless Lord!
—Yet is the Creature rational—endowed
With foresight; hears, too, every Sabbath day,
The christian promise with attentive ear, 595
Nor disbelieves the tidings which he hears.
Meanwhile the incense offered up by him
Is of the kind which beasts and birds present
In grove or pasture; chearfulness of soul,
From trepidation and repining free. 600
How many scrupulous worshippers fall down
Upon their knees, and daily homage pay
Less worthy, less religious even, than his!

    This qualified respect, the Old Man's due,
Is paid without reluctance; but in truth" 605
(Said the good Vicar with a fond half-smile)
"I feel at times a motion of despite
Towards One, whose bold contrivances and skill,
As you have seen, bear such conspicuous part
In works of havoc; taking from these vales, 610
One after one, their proudest ornaments.
Full oft his doings leave me to deplore
Tall ash-tree sown by winds, by vapours nursed,
In the dry crannies of the pendant rocks;
Light birch, aloft upon the horizon's edge, 615
Transparent texture, framing in the east
A veil of glory for the ascending moon;
And oak whose roots by noontide dew were damped,
And on whose forehead inaccessible

The raven lodged in safety.—Many a ship 620
Launched into Morecamb bay, hath owed to him
Her strong knee-timbers, and the mast that bears
The loftiest of her pendants. Help he gives
To lordly mansion rising far or near;
The enormous wheel that turns ten thousand spindles, 625
And the vast engine labouring in the mine,
Content with meaner prowess, must have lacked
The trunk and body of their marvellous strength,
If his undaunted enterprize had failed
Among the mountain coves, or keen research 630
In forest, park, or chace. Yon household Fir,
A guardian planted to fence off the blast,
But towering high the roof above, as if
Its humble destination were forgot;
That Sycamore, which annually holds 635
Within its shade, as in a stately tent[1]
On all sides open to the fanning breeze,
A grave assemblage, seated while they shear
The fleece-incumbered flock;— the JOYFUL ELM
Around whose trunk the lasses dance in May;— 640
And the LORD'S OAK;—would plead their several rights
In vain, if He were master of their fate.
Not one would have his pitiful regard,
For prized accommodation, pleasant use,
For dignity, for old acquaintance sake, 645
For ancient custom or distinguished name.
His sentence to the axe would doom them all!
—But, green in age and lusty as he is
And promising to stand from year to year,
Less, as might seem, in rivalship with men 650
Than with the forest's more enduring growth,
His own appointed hour will come at last;

---

[1] "This Sycamore oft musical with Bees;
   Such Tents the Patriarchs loved.
            S. T. Coleridge."
   WW quotes from Coleridge's *Inscription for a Fountain on a Heath*, ll. 1–2.

And, like the haughty Spoilers of the world,
This keen Destroyer, in his turn, must fall.

    Now from the living pass we once again;   655
From Age," the Priest continued, "turn your thoughts;—
From Age, that often unlamented drops,
And mark that daisied hillock, three spans long.
—Seven lusty Sons sate daily round the board
Of Gold-rill side; and when the hope had ceased   660
Of other progeny, a Daughter then
Was given, the crown and glory of the whole!
Welcomed with joy, whose penetrating power
Was not unfelt amid that heavenly calm
With which by nature every Mother's Soul   665
Is stricken, in the moment when her throes
Are ended, and her ears have heard the cry
Which tells her that a living Child is born,—
And she lies conscious in a blissful rest
That the dread storm is weathered by them both.   670
—The Father—Him at this unlooked-for gift
A bolder transport seizes. From the side
Of his bright hearth, and from his open door,
And from the laurel-shaded seat thereby,
Day after day the gladness is diffused   675
To all that come, and almost all that pass;
Invited, summoned, to partake the cheer
Spread on the never-empty board, and drink
Health and good wishes to his new-born Girl,
From cups replenished by his joyous hand.   680
—Those seven fair Brothers variously were moved
Each by the thoughts best suited to his years:
But most of all and with most thankful mind
The hoary Grand-sire felt himself enriched;
A happiness that ebbed not, but remained   685
To fill the total measure of the soul!
—From the low tenement, his own abode,
Whither, as to a little private cell,

He had withdrawn from bustle, care, and noise,
To spend the Sabbath of old age in peace, 690
Once every day he duteously repaired
To rock the cradle of the slumbering Babe:
For in that female Infant's name he heard
The silent Name of his departed Wife;
Heart-stirring music! hourly heard that name; 695
Full blest he was, "Another Margaret Green,"
Oft did he say, "was come to Gold-rill side."
—Oh! pang unthought of, as the precious boon
Itself had been unlooked for;—oh! dire stroke
Of desolating anguish for them all! 700
—Just as the Child could totter on the floor,
And, by some friendly finger's help upstayed,
Range round the garden-walk, whose low ground-flowers
Were peeping forth, shy messengers of spring,—
Even at that hopeful time,—the winds of March, 705
One sunny day, smiting insidiously,
Raised in the tender passage of the throat
Viewless obstruction; whence—all unforewarned,
The Household lost their hope and soul's delight.
—But Providence, that gives and takes away 710
By his own law, is merciful and just;
Time wants not power to soften all regrets,
And prayer and thought can bring to worst distress
Due resignation. Therefore, though some tears
Fail not to spring from either Parent's eye 715
Oft as they hear of sorrow like their own,
Yet this departed Little-one, too long
The innocent troubler of their quiet, sleeps
In what may now be called a peaceful grave.

On a bright day, the brightest of the year, 720
These mountains echoed with an unknown sound,
A volley, thrice repeated o'er the Corse
Let down into the hollow of that Grave,
Whose shelving sides are red with naked mold.

Ye Rains of April, duly wet this earth! 725
Spare, burning Sun of Midsummer, these sods,
That they may knit together, and therewith
Our thoughts unite in kindred quietness!
Nor so the Valley shall forget her loss.
Dear Youth! by young and old alike beloved, 730
To me as precious as my own!—Green herbs
May creep (I wish that they would softly creep)
Over thy last abode, and we may pass
Reminded less imperiously of thee;—
The ridge itself may sink into the breast 735
Of earth, the great abyss, and be no more;
Yet shall not thy remembrance leave our hearts,
Thy image disappear. The mountain Ash,
Decked with autumnal berries that outshine
Spring's richest blossoms, yields a splendid show, 740
Amid the leafy woods; and ye have seen,
By a brook side or solitary tarn,
How she her station doth adorn,—the pool
Glows at her feet, and all the gloomy rocks
Are brightened round her. In his native Vale 745
Such and so glorious did this Youth appear;
A sight that kindled pleasure in all hearts
By his ingenuous beauty, by the gleam
Of his fair eyes, by his capacious brow,
By all the graces with which nature's hand 750
Had bounteously arrayed him. As old Bards
Tell in their idle songs of wandering Gods,
Pan or Apollo, veiled in human form;
Yet, like the sweet-breathed violet of the shade,
Discovered in their own despite to sense 755
Of Mortals, (if such fables without blame
May find chance-mention on this sacred ground)
So, through a simple rustic garb's disguise,
And through the impediment of rural cares,
In him revealed a Scholar's genius shone; 760

And so, not wholly hidden from men's sight,
In him the spirit of a Hero walked
Our unpretending valley.—How the coit
Whizzed from the Stripling's arm! If touched by him
The inglorious foot-ball mounted to the pitch   765
Of the Lark's flight,—or shaped a rain-bow curve,
Aloft, in prospect of the shouting field!
The indefatigable Fox had learned
To dread his perseverance in the chace.
With admiration he could lift his eyes   770
To the wide-ruling Eagle, and his hand
Was loth to assault the majesty he loved;
Else had the strongest fastnesses proved weak
To guard the royal brood. The sailing glead,
The wheeling swallow, and the darting snipe,   775
The sportive sea-gull dancing with the waves,
And cautious water-fowl, from distant climes,
Fixed at their seat—the centre of the Mere,
Were subject to young Oswald's steady aim.

   From Gallia's coast a Tyrant's threats were hurled;   780
Our Country marked the preparations vast
Of hostile Forces; and she called—with voice
That filled her plains and reached her utmost shores
And in remotest vales was heard—to Arms!
—Then, for the first time, here you might have seen   785
The Shepherd's grey to martial scarlet changed,
That flashed uncouthly through the woods and fields.
Ten hardy Striplings, all in bright attire
And graced with shining weapons, weekly marched,
From this lone valley, to a central spot   790
Where, in assemblage with the Flower and Choice
Of the surrounding district, they might learn
The rudiments of war; ten—hardy, strong,
And valiant; but young Oswald, like a Chief
And yet a modest Comrade, led them forth   795
From their shy solitude, to face the world,

With a gay confidence and seemly pride;
Measuring the soil beneath their happy feet
Like youths released from labour and yet bound
To most laborious service, though to them   800
A festival of unencumbered ease;
The inner spirit keeping holiday,
Like vernal ground to sabbath sunshine left.

   Oft have I marked him, at some leisure hour,
Stretched on the grass or seated in the shade   805
Among his Fellows, while an ample Map
Before their eyes lay carefully outspread,
From which the gallant Teacher would discourse,
Now pointing this way and now that.—"Here flows,"
Thus would he say, "the Rhine, that famous Stream!   810
"Eastward, the Danube tow'rds this inland sea,
"A mightier river, winds from realm to realm;—
"And, like a serpent, shews his glittering back
"Bespotted with innumerable isles.
"Here reigns the Russian, there the Turk; observe   815
"His capital city!"—Thence—along a tract
Of livelier interest to his hopes and fears
His finger moved, distinguishing the spots
Where wide-spread conflict then most fiercely raged;
Nor left unstigmatized those fatal Fields   820
On which the Sons of mighty Germany
Were taught a base submission.—"Here behold
"A nobler race, the Switzers, and their Land;
"Vales deeper far than these of ours, huge woods,
"And mountains white with everlasting snow!"   825
—And, surely, he, that spake with kindling brow,
Was a true Patriot, hopeful as the best
Of that young Peasantry, who, in our days,
Have fought and perished for Helvetia's rights,—
Ah not in vain!—or those who, in old time,   830
For work of happier issue, to the side
Of Tell came trooping from a thousand huts,

When he had risen alone! No braver Youth
Descended from Judea's heights, to march
With righteous Joshua; or appeared in arms 835
When grove was felled, and altar was cast down,
And Gideon blew the trumpet, soul-enflamed,
And strong in hatred of Idolatry."

    This spoken, from his seat the Pastor rose,
And moved towards the grave;—instinctively 840
His steps we followed; and my voice exclaimed,
"Power to the Oppressors of the world is given,
A might of which they dream not. Oh! the curse,
To be the Awakener of divinest thoughts,
Father and Founder of exalted deeds, 845
And to whole Nations bound in servile straits
The liberal Donor of capacities
More than heroic! this to be, nor yet
Have sense of one connatural wish, nor yet
Deserve the least return of human thanks; 850
Winning no recompence but deadly hate
With pity mixed, astonishment with scorn!"

    When these involuntary words had ceased,
The Pastor said, "So Providence is served;
The forked weapon of the skies can send 855
Illumination into deep, dark Holds,
Which the mild sunbeam hath not power to pierce.
Why do ye quake, intimidated Thrones?
For, not unconscious of the mighty debt
Which to outrageous Wrong the Sufferer owes, 860
Europe, through all her habitable Seats,
Is thirsting for *their* overthrow, who still
Exist, as Pagan Temples stood of old,
By very horror of their impious rites
Preserved; are suffered to extend their pride, 865
Like Cedars on the top of Lebanon
Darkening the sun.—But less impatient thoughts,

And love "all hoping and expecting all,"
This hallowed Grave demands; where rests in peace
A humble Champion of the better Cause;   870
A Peasant-youth, so call him, for he asked
No higher name; in whom our Country shewed,
As in a favourite Son, most beautiful.
In spite of vice, and misery, and disease,
Spread with the spreading of her wealthy arts,   875
England, the ancient and the free, appeared,
In him, to stand before my swimming eyes
Unconquerably virtuous and secure.
—No more of this, lest I offend his dust:
Short was his life, and a brief tale remains.   880

   One summer's day, a day of annual pomp
And solemn chace; from morn to sultry noon
His steps had followed, fleetest of the fleet,
The red-deer driven along its native heights
With cry of hound and horn: and, from that toil   885
Returned with sinews weakened and relaxed,
This generous Youth, too negligent of self,
(A natural failing which maturer years
Would have subdued) took fearlessly—and kept—
His wonted station in the chilling flood,   890
Among a busy company convened
To wash his Father's flock. Convulsions dire
Seized him, that self-same night; and through the space
Of twelve ensuing days his frame was wrenched,
Till nature rested from her work in death.   895
—To him, thus snatched away, his Comrades paid
A Soldier's honours. At his funeral hour
Bright was the sun, the sky a cloudless blue,
A golden lustre slept upon the hills;
And if by chance a Stranger, wandering there,   900
From some commanding eminence had looked
Down on this spot, well pleased would he have seen
A glittering Spectacle; but every face

Was pallid,—seldom hath that eye been moist
With tears—that wept not then; nor were the few 905
Who from their Dwellings came not forth to join
In this sad service, less disturbed than we.
They started at the tributary peal
Of instantaneous thunder, which announced
Through the still air the closing of the Grave; 910
And distant mountains echoed with a sound
Of lamentation, never heard before!"

    The Pastor ceased.—My venerable Friend
Victoriously upraised his clear bright eye;
And, when that eulogy was ended, stood 915
Enwrapt,—as if his inward sense perceived
The prolongation of some still response,
Sent by the ancient soul of this wide Land,
The spirit of its mountains and its seas,
Its cities, temples, fields, its awful power, 920
Its rights and virtues—by that Deity
Descending; and supporting his pure heart
With patriotic confidence and joy.
And, at the last of those memorial words,
The pining Solitary turned aside, 925
Whether through manly instinct to conceal
Tender emotions spreading from the heart
To his worn cheek; or with uneasy shame
For those cold humours of habitual spleen,
Which, fondly seeking in dispraise of Man 930
Solace and self-excuse, had sometimes urged
To self-abuse, a not ineloquent tongue.
—Right tow'rds the sacred Edifice his steps
Had been directed; and we saw him now
Intent upon a monumental Stone, 935
Whose uncouth Form was grafted on the wall
Or rather seemed to have grown into the side
Of the rude Pile; as oft-times trunks of trees,
Where Nature works in wild and craggy spots,

Are seen incorporate with the living rock; 940
To endure for aye. The Vicar, taking note
Of his employment, with a courteous smile
Exclaimed, "The sagest Antiquarian's eye
That task would foil." And, with these added words,
He thitherward advanced, "Tradition tells 945
That, in Eliza's golden days, a Knight
Came on a War-horse sumptuously attired,
And fixed his home in this sequestered Vale.
'Tis left untold if here he first drew breath,
Or as a Stranger reached this deep recess, 950
Unknowing and unknown. A pleasing thought
I sometimes entertain, that, haply bound
To Scotland's court in service of his Queen,
Or sent on mission to some northern Chief
Of England's Realm, this Vale he might have seen 955
With transient observation; and thence caught
An Image fair, which, brightening in his soul
When years admonished him of failing strength
And he no more rejoiced in war's delights,
Had power to draw him from the world—resolved 960
To make that paradise his chosen home
To which his peaceful Fancy oft had turned.
—Vague thoughts are these; but, if belief may rest
Upon unwritten story fondly traced
From sire to son, in this obscure Retreat 965
The Knight arrived, with pomp of spear and shield,
And borne upon a Charger covered o'er
With gilded housings. And the lofty Steed—
His sole companion, and his faithful friend,
Whom he, in gratitude, let loose to range 970
In fertile pastures—was beheld with eyes
Of admiration and delightful awe,
By those untravelled Dalesmen. With less pride,
Yet free from touch of envious discontent,
They saw a Mansion at his bidding rise, 975

Like a bright star, amid the lowly band
Of their rude Homesteads. Here the Warrior dwelt,
And in that Mansion Children of his own,
Or Kindred, gathered round him. As a Tree
That falls and disappears, the House is gone; 980
And, through improvidence, or want of love
For ancient worth and honourable things,
The spear and shield are vanished, which the Knight
Hung in his rustic Hall. One ivied arch
Myself have seen, a gateway, last remains 985
Of that Foundation in domestic care
Raised by his hands. And now no trace is left
Of the mild-hearted Champion, save this Stone,
Faithless memorial! and his family name
Borne by yon clustering cottages, that sprang 990
From out the ruins of his stately Lodge:
These, and the name and title at full length,—
Sir Alfred Irthing, with appropriate words
Accompanied, still extant, in a wreath
Or posy—girding round the several fronts 995
Of three clear-sounding and harmonious bells,
That in the steeple hang, his pious gift."

"So fails, so languishes, grows dim, and dies,"
The grey-haired Wanderer pensively exclaimed,
"All that this World is proud of. From their spheres 1000
The stars of human glory are cast down;
Perish the roses and the flowers of Kings,[1]
Princes and Emperors, and the crowns and palms
Of all the Mighty, withered and consumed!

---

1 "The 'Transit gloria mundi' is finely expressed in the Introduction to the Foundation Charters of some of the ancient Abbies. Some expressions here used are taken from that of the Abbey of St. Mary's Furness, the translation of which is as follows.

'Considering every day the uncertainty of life, that the roses and flowers of Kings, Emperors, and Dukes, and the crowns and palms of all the great, wither and decay; and that all things with an uninterrupted course, tend to dissolution and death: I therefore,' &c." WW

Nor is power given to lowliest Innocence   1005
Long to protect her own. The Man himself
Departs; and soon is spent the Line of those
Who, in the bodily image, in the mind,
In heart or soul, in station or pursuit,
Did most resemble him. Degrees and Ranks,   1010
Fraternities and Orders—heaping high
New wealth upon the burthen of the old,
And placing trust in privilege confirmed
And re-confirmed—are scoffed at with a smile
Of greedy foretaste, from the secret stand   1015
Of Desolation, aimed: to slow decline
These yield, and these to sudden overthrow;
Their virtue, service, happiness, and state
Expire; and Nature's pleasant robe of green,
Humanity's appointed shroud, enwraps   1020
Their monuments and their memory. The vast Frame
Of social nature changes evermore
Her organs and her members, with decay
Restless, and restless generation, powers
And functions dying and produced at need,—   1025
And by this law the mighty Whole subsists:
With an ascent and progress in the main;
Yet oh! how disproportioned to the hopes
And expectations of self-flattering minds!
—The courteous Knight, whose bones are here interred,   1030
Lived in an age conspicuous as our own
For strife and ferment in the minds of men;
Whence alteration, in the forms of things,
Various and vast. A memorable age!
Which did to him assign a pensive lot,   1035
—To linger mid the last of those bright Clouds,
That, on the steady breeze of honour, sailed
In long procession calm and beautiful.
He, who had seen his own bright Order fade,
And its devotion gradually decline,   1040

(While War, relinquishing the lance and shield,
Her temper changed and bowed to other laws)
Had also witnessed, in his morn of life,
That violent Commotion, which o'erthrew,
In town, and city, and sequestered glen,   1045
Altar, and Cross, and Church of solemn roof,
And old religious House—Pile after Pile;
And shook the Tenants out into the fields,
Like wild Beasts without home! Their hour was come;
But why no softening thought of gratitude,   1050
No just remembrance, scruple, or wise doubt?
Benevolence is mild; nor borrows help,
Save at worst need, from bold impetuous force,
Fitliest allied to anger and revenge.
But Human-kind rejoices in the might   1055
Of Mutability, and airy Hopes,
Dancing around her, hinder and disturb
Those meditations of the soul, which feed
The retrospective Virtues. Festive songs
Break from the maddened Nations at the sight   1060
Of sudden overthrow; and cold neglect
Is the sure consequence of slow decay.
—Even," said the Wanderer, "as that courteous Knight,
Bound by his vow to labour for redress
Of all who suffer wrong, and to enact   1065
By sword and lance the law of gentleness,
If I may venture of myself to speak,
Trusting that not incongruously I blend
Low things with lofty, I too shall be doomed
To outlive the kindly use and fair esteem   1070
Of the poor calling which my Youth embraced
With no unworthy prospect. But enough;
—Thoughts crowd upon me—and 'twere seemlier now
To stop, and yield our gracious Teacher thanks
For the pathetic Records which his voice   1075
Hath here delivered; words of heartfelt truth,

Tending to patience when Affliction strikes;
To hope and love; to confident repose
In God; and reverence for the dust of Man."

END OF THE SEVENTH BOOK.

BOOK THE EIGHTH

THE PARSONAGE

The pensive Sceptic of the lonely Vale
To those acknowledgments subscribed his own
With a sedate compliance, which the Priest
Failed not to notice inly pleased, and said,
"If Ye, by whom invited I commenced   5
Those Narratives of calm and humble life,
Be satisfied, 'tis well,—the end is gained;
And, in return for sympathy bestowed
And patient listening, thanks accept from me.
—Life, Death, Eternity! momentous themes   10
Are these—and might demand a Seraph's tongue,
Were they not equal to their own support;
And therefore no incompetence of mine
Could do them wrong. The universal Forms
Of human nature, in a Spot like this,   15
Present themselves, at once to all Men's view:
Ye wished for act and circumstance, that make
The Individual known and understood;
And such as my best judgment could select
From what the Place afforded have been given;   20
Though apprehensions crossed me, in the course
Of this self-pleasing exercise, that Ye
My zeal to his would liken, who, possessed
Of some rare gems, or pictures finely wrought,
Unlocks his Cabinet, and draws them forth   25
One after one,—soliciting regard

To this—and this, as worthier than the last,
Till the Spectator, who a while was pleased
More than the Exhibitor himself, becomes
Weary and faint, and longs to be released.   30
—But let us hence! my Dwelling is in sight,
And there—"
                    At this the Solitary shrunk
With backward will; but, wanting not address
That inward motion to disguise, he said
To his Compatriot, smiling as he spake;   35
—"The peaceable Remains of this good Knight
Would be disturbed, I fear, with wrathful scorn,
If consciousness could reach him where he lies
That One, albeit of these degenerate times,
Deploring changes past, or dreading change   40
Foreseen, had dared to couple, even in thought,
The fine Vocation of the sword and lance
With the gross aims and body-bending toil
Of a poor Brotherhood who walk the earth
Pitied, and where they are not known, despised.   45
—Yet, by the good Knight's leave, the two Estates
Are graced with some resemblance. Errant Those,
Exiles and Wanderers—and the like are These;
Who, with their burthen, traverse hill and dale,
Carrying relief for Nature's simple wants.   50
—What though no higher recompence they seek
Than honest maintenance, by irksome toil
Full oft procured! Yet Such may claim respect,
Among the Intelligent, for what this course
Enables them to be, and to perform.   55
Their tardy steps give leisure to observe;
While solitude permits the mind to feel;
And doth instruct her to supply defects
By the division of her inward self,
For grateful converse: and to these poor Men,   60
(As I have heard you boast with honest pride)

Nature is bountiful, where'er they go;
Kind Nature's various wealth is all their own.
Versed in the characters of men; and bound,
By tie of daily interest, to maintain 65
Conciliatory manners and smooth speech;
Such have been, and still are in their degree,
Examples efficacious to refine
Rude intercourse; apt Instruments to excite,
By importation of unlooked-for Arts, 70
Barbarian torpor, and blind prejudice;
Raising, through just gradation, savage life
To rustic, and the rustic to urbane.
—Within their moving magazines is lodged
Power that comes forth to quicken and exalt 75
The affections seated in the Mother's breast,
And in the Lover's fancy; and to feed
The sober sympathies of long tried Friends.
—By these Itinerants, as experienced Men,
Counsel is given; contention they appease 80
With healing words; and in remotest Wilds
Tears wipe away, and pleasant tidings bring;
Could the proud quest of Chivalry do more?"

  "Happy," rejoined the Wanderer, "They who gain
A panegyric from your generous tongue! 85
But, if to these Wayfarers once pertained
Aught of romantic interest, 'tis gone;
Their purer service, in this realm at least,
Is past for ever.—An inventive Age
Has wrought, if not with speed of magic, yet 90
To most strange issues. I have lived to mark
A new and unforeseen Creation rise
From out the labours of a peaceful Land,
Wielding her potent Enginery to frame
And to produce, with appetite as keen 95
As that of War, which rests not night or day,
Industrious to destroy! With fruitless pains

Might One like me *now* visit many a tract
Which, in his youth, he trod, and trod again,
A lone Pedestrian with a scanty freight,   100
Wished for, or welcome, wheresoe'er he came,
Among the Tenantry of Thorpe and Vill;
Or straggling Burgh, of ancient charter proud,
And dignified by battlements and towers
Of some stern Castle, mouldering on the brow   105
Of a green hill or bank of rugged stream.
The foot-path faintly marked, the horse-track wild,
And formidable length of plashy lane,
(Prized avenues ere others had been shaped
Or easier links connecting place with place)   110
Have vanished,—swallowed up by stately roads
Easy and bold, that penetrate the gloom
Of England's farthest Glens. The Earth has lent
Her waters, Air her breezes;[1] and the Sail
Of traffic glides with ceaseless interchange,   115
Glistening along the low and woody dale,
Or on the naked mountain's lofty side.
Meanwhile, at social Industry's command,
How quick, how vast an increase! From the germ
Of some poor Hamlet, rapidly produced   120
Here a huge Town, continuous and compact,
Hiding the face of earth for leagues—and there,
Where not a Habitation stood before,
The Abodes of men irregularly massed
Like trees in forests—spread through spacious tracts,   125
O'er which the smoke of unremitting fires
Hangs permanent, and plentiful as wreaths

---

1 "In treating this subject, it was impossible not to recollect, with gratitude, the pleasing picture, which in his Poem of the Fleece, the excellent and amiable Dyer has given of the influences of manufacturing industry, upon the face of this Island. He wrote at a time when machinery was first beginning to be introduced, and his benevolent heart prompted him to augur from it nothing but good. Truth has compelled me to dwell upon the baneful effects arising out of an ill-regulated and excessive application of powers so admirable in themselves." WW refers to John Dyer's poem *The Fleece* (1757).

Of vapour glittering in the morning sun.
And, wheresoe'er the Traveller turns his steps,
He sees the barren wilderness erased,   130
Or disappearing; triumph that proclaims
How much the mild Directress of the plough
Owes to alliance with these new-born Arts!
—Hence is the wide Sea peopled,—and the Shores
Of Britain are resorted to by Ships   135
Freighted from every climate of the world
With the world's choicest produce. Hence that sum
Of Keels that rest within her crowded ports,
Or ride at anchor in her sounds and bays;
That animating spectacle of Sails   140
Which through her inland regions, to and fro
Pass with the respirations of the tide,
Perpetual, multitudinous! Finally,
Hence a dread arm of floating Power, a voice
Of Thunder, daunting those who would approach   145
With hostile purposes the blessed Isle,
Truth's consecrated residence, the seat
Impregnable, of Liberty and Peace.

   And yet, O happy Pastor of a Flock
Faithfully watched, and by that loving care   150
And heaven's good providence preserved from taint!
With You I grieve, when on the darker side
Of this great change I look; and there behold,
Through strong temptation of those gainful Arts,
Such outrage done to Nature as compels   155
The indignant Power to justify herself;
Yea to avenge her violated rights
For England's bane.—When soothing darkness spreads
O'er hill and vale," the Wanderer thus expressed
His recollections, "and the punctual stars,   160
While all things else are gathering to their homes,
Advance, and in the firmament of heaven
Glitter—but undisturbing, undisturbed,

As if their silent company were charged
With peaceful admonitions for the heart 165
Of all-beholding Man, earth's thoughtful Lord;
Then, in full many a region, once like this
The assured domain of calm simplicity
And pensive quiet, an unnatural light,
Prepared for never-resting Labour's eyes, 170
Breaks from a many-windowed Fabric huge;
And at the appointed hour a Bell is heard—
Of harsher import than the Curfew-knoll
That spake the Norman Conqueror's stern behest,
A local summons to unceasing toil! 175
Disgorged are now the Ministers of day;
And, as they issue from the illumined Pile,
A fresh Band meets them, at the crowded door,—
And in the Courts—and where the rumbling Stream,
That turns the multitude of dizzy wheels, 180
Glares, like a troubled Spirit, in its bed
Among the rocks below. Men, Maidens, Youths,
Mother and little Children, Boys and Girls,
Enter, and each the wonted task resumes
Within this Temple—where is offered up 185
To Gain—the Master Idol of the Realm,
Perpetual sacrifice. Even thus of old
Our Ancestors, within the still domain
Of vast Cathedral or Conventual Church,
Their vigils kept; where tapers day and night 190
On the dim altar burned continually,
In token that the House was evermore
Watching to God. Religious Men were they;
Nor would their Reason, tutored to aspire
Above this transitory world, allow 195
That there should pass a moment of the year,
When in their land the Almighty's Service ceased.

   Triumph who will in these profaner rites
Which We, a generation self-extolled,

As zealously perform! I cannot share 200
His proud complacency; yet I exult,
Casting reserve away, exult to see
An Intellectual mastery exercised
O'er the blind Elements; a purpose given,
A perseverance fed; almost a soul 205
Imparted—to brute Matter. I rejoice,
Measuring the force of those gigantic powers,
Which by the thinking Mind have been compelled
To serve the Will of feeble-bodied Man.
For with the sense of admiration blends 210
The animating hope that time may come
When strengthened, yet not dazzled, by the might
Of this dominion over Nature gained,
Men of all lands shall exercise the same
In due proportion to their Country's need; 215
Learning, though late, that all true glory rests,
All praise, all safety, and all happiness,
Upon the Moral law. Egyptian Thebes;
Tyre by the margin of the sounding waves;
Palmyra, central in the Desart, fell; 220
And the Arts died by which they had been raised.
—Call Archimedes from his buried Tomb
Upon the plain of vanished Syracuse,
And feelingly the Sage shall make report
How insecure, how baseless in itself, 225
Is that Philosophy, whose sway is framed
For mere material instruments:—how weak
Those Arts, and high Inventions, if unpropped
By Virtue.—He with sighs of pensive grief,
Amid his calm abstractions, would admit 230
That not the slender privilege is theirs
To save themselves from blank forgetfulness!"

   When from the Wanderer's lips these words had fallen,
I said, "And, did in truth these vaunted Arts
Possess such privilege, how could we escape 235

Regret and painful sadness, who revere,
And would preserve as things above all price,
The old domestic morals of the land,
Her simple manners, and the stable worth
That dignified and cheered a low estate. 240
Oh! where is now the character of peace,
Sobriety, and order, and chaste love,
And honest dealing, and untainted speech,
And pure good-will, and hospitable cheer;
That made the very thought of Country-life 245
A thought of refuge, for a Mind detained
Reluctantly amid the bustling crowd?
Where now the beauty of the Sabbath kept
With conscientious reverence, as a day
By the Almighty Law-giver pronounced 250
Holy and blest? and where the winning grace
Of all the lighter ornaments attached
To time and season, as the year rolled round?"

"Fled!" was the Wanderer's passionate response,
"Fled utterly! or only to be traced 255
In a few fortunate Retreats like this;
Which I behold with trembling, when I think
What lamentable change, a year—a month—
May bring; that Brook converting as it runs
Into an Instrument of deadly bane 260
For those, who, yet untempted to forsake
The simple occupations of their Sires,
Drink the pure water of its innocent stream
With lip almost as pure.—Domestic bliss,
(Or call it comfort, by a humbler name,) 265
How art thou blighted for the poor Man's heart!
Lo! in such neighbourhood, from morn to eve,
The Habitations empty! or perchance
The Mother left alone,—no helping hand
To rock the cradle of her peevish babe; 270
No daughters round her, busy at the wheel,

Or in dispatch of each day's little growth
Of household occupation; no nice arts
Of needle-work; no bustle at the fire,
Where once the dinner was prepared with pride;   275
Nothing to speed the day, or cheer the mind;
Nothing to praise, to teach, or to command!
—The Father, if perchance he still retain
His old employments, goes to field or wood,
No longer led or followed by his Sons;   280
Idlers perchance they were,—but in his sight;
Breathing fresh air, and treading the green earth;
'Till their short holiday of childhood ceased,
Ne'er to return! That birth-right now is lost.
Economists will tell you that the State   285
Thrives by the forfeiture—unfeeling thought,
And false as monstrous! Can the Mother thrive
By the destruction of her innocent Sons?
In whom a premature Necessity
Blocks out the forms of Nature, preconsumes   290
The reason, famishes the heart, shuts up
The infant Being in itself, and makes
Its very spring a season of decay?
The lot is wretched, the condition sad,
Whether a pining discontent survive,   295
And thirst for change; or habit hath subdued
The soul depressed; dejected—even to love
Of her dull tasks, and close captivity.
—Oh, banish far such Wisdom as condemns
A native Briton to these inward chains,   300
Fixed in his soul, so early and so deep,
Without his own consent, or knowledge, fixed!
He is a Slave to whom release comes not,
And cannot come. The Boy, where'er he turns,
Is still a prisoner; when the wind is up   305
Among the clouds and in the ancient woods;
Or when the sun is rising in the heavens,

Quiet and calm. Behold him—in the school
Of his attainments? no; but with the air
Fanning his temples under heaven's blue arch. 310
His raiment, whitened o'er with cotton flakes,
Or locks of wool, announces whence he comes.
Creeping his gait and cowering—his lip pale—
His respiration quick and audible;
And scarcely could you fancy that a gleam 315
From out those languid eyes could break, or blush
Mantle upon his cheek. Is this the form,
Is that the countenance, and such the port,
Of no mean Being? One who should be clothed
With dignity befitting his proud hope; 320
Who, in his very childhood, should appear
Sublime—from present purity and joy!
The limbs increase; but, liberty of mind
Thus gone for ever, this organic Frame,
Which from heaven's bounty we receive, instinct 325
With light, and gladsome motions, soon becomes
Dull, to the joy of her own motions dead;
And even the Touch, so exquisitely poured
Through the whole body, with a languid Will
Performs its functions; rarely competent 330
To impress a vivid feeling on the mind
Of what there is delightful in the breeze,
The gentle visitations of the sun,
Or lapse of liquid element—by hand,
Or foot, or lip, in summer's warmth—perceived. 335
—Can hope look forward to a manhood raised
On such foundations?"
                    "Hope is none for him,"
The pale Recluse indignantly exclaimed,
"And tens of thousands suffer wrong as deep.
Yet be it asked, in justice to our age, 340
If there were not, before those Arts appeared,
These Structures rose, commingling old and young,

And unripe sex with sex, for mutual taint;
Then, if there were not, in our far-famed Isle,
Multitudes, who from infancy had breathed 345
Air unimprisoned, and had lived at large;
Yet walked beneath the sun, in human shape,
As abject, as degraded? At this day,
Who shall enumerate the crazy huts
And tottering hovels, whence do issue forth 350
A ragged Offspring, with their own blanched hair
Crowned like the image of fantastic Fear;
Or wearing, we might say, in that white growth
An ill-adjusted turban, for defence
Or fierceness, wreathed around their sun-burnt brows, 355
By savage Nature's unassisted care.
Naked and coloured like the soil, the feet
On which they stand; as if thereby they drew
Some nourishment, as Trees do by their roots,
From Earth the common Mother of us all. 360
Figure and mien, complexion and attire,
Are framed to strike dismay, but the outstretched hand
And whining voice denote them Supplicants
For the least boon that pity can bestow.
Such on the breast of darksome heaths are found; 365
And with their Parents dwell upon the skirts
Of furze-clad commons; and are born and reared
At the mine's mouth, beneath impending rocks,
Or in the chambers of some natural cave;
And where their Ancestors erected huts, 370
For the convenience of unlawful gain,
In forest purlieus; and the like are bred,
All England through, where nooks and slips of ground,
Purloined in times less jealous than our own,
From the green margin of the public way, 375
A residence afford them, mid the bloom
And gaiety of cultivated fields.
—Such (we will hope the lowest in the scale)

Do I remember oft-times to have seen
'Mid Buxton's dreary heights. Upon the watch,   380
Till the swift vehicle approach, they stand;
Then, following closely with the cloud of dust,
An uncouth feat exhibit, and are gone
Heels over head like Tumblers on a Stage.
—Up from the ground they snatch the copper coin,   385
And, on the freight of merry Passengers
Fixing a steady eye, maintain their speed;
And spin—and pant—and overhead again,
Wild Pursuivants! until their breath is lost,
Or bounty tires,—and every face, that smiled   390
Encouragement, hath ceased to look that way.
—But, like the Vagrants of the Gypsy tribe,
These, bred to little pleasure in themselves,
Are profitless to others. Turn we then
To Britons born and bred within the pale   395
Of civil polity, and early trained
To earn, by wholesome labour in the field,
The bread they eat. A sample should I give
Of what this stock produces to enrich
And beautify the tender age of life,   400
A sample fairly culled, ye would exclaim,
"Is this the whistling Plough-boy whose shrill notes
Impart new gladness to the morning air?"
"Forgive me! if I venture to suspect
That many, sweet to hear of in soft verse,   405
Are of no finer frame:—his joints are stiff;
Beneath a cumbrous frock that to the knees
Invests the thriving churl, his legs appear,
Fellows to those which lustily upheld
The wooden stools, for everlasting use,   410
On which our Fathers sate. And mark his brow!
Under whose shaggy canopy are set
Two eyes, not dim, but of a healthy stare;
Wide, sluggish, blank, and ignorant, and strange;

Proclaiming boldly that they never drew 415
A look or motion of intelligence
From infant conning of the Christ-cross-row,
Or puzzling through a Primer, line by line,
Till perfect mastery crown the pains at last.
—What kindly warmth from touch of fostering hand, 420
What penetrating power of sun or breeze,
Shall e'er dissolve the crust wherein his soul
Sleeps, like a caterpillar sheathed in ice?
This torpor is no pitiable work
Of modern ingenuity; no Town 425
Nor crowded City may be taxed with aught
Of sottish vice or desperate breach of law,
To which in after years he may be rouzed.
—This Boy the Fields produce: his spade and hoe,
The Carter's whip which on his shoulder rests 430
In air high-towering with a boorish pomp,
The sceptre of his sway; his Country's name,
Her equal rights, her churches and her schools,
What have they done for him? And, let me ask,
For tens of thousands uninformed as he? 435
In brief, what liberty of mind is here?"

    This cheerful sally pleased the mild good Man,
To whom the appeal couched in those closing words
Was pointedly addressed; and to the thoughts
Which, in assent or opposition, rose 440
Within his mind, he seemed prepared to give
Prompt utterance; but, rising from our seat,
The hospitable Vicar interposed
With invitation earnestly renewed.
—We followed, taking as he led, a Path 445
Along a Hedge of stately hollies framed,
Whose flexile boughs, descending with a weight
Of leafy spray, concealed the stems and roots
That gave them nourishment. How sweet methought,
When the fierce wind comes howling from the north, 450

How grateful, this impenetrable screen!
Not shaped by simple wearing of the foot
On rural business passing to and fro
Was the commodious Walk; a careful hand
Had marked the line, and strewn the surface o'er   455
With pure cerulean gravel, from the heights
Fetched by the neighbouring brook.—Across the Vale
The stately Fence accompanied our steps;
And thus the Pathway, by perennial green
Guarded and graced, seemed fashioned to unite,   460
As by a beautiful yet solemn chain,
The Pastor's Mansion with the House of Prayer.

   Like Image of solemnity conjoined
With feminine allurement soft and fair
The Mansion's self displayed;—a reverend Pile   465
With bold projections and recesses deep;
Shadowy, yet gay and lightsome as it stood
Fronting the noon-tide Sun. We paused to admire
The pillared Porch, elaborately embossed;
The low wide windows with their mullions old;   470
The cornice richly fretted, of grey stone;
And that smooth slope from which the Dwelling rose,
By beds and banks Arcadian of gay flowers
And flowering shrubs, protected and adorned.
Profusion bright! and every flower assuming   475
A more than natural vividness of hue,
From unaffected contrast with the gloom
Of sober cypress, and the darker foil
Of yew, in which survived some traces, here
Not unbecoming, of grotesque device   480
And uncouth fancy. From behind the roof
Rose the slim ash and massy sycamore,
Blending their diverse foliage with the green
Of ivy, flourishing and thick, that clasped
The huge round chimneys, harbour of delight   485
For wren and red-breast,—where they sit and sing

Their slender ditties when the trees are bare.
Nor must I pass unnoticed (leaving else
The picture incomplete, as it appeared
Before our eyes) a relique of old times 490
Happily spared, a little gothic niche
Of nicest workmanship; which once had held
The sculptured Image of some Patron Saint,
Or of the blessed Virgin, looking down
On all who entered those religious doors. 495

   But lo! where from the rocky garden mount
Crowned by its antique summer-house—descends,
Light as the silver fawn, a radiant Girl;
For she hath recognized her honoured Friend,
The Wanderer ever welcome! A prompt kiss 500
The gladsome Child bestows at his request,
And, up the flowery lawn as we advance,
Hangs on the Old Man with a happy look,
And with a pretty restless hand of love.
—We enter;—need I tell the courteous guise 505
In which the Lady of the place received
Our little Band, with salutation meet
To each accorded? Graceful was her port;
A lofty stature undepressed by Time,
Whose visitation had not spared to touch 510
The finer lineaments of frame and face;
To that complexion brought which prudence trusts in
And wisdom loves.—But when a stately Ship
Sails in smooth weather by the placid coast
On homeward voyage, what—if wind and wave, 515
And hardship undergone in various climes,
Have caused her to abate the virgin pride,
And that full trim of inexperienced hope
With which she left her haven—not for this,
Should the sun strike her, and the impartial breeze 520
Play on her streamers, doth she fail to assume
Brightness and touching beauty of her own,

That charm all eyes. So bright to us appeared
This goodly Matron, shining in the beams
Of unexpected pleasure. Soon the board 525
Was spread, and we partook a plain repast.

    Here in cool shelter, while the scorching heat
Oppressed the fields, we sate, and entertained
The mid-day hours with desultory talk;
From trivial themes to general argument 530
Passing, as accident or fancy led,
Or courtesy prescribed. While question rose
And answer flowed, the fetters of reserve
Dropped from our minds; and even the shy Recluse
Resumed the manners of his happier days. 535
He in the various conversation bore
A willing, and, at times, a forward part;
Yet with the grace of one who in the world
Had learned the art of pleasing, and had now
Occasion given him to display his skill 540
Upon the stedfast 'vantage ground of truth.
He gazed with admiration unsuppressed
Upon the landscape of the sun-bright vale,
Seen, from the shady room in which we sate,
In softened pèrspective; and more than once 545
Praised the consummate harmony serene
Of gravity and elegance—diffused
Around the Mansion and its whole domain;
Not, doubtless, without help of female taste
And female care.—"A blessed lot is yours!" 550
He said, and with that exclamation breathed
A tender sigh;—but, suddenly the door
Opening, with eager haste two lusty Boys
Appeared,—confusion checking their delight.
—Not Brothers they in feature or attire, 555
But fond Companions, so I guessed, in field,
And by the river-side—from which they come,
A pair of Anglers, laden with their spoil.

One bears a willow-pannier on his back,
The Boy of plainer garb, and more abashed 560
In countenance,—more distant and retired.
Twin might the Other be to that fair Girl
Who bounded tow'rds us from the garden mount.
Triumphant entry this to him!—for see,
Between his hands he holds a smooth blue stone, 565
On whose capacious surface is outspread
Large store of gleaming crimson-spotted trouts;
Ranged side by side, in regular ascent,
One after one, still lessening by degrees
Up to the dwarf that tops the pinnacle. 570
Upon the Board he lays the sky-blue stone
With its rich spoil;—their number he proclaims;
Tells from what pool the noblest had been dragged;
And where the very monarch of the brook,
After long struggle, had escaped at last— 575
Stealing alternately at them and us
(As doth his Comrade too) a look of pride.
And, verily, the silent Creatures made
A splendid sight, together thus exposed;
Dead—but not sullied or deformed by Death, 580
That seemed to pity what he could not spare.

 But oh! the animation in the mien
Of those two Boys! Yea in the very words
With which the young Narrator was inspired,
When, as our questions led, he told at large 585
Of that day's prowess! Him might I compare,
His look, tones, gestures, eager eloquence,
To a bold Brook which splits for better speed,
And, at the self-same moment, works its way
Through many channels, ever and anon 590
Parted and reunited: his Compeer
To the still Lake, whose stillness is to the eye
As beautiful, as grateful to the mind.
—But to what object shall the lovely Girl

Be likened? She whose countenance and air 595
Unite the graceful qualities of both,
Even as she shares the pride and joy of both.

   My grey-haired Friend was moved; his vivid eye
Glistened with tenderness; his Mind, I knew,
Was full; and had, I doubted not, returned, 600
Upon this impulse, to the theme—erewhile
Abruptly broken-off. The ruddy Boys
Did now withdraw to take their well-earned meal;
And He—(to whom all tongues resigned their rights
With willingness, to whom the general ear 605
Listened with readier patience than to strain
Of music, lute or harp,—a long delight
That ceased not when his voice had ceased) as One
Who from truth's central point serenely views
The compass of his argument,—began 610
Mildly, and with a clear and steady tone.

END OF THE EIGHTH BOOK.

BOOK THE NINTH

DISCOURSE OF THE WANDERER, AND AN EVENING VISIT TO THE LAKE

"To every Form of Being is assigned,"
Thus calmly spake the venerable Sage,
"An *active* principle:—howe'er removed
From sense and observation, it subsists
In all things, in all natures, in the stars 5
Of azure heaven, the unenduring clouds,
In flower and tree, in every pebbly stone
That paves the brooks, the stationary rocks,
The moving waters, and the invisible air.
Whate'er exists hath properties that spread 10
Beyond itself, communicating good,

A simple blessing, or with evil mixed;
Spirit that knows no insulated spot,
No chasm, no solitude; from link to link
It circulates, the Soul of all the Worlds. 15
This is the freedom of the Universe;
Unfolded still the more, more visible,
The more we know; and yet is reverenced least,
And least respected, in the human Mind,
Its most apparent home. The food of hope 20
Is meditated action; robbed of this,
Her sole support, she languishes and dies.
We perish also; for we live by hope
And by desire; we see by the glad light,
And breathe the sweet air of futurity, 25
And so we live, or else we have no life.
To-morrow—nay perchance this very hour,
(For every moment has its own to-morrow!)
—Those blooming Boys, whose hearts are almost sick
With present triumph, will be sure to find 30
A field before them freshened with the dew
Of other expectations;—in which course
Their happy year spins round. The Youth obeys
A like glad impulse; and so moves the Man
Mid all his apprehensions, cares, and fears,— 35
Or so he ought to move. Ah! why in age
Do we revert so fondly to the walks
Of Childhood—but that there the Soul discerns
The dear memorial footsteps unimpaired
Of her own native vigour—but for this, 40
That it is given her thence in age to hear
Reverberations; and a choral song,
Commingling with the incense that ascends
Undaunted, tow'rds the imperishable heavens,
From her own lonely altar?—Do not think 45
That Good and Wise will ever be allowed,
Though strength decay, to breathe in such estate

As shall divide them wholly from the stir
Of hopeful nature. Rightly is it said
That Man descends into the Vale of years; 50
Yet have I thought that we might also speak,
And not presumptuously I trust, of Age,
As of a final Eminence, though bare
In aspect and forbidding, yet a Point
On which 'tis not impossible to sit 55
In awful sovereignty—a place of power—
—A Throne, which may be likened unto his,
Who, in some placid day of summer, looks
Down from a mountain-top,—say one of those
High peaks, that bound the Vale where now we are. 60
Faint, and diminished to the gazing eye,
Forest and field, and hill and dale appear,
With all the shapes upon their surface spread.
But, while the gross and visible frame of things
Relinquishes its hold upon the sense, 65
Yea almost on the mind itself, and seems
All unsubstantialized,—how loud the voice
Of waters, with invigorated peal
From the full River in the vale below,
Ascending!—For on that superior height 70
Who sits, is disencumbered from the press
Of near obstructions, and is privileged
To breathe in solitude above the host
Of ever-humming insects, mid thin air
That suits not them. The murmur of the leaves 75
Many and idle, touches not his ear;
This he is freed from, and from thousand notes
Not less unceasing, not less vain than these,—
By which the finer passages of sense
Are occupied; and the Soul, that would incline 80
To listen, is prevented or deterred.

   And may it not be hoped, that, placed by Age
In like removal tranquil though severe,

We are not so removed for utter loss;
But for some favour, suited to our need? 85
What more than this, that we thereby should gain
Fresh power to commune with the invisible world,
And hear the mighty stream of tendency
Uttering, for elevation of our thought,
A clear sonorous voice, inaudible 90
To the vast multitude; whose doom it is
To run the giddy round of vain delight,
Or fret and labour on the Plain below.

   But, if to such sublime ascent the hopes
Of Man may rise, as to a welcome close 95
And termination of his mortal course,
Them only can such hope inspire whose minds
Have not been starved by absolute neglect;
Nor bodies crushed by unremitting toil;
To whom kind Nature, therefore, may afford 100
Proof of the sacred love she bears for all;
Whose birth-right Reason, therefore, may ensure.
For me, consulting what I feel within
In times when most existence with herself
Is satisfied, I cannot but believe, 105
That, far as kindly Nature hath free scope
And Reason's sway predominates, even so far,
Country, society, and time itself,
That saps the Individual's bodily frame
And lays the generations low in dust, 110
Do, by the Almighty Ruler's grace, partake
Of one maternal spirit, bringing forth
And cherishing with ever-constant love,
That tires not, nor betrays. Our Life is turned
Out of her course, wherever Man is made 115
An offering, or a sacrifice, a tool
Or implement, a passive Thing employed
As a brute mean, without acknowledgment
Of common right or interest in the end;

Used or abused, as selfishness may prompt. 120
Say, what can follow for a rational Soul
Perverted thus, but weakness in all good,
And strength in evil? Hence an after-call
For chastisement, and custody, and bonds,
And oft-times Death, avenger of the past, 125
And the sole guardian in whose hands we dare
Entrust the future.—Not for these sad issues
Was Man created; but to obey the law
Of life, and hope, and action. And 'tis known
That when we stand upon our native soil, 130
Unelbowed by such objects as oppress
Our active powers, those powers themselves become
Strong to subvert our noxious qualities:
They sweep away infection from the heart;
And, by the substitution of delight, 135
Suppress all evil; whence the Being moves
In beauty through the world; and all who see
Bless him, rejoicing in his neighbourhood."

   "Then," said the Solitary, "by what power
Of language shall a feeling Heart express 140
Her sorrow for that multitude in whom
We look for health from seeds that have been sown
In sickness and for increase in a power
That works but by extinction. On themselves
They cannot lean, nor turn to their own hearts 145
To know what they must do; their wisdom is
To look into the eyes of others, thence
To be instructed what they must avoid:
Or rather let us say, how least observed,
How with most quiet and most silent death, 150
With the least taint and injury to the air
The Oppressor breathes, their human Form divine,
And their immortal Soul, may waste away."

   The Sage rejoined, "I thank you—you have spared

My voice the utterance of a keen regret,   155
A wide compassion which with you I share.
When, heretofore, I placed before your sight
A most familiar object of our days,
A Little-one, subjected to the Arts
Of modern ingenuity, and made   160
The senseless member of a vast machine,
Serving as doth a spindle or a wheel;
Think not, that, pitying him, I could forget
The rustic Boy, who walks the fields, untaught;
The Slave of ignorance, and oft of want,   165
And miserable hunger. Much too much
Of this unhappy lot, in early youth
We both have witnessed, lot which I myself
Shared, though in mild and merciful degree:
Yet was my mind to hindrances exposed,   170
Through which I struggled, not without distress
And sometimes injury, like a Sheep enthralled
Mid thorns and brambles; or a Bird that breaks
Through a strong net, and mounts upon the wind,
Though with her plumes impaired. If they, whose souls   175
Should open while they range the richer fields
Of merry England, are obstructed less
By indigence, their ignorance is not less
Nor less to be deplored. For who can doubt
That tens of thousands at this day exist   180
Such as the Boy you painted, lineal Heirs
Of those who once were Vassals of her soil,
Following its fortunes like the beasts or trees
Which it sustained. But no one takes delight
In this oppression; none are proud of it;   185
It bears no sounding name nor ever bore;
A standing grievance, an indigenous vice
Of every country under heaven. My thoughts
Were turned to evils that are new and chosen,
A Bondage lurking under shape of good,—   190

Arts, in themselves beneficent and kind,
But all too fondly followed and too far;
To Victims, which the merciful can see
Nor think that they are Victims; turned to wrongs
Which Women who have Children of their own   195
Regard without compassion, yea with praise!
I spake of mischief which the wise diffuse
With gladness, thinking that the more it spreads
The healthier, the securer we become;
Delusion which a moment may destroy!   200
Lastly I mourned for those whom I had seen
Corrupted and cast down, on favoured ground,
Where circumstance and nature had combined
To shelter innocence, and cherish love;
Who, but for this intrusion, would have lived,   205
Possessed of health, and strength, and peace of mind;
Thus would have lived, or never have been born.

   Alas! what differs more than man from man!
And whence that difference? whence but from himself?
For see the universal Race endowed   210
With the same upright form!—The sun is fixed,
And the infinite magnificence of heaven,
Within the reach of every human eye;
The sleepless Ocean murmurs for all ears;
The vernal field infuses fresh delight   215
Into all hearts. Throughout the world of sense
Even as an object is sublime or fair,
That object is laid open to the view
Without reserve or veil; and as a power
Is salutary, or an influence sweet,   220
Are each and all enabled to perceive
That power, that influence, by impartial law.
Gifts nobler are vouchsafed alike to all;
Reason,—and, with that reason, smiles and tears;
Imagination, freedom in the will,   225
Conscience to guide and check; and death to be

Foretasted, immortality presumed.
Strange, then, nor less than monstrous might be deemed
The failure, if the Almighty, to this point
Liberal and undistinguishing, should hide 230
The excellence of moral qualities
From common understanding; leaving truth
And virtue, difficult, abstruse, and dark;
Hard to be won, and only by a few;
Strange, should he deal herein with nice respects, 235
And frustrate all the rest! Believe it not:
The primal duties shine aloft—like stars;
The charities that soothe, and heal, and bless,
Are scattered at the feet of Man—like flowers.
The generous inclination, the just rule, 240
Kind wishes, and good actions, and pure thoughts—
No mystery is here; no special boon
For high and not for low, for proudly graced
And not for meek of heart. The smoke ascends
To heaven as lightly from the Cottage hearth 245
As from the haughty palace. He, whose soul
Ponders this true equality, may walk
The fields of earth with gratitude and hope;
Yet, in that meditation, will he find
Motive to sadder grief, as we have found,— 250
Lamenting ancient virtues overthrown,
And for the injustice grieving, that hath made
So wide a difference betwixt Man and Man.

   But let us rather fix our gladdened thoughts
Upon the brighter scene. How blest that Pair 255
Of blooming Boys (whom we beheld even now)
Blest in their several and their common lot!
A few short hours of each returning day
The thriving Prisoners of their Village school;
And thence let loose, to seek their pleasant homes, 260
Or range the grassy lawn in vacancy,
To breathe and to be happy, run and shout

Idle,—but no delay, no harm, no loss;
For every genial Power of heaven and earth,
Through all the seasons of the changeful year, 265
Obsequiously doth take upon herself
To labour for them; bringing each in turn
The tribute of enjoyment, knowledge, health,
Beauty, or strength! Such privilege is theirs,
Granted alike in the outset of their course 270
To both; and, if that partnership must cease,
I grieve not," to the Pastor here he turned,
"Much as I glory in that Child of yours,
Repine not, for his Cottage-comrade, whom
Belike no higher destiny awaits 275
Than the old hereditary wish fulfilled,
The wish for liberty to live—content
With what heaven grants, and die—in peace of mind,
Within the bosom of his native Vale.
At least, whatever fate the noon of life 280
Reserves for either, this is sure, that both
Have been permitted to enjoy the dawn;
Whether regarded as a jocund time
That in itself may terminate, or lead
In course of nature to a sober eve. 285
Both have been fairly dealt with; looking back
They will allow that justice has in them
Been shewn—alike to body and to mind."

   He paused, as if revolving in his soul
Some weighty matter, then, with fervent voice 290
And an impassioned majesty, exclaimed,
"Oh for the coming of that glorious time
When, prizing knowledge as her noblest wealth
And best protection, this Imperial Realm,
While she exacts allegiance, shall admit 295
An obligation, on her part, to *teach*
Them who are born to serve her and obey;

Binding herself by Statute[1] to secure
For all the Children whom her soil maintains
The rudiments of Letters, and to inform   300
The mind with moral and religious truth,
Both understood, and practised,—so that none,
However destitute, be left to droop
By timely culture unsustained, or run
Into a wild disorder; or be forced   305
To drudge through weary life without the aid
Of intellectual implements and tools;
A savage Horde among the civilized,
A servile Band among the lordly free!
This right, as sacred almost as the right   310
To exist and be supplied with sustenance
And means of life, the lisping Babe proclaims
To be inherent in him, by Heaven's will,
For the protection of his innocence;
And the rude Boy—who, having overpast   315
The sinless age, by conscience is enrolled,
Yet mutinously knits his angry brow,
And lifts his wilful hand on mischief bent,
Or turns the sacred faculty of speech
To impious use—by process indirect   320
Declares his due, while he makes known his need.
—This sacred right is fruitlessly announced,
This universal plea in vain addressed,
To eyes and ears of Parents who themselves
Did, in the time of their necessity,   325
Urge it in vain; and, therefore, like a prayer
That from the humblest floor ascends to heaven,
It mounts, to reach the State's parental ear;
Who, if indeed she own a Mother's heart,

---

[1] "The discovery of Dr. Bell affords marvellous facilities for carrying this into effect, and it is impossible to overrate the benefit which might accrue to humanity from the universal application of this simple engine under an enlightened and conscientious government." WW refers to Andrew Bell and his educational system built on the notion of pupil-teachers teaching one another.

And be not most unfeelingly devoid 330
Of gratitude to Providence, will grant
The unquestionable good; which, England, safe
From interference of external force,
May grant at leisure; without risk incurred
Tlaat what in wisdom for herself she doth, 335
Others shall e'er be able to undo.

   Look! and behold, from Calpe's sunburnt cliffs
To the flat margin of the Baltic sea,
Long-reverenced Titles cast away as weeds;
Laws overturned,—and Territory split; 340
Like fields of ice rent by the polar wind
And forced to join in less obnoxious shapes,
Which, ere they gain consistence, by a gust
Of the same breath are shattered and destroyed.
Meantime, the Sovereignty of these fair Isles 345
Remains entire and indivisible;
And, if that ignorance were removed, which acts
Within the compass of their several shores
To breed commotion and disquietude,
Each might preserve the beautiful repose 350
Of heavenly Bodies shining in their spheres.
—The discipline of slavery is unknown
Amongst us,—hence the more do we require
The discipline of virtue; order else
Cannot subsist, nor confidence, nor peace. 355
Thus, duties rising out of good possessed,
And prudent caution needful to avert
Impending evil, do alike require
That permanent provision should be made
For the whole people to be taught and trained. 360
So shall licentiousness and black resolve
Be rooted out, and virtuous habits take
Their place; and genuine piety descend,
Like an inheritance, from age to age.

     With such foundations laid, avaunt the fear 365
Of numbers crowded on their native soil,
To the prevention of all healthful growth
Through mutual injury! Rather in the law
Of increase and the mandate from above
Rejoice!—and Ye have special cause for joy. 370
—For, as the element of air affords
An easy passage to the industrious bees
Fraught with their burthens; and a way as smooth
For those ordained to take their sounding flight
From the thronged hive, and settle where they list 375
In fresh abodes, their labour to renew;
So the wide waters, open to the power,
The will, the instincts, and appointed needs
Of Britain, do invite her to cast off
Her swarms, and in succession send them forth; 380
Bound to establish new communities
On every shore whose aspect favours hope
Or bold adventure; promising to skill
And perseverance their deserved reward.
—"Yes," he continued, kindling as he spake, 385
"Change wide, and deep, and silently performed,
This Land shall witness; and, as days roll on,
Earth's universal Frame shall feel the effect
Even 'till the smallest habitable Rock,
Beaten by lonely billows, hear the songs 390
Of humanized Society; and bloom
With civil arts, and send their fragrance forth,
A grateful tribute to all-ruling Heaven.
From Culture, universally bestowed
On Britain's noble Race in freedom born; 395
From Education, from that humble source,
Expect these mighty issues; from the pains
And quiet care of unambitious Schools
Instructing simple Childhood's ready ear:
Thence look for these magnificent results! 400

Vast the circumference of hope—and Ye
Are at its centre, British Lawgivers,
Ah! sleep not there in shame! Shall Wisdom's voice,
From out the bosom of these troubled Times
Repeat the dictates of her calmer mind, 405
And shall the venerable Halls ye fill
Refuse to echo the sublime decree?
Trust not to partial care a general good;
Transfer not to Futurity a work
Of urgent need.—Your Country must complete 410
Her glorious destiny.—Begin even now,
Now, when Oppression, like the Egyptian plague
Of darkness stretched o'er guilty Europe, makes
The brightness more conspicuous, that invests
The happy Island where ye think and act: 415
Now, when destruction is a prime pursuit,
Shew to the wretched Nations for what end
The Powers of civil Polity were given!"

   Abruptly here, but with a graceful air
The Sage broke off. No sooner had he ceased 420
Than, looking forth, the gentle Lady said,
"Behold, the shades of afternoon have fallen
Upon this flowery slope; and see—beyond—
The Lake, though bright, is of a placid blue;
As if preparing for the peace of evening. 425
How temptingly the landscape shines!—The air
Breathes invitation; easy is the walk
To the Lake's margin, where a Boat lies moored
Beneath her sheltering tree."—Upon this hint
We rose together: all were pleased—but most 430
The beauteous Girl, whose cheek was flushed with joy.
Light as a sun-beam glides along the hills
She vanished—eager to impart the scheme
To her loved Brother and his shy Compeer,
—Now was there bustle in the Vicar's house 435
And earnest preparation.—Forth we went,

And down the Valley on the Streamlet's bank
Pursued our way, a broken Company,
Mute or conversing, single or in pairs.
Thus having reached a bridge, that overarched 440
The hasty rivulet where it lay becalmed
In a deep pool, by happy chance we saw
A two-fold Image; on a grassy bank
A snow-white Ram, and in the crystal flood
Another and the same! Most beautiful, 445
On the green turf, with his imperial front
Shaggy and bold, and wreathed horns superb,
The breathing Creature stood; as beautiful,
Beneath him, shewed his shadowy Counterpart.
Each had his glowing mountains, each his sky, 450
And each seemed centre of his own fair world:
Antipodes unconscious of each other,
Yet, in partition, with their several spheres,
Blended in perfect stillness, to our sight!

   "Ah! what a pity were it to disperse, 455
Or to disturb, so fair a spectacle,
And yet a breath can do it!"
                        These few words
The Lady whispered, while we stood and gazed
Gathered together, all, in still delight,
Not without awe. Thence passing on, she said 460
In like low voice to my particular ear,
"I love to hear that eloquent Old Man
Pour forth his meditations, and descant
On human life from infancy to age.
How pure his spirit! in what vivid hues 465
His mind gives back the various forms of things,
Caught in their fairest, happiest attitude!
While he is speaking I have power to see
Even as he sees; but when his voice hath ceased,
Then, with a sigh I sometimes feel, as now, 470
That combinations so serene and bright,

Like those reflected in yon quiet Pool,
Cannot be lasting in a world like ours,
To great and small disturbances exposed."
More had she said—but sportive shouts were heard; 475
Sent from the jocund hearts of those two Boys,
Who, bearing each a basket on his arm,
Down the green field came tripping after us.
—When we had cautiously embarked, the Pair
Now for a prouder service were addrest; 480
But an inexorable law forbade,
And each resigned the oar which he had seized.
Whereat, with willing hand I undertook
The needful labour; grateful task!—to me
Pregnant with recollections of the time 485
When, on thy bosom, spacious Windermere!
A Youth, I practised this delightful art;
Tossed on the waves alone, or mid a crew
Of joyous Comrades.—Now the reedy marge
Cleared, with a strenuous arm I dipped the oar, 490
Free from obstruction; and the Boat advanced
Through crystal water, smoothly as a Hawk,
That, disentangled from the shady boughs
Of some thick wood, her place of covert, cleaves
With correspondent wings the abyss of air. 495
—"Observe," the Vicar said, "yon rocky Isle
With birch-trees fringed; my hand shall guide the helm,
While thitherward we bend our course; or while
We seek that other, on the western shore,—
Where the bare Columns of those lofty Firs, 500
Supporting gracefully a massy Dome
Of sombre foliage, seem to imitate
A Grecian Temple rising from the Deep."

"Turn where we may," said I, we cannot err
In this delicious Region."—Cultured slopes, 505
Wild tracts of forest-ground, and scattered groves,
And mountains bare—or clothed with ancient woods,

Surrounded us; and, as we held our way
Along the level of the glassy flood,
They ceased not to surround us; change of place,   510
From kindred features diversly combined,
Producing change of beauty ever new.
—Ah! that such beauty, varying in the light
Of living nature, cannot be pourtrayed
By words, nor by the pencil's silent skill;   515
But is the property of him alone
Who hath beheld it, noted it with care,
And in his mind recorded it with love!
Suffice it, therefore, if the rural Muse
Vouchsafe sweet influence, while her Poet speaks   520
Of trivial occupations well devised,
And unsought pleasures springing up by chance;
As if some friendly Genius had ordained
That, as the day thus far had been enriched
By acquisition of sincere delight,   525
The same should be continued to its close.

   One spirit animating old and young,
A gypsy fire we kindled on the shore
Of the fair Isle with birch-trees fringed—and there
Merrily seated in a ring, partook   530
The beverage drawn from China's fragrant herb.
—Launched from our hands the smooth stone skimmed the Lake;
With shouts we roused the echoes;—stiller sounds
The lovely Girl supplied—a simple song,
Whose low tones reached not to the distant rocks   535
To be repeated there, but gently sank
Into our hearts; and charmed the peaceful flood.
Rapaciously we gathered flowery spoils
From land and water; Lillies of each hue—
Golden and white, that float upon the waves   540
And court the wind; and leaves of that shy Plant,
(Her flowers were shed) the Lilly of the Vale,
That loves the ground, and from the sun withholds

Her pensive beauty, from the breeze her sweets.

    Such product, and such pastime did the place 545
And season yield; but, as we re-embarked,
Leaving, in quest of other scenes, the shore
Of that wild Spot, the Solitary said
In a low voice, yet careless who might hear,
"The Fire, that burned so brightly to our wish, 550
Where is it now? Deserted on the beach
It seems extinct; nor shall the fanning breeze
Revive its ashes. What care we for this,
Whose ends are gained? Behold an emblem here
Of one day's pleasure, and all mortal joys! 555
And, in this unpremeditated slight
Of that which is no longer needed, see
The common course of human gratitude!"

    This plaintive note disturbed not the repose
Of the still evening. Right across the Lake 560
Our pinnace moves: then, coasting creek and bay,
Glades we behold—and into thickets peep—
Where couch the spotted deer; or raised our eyes
To shaggy steeps on which the careless goat
Browzed by the side of dashing waterfalls. 565
Thus did the Bark, meandering with the shore,
Pursue her voyage, till a point was gained
Where a projecting line of rock, that framed
A natural pier, invited us to land.
—Alert to follow as the Pastor led 570
We clomb a green hill's side; and thence obtained,
Slowly, a less and less obstructed sight
Of the flat meadows, and indented coast
Of the whole lake—in compass seen! Far off,
And yet conspicuous, stood the old Church-tower, 575
In majesty presiding o'er the Vale
And all her Dwellings; seemingly preserved
From the intrusion of a restless world

By rocks impassable and mountains huge.

   Soft heath this elevated spot supplied, 580
With resting-place of mossy stone;—and there
We sate reclined—admiring quietly
The frame and general aspect of the scene;
And each not seldom eager to make known
His own discoveries; or to favourite points 585
Directing notice, merely from a wish
To impart a joy, imperfect while unshared.
That rapturous moment ne'er shall I forget
When these particular interests were effaced
From every mind!—Already had the sun, 590
Sinking with less than ordinary state,
Attained his western bound; but rays of light—
Now suddenly diverging from the orb
Retired behind the mountain tops or veiled
By the dense air—shot upwards to the crown 595
Of the blue firmament—aloft—and wide:
And multitudes of little floating clouds,
Pierced through their thin etherial mould, ere we,
Who saw, of change were conscious, had become
Vivid as fire—clouds separately poized, 600
Innumerable multitude of Forms
Scattered through half the circle of the sky;
And giving back, and shedding each on each,
With prodigal communion, the bright hues
Which from the unapparent Fount of glory 605
They had imbibed, and ceased not to receive.
That which the heavens displayed, the liquid deep
Repeated; but with unity sublime!

   While from the grassy mountain's open side
We gazed, in silence hushed, with eyes intent 610
On the refulgent spectacle—diffused
Through earth, sky, water, and all visible space,
The Priest in holy transport thus exclaimed—

"Eternal Spirit! universal God!
Power inaccessible to human thought   615
Save by degrees and steps which Thou hast deigned
To furnish; for this Image of Thyself,
To the infirmity of mortal sense
Vouchsafed; this local, transitory type
Of thy paternal splendors, and the pomp   620
Of those who fill thy courts in highest heaven,
The radiant Cherubim;—accept the thanks
Which we, thy humble Creatures, here convened,
Presume to offer; we, who from the breast
Of the frail earth, permitted to behold   625
The faint reflections only of thy face,
Are yet exalted, and in Soul adore!
Such as they are who in thy presence stand
Unsullied, incorruptible, and drink
Imperishable majesty streamed forth   630
From thy empyreal Throne, the elect of Earth
Shall be—divested at the appointed hour
Of all dishonour—cleansed from mortal stain.
—Accomplish, then, their number; and conclude
Time's weary course! Or, if by thy decree   635
The consummation that will come by stealth
Be yet far distant, let thy Word prevail,
Oh! let thy Word prevail, to take away
The sting of human nature. Spread the law,
As it is written in thy holy book,   640
Throughout all Lands; let every nation hear
The high behest, and every heart obey;
Both for the love of purity, and hope
Which it affords, to such as do thy will
And persevere in good, that they shall rise,   645
To have a nearer view of Thee, in heaven.
—Father of Good! this prayer in bounty grant,
In mercy grant it to thy wretched Sons.
Then, nor till then, shall persecution cease,

And cruel Wars expire. The way is marked,   650
The guide appointed, and the ransom paid.
Alas! the Nations, who of yore received
These tidings, and in Christian Temples meet
The sacred truth to acknowledge, linger still;
Preferring bonds and darkness to a state   655
Of holy freedom, by redeeming love
Proffered to all, while yet on earth detained.
So fare the many; and the thoughtful few,
Who in the anguish of their souls bewail
This dire perverseness, cannot choose but ask,   660
Shall it endure?—Shall enmity and strife,
Falsehood and guile, be left to sow their seed;
And the kind never perish? Is the hope
Fallacious, or shall Righteousness obtain
A peaceable dominion, wide as earth   665
And ne'er to fail? Shall that blest day arrive
When they, whose choice or lot it is to dwell
In crowded cities, without fear shall live
Studious of mutual benefit; and he,
Whom morning wakes, among sweet dews and flowers   670
Of every clime, to till the lonely field,
Be happy in himself?—The law of faith
Working through love, such conquest shall it gain,
Such triumph over sin and guilt achieve?
Almighty Lord, thy further grace impart!   675
And with that help the wonder shall be seen
Fulfilled, the hope accomplished; and thy praise
Be sung with transport and unceasing joy.

   Once, while the Name, Jehovah, was a sound,
Within the circuit of this sea-girt isle,   680
Unheard, the savage Nations bowed their heads
To Gods delighting in remorseless deeds;
Gods which themselves had fashioned, to promote
Ill purposes, and flatter foul desires.
Then, in the bosom of yon mountain cove,   685

To those inventions of corrupted Man
Mysterious rites were solemnized; and there,
Amid impending rocks and gloomy woods,
Of those dread Idols, some, perchance, received
Such dismal service, that the loudest voice   690
Of the swoln cataracts (which now are heard
Soft murmuring) was too weak to overcome,
Though aided by wild winds, the groans and shrieks
Of human Victims, offered up to appease
Or to propitiate. And, if living eyes   695
Had visionary faculties to see
The thing that hath been as the thing that is,
Aghast we might behold this spacious Mere
Bedimmed with smoke, in wreaths voluminous,
Flung from the body of devouring fires,   700
To Taranis erected on the heights
By priestly hands, for sacrifice, performed
Exultingly, in view of open day
And full assemblage of a barbarous Host;
Or to Andates, Female Power! who gave   705
(For so they fancied) glorious Victory.
—A few rude Monuments of mountain-stone
Survive; all else is swept away.—How bright
The appearances of things! From such, how changed
The existing worship; and, with those compared,   710
The Worshippers how innocent and blest!
So wide the difference, a willing mind,
At this affecting hour, might almost think
That Paradise, the lost abode of man,
Was raised again; and to a happy Few,   715
In its original beauty, here restored.
—Whence but from Thee, the true and only God,
And from the faith derived through Him who bled
Upon the Cross, this marvellous advance
Of good from evil; as if one extreme   720
Were left—the other gained.—O Ye, who come

To kneel devoutly in yon reverend Pile,
Called to such office by the peaceful sound
Of Sabbath bells; and Ye, who sleep in earth,
All cares forgotten, round its hallowed walls!   725
For You, in presence of this little Band
Gathered together on the green hill-side,
Your Pastor is emboldened to prefer
Vocal thanksgivings to the eternal King;
Whose love, whose counsel, whose commands have made   730
Your very poorest rich in peace of thought
And in good works; and Him, who is endowed
With scantiest knowledge, Master of all truth
Which the salvation of his soul requires.
Conscious of that abundant favour shower'd   735
On you, the Children of my humble care;—
On your Abodes, and this beloved Land,
Our birth-place, home, and Country, while on Earth
We sojourn,—loudly do I utter thanks
With earnest joy, that will not be suppressed.   740
These barren rocks, your stern inheritance;
These fertile fields, that recompence your pains;
The shadowy vale, the sunny mountain-top;
Woods waving in the wind their lofty heads,
Or hushed; the roaring waters, or the still;   745
They see the offering of my lifted hands—
They hear my lips present their sacrifice—
They know if I be silent, morn or even:
For, though in whispers speaking, the full heart
Will find a vent; and Thought is praise to Him,   750
Audible praise, to Thee, Omniscient Mind,
From Whom all gifts descend, all blessings flow!"

   This Vesper service closed, without delay,
From that exalted station, to the plain
Descending, we pursued our homeward course,   755
In mute composure, o'er the shadowy lake,
Beneath a faded sky. No trace remained

Of those celestial splendors; grey the vault,
Pure, cloudless ether; and the Star of Eve
Was wanting;—but inferior Lights appeared 760
Faintly, too faint almost for sight; and some
Above the darkened hills stood boldly forth
In twinkling lustre, ere the Boat attained
Her mooring-place;—where, to the sheltering tree
Our youthful Voyagers bound fast her prow, 765
With prompt yet careful hands. This done, we paced
The dewy fields; but ere the Vicar's door
Was reached, the Solitary checked his steps;
Then, intermingling thanks, on each bestowed
A farewell salutation,—and, the like 770
Receiving, took the slender path that leads
To the one Cottage in the lonely dell,
His chosen residence. But, ere he turned
Aside, a welcome promise had been given,
That he would share the pleasures and pursuits 775
Of yet another summer's day, consumed
In wandering with us through the Vallies fair,
And o'er the Mountain-wastes. "Another sun,"
Said he, "shall shine upon us, ere we part,—
Another sun, and peradventure more; 780
If time, with free consent, be yours to give,—
And season favours."
      To enfeebled Power,
From this conmunion with uninjured Minds,
What renovation had been brought; and what
Degree of healing to a wounded spirit, 785
Dejected, and habitually disposed
To seek, in degradation of the Kind,
Excuse and solace for her own defects;
How far those erring notions were reformed;
And whether aught, of tendency as good 790
And pure, from further intercourse ensued;
This—(if delightful hopes, as heretofore,

Inspire the serious song, and gentle Hearts
Cherish, and lofty Minds approve the past)
My future Labours may not leave untold. 795

[POEMS EXTRACTED FROM THE EXCURSION]

[The Peasant's Life][1]

              To the Yoke he bends,
Receives the chain from Nature's conquering hand,
Not loth, nor sad; but inwardly rejoiced
E'en like the Blackbird whistling in the grove
Or lordly Eagle in the rocky wild   5
Subdued. His day shews little, by that light
You cannot read him; into the hours of rest
His Spirit and course of action overflow.
No ghost familiar with the night like Him.
   To this new service bound, his fervent Zeal   10
The liveliest star outwatches, in mid heaven
Fix'd or slow travelling on the horizon's bound.
Happy if she for whom he wakes abide
Within the limits of his native Vale,
The native vale of both, or common Home;   15
And not less happy if need be, the Youth
Posts over Hill and dale and mountain top
Through wood, and brook across, by shortest line
Hasting, and chiding oft the wat'ry clouds
Which the sky breeds to blind his eager steps.   20
What sundry shapes of hazard, paths obscure
And length of indefatigable march,
Ere at the door the soft low tap be giv'n

---

1 WW never published these verses and the ones following as separate poems. His account here of the life of the typical peasant, part of *The Excursion* in DC MS. 74, was for the most part excluded from the published poem. MW copied it as an independent poem into a second manuscript, MS. 80. Gaps in this text have been filled by reference to the earlier manuscript.

Or from beneath the cottage eaves ascend
The stifled Cough—warning his chosen Maid 25
That now when sleep has hushed the world he comes
For a brief taste of stealthy intercourse.
Ten thousand sparks do from this covert fire
Spring up at each incitement of the breeze
Vivid, though noiseless, blessed hours if doubt 30
Be not nor jealousy; but hours they are
And Time has wings and Pleasure is Time's slave.
He must depart—ere blush of morning's light—
With the far wandering Fox slink to his home,
For short repose or haply to commence 35
A long day's labour with the sun new risen.
   Each current stemm'd of adverse circumstance,
The rock of absence either shunned or touch[ed]
Without a fatal shock, the insidious shoals
[?Of] jealousy triumphantly escaped, 40
And fancy's cross-winds and her peevish squalls
All stoutly weather'd, the trim vessel holds
Her port in open view.— It dawns; the day,
The important day of lasting recompense,
Not unproceeded by a throng of cares 45
Of frugal preparations intermix'd
With inoffensive vanity and show.
And see the orb, that animates the earth
And cheers the frame and fills the Spirit of man
With genial thoughts upon that morning shine 50
In splendour, so that Hill and dale reflect
The satisfaction of the festive troop
As they advance, or from the Church return
Blithe company of Elders, Maids and Youths
And the blest pair for life's remaining course 55
Each gives to each indissolubly bound.
This natural wedlock yields in season due
Fair fruit, a gift by either Parent prized
From the first hour—but to the father's heart

Doubly endeared, soon as the tender Babe 60
By creeping Time is strengthen'd to endure
Rough fondness and the gaiety of love
In boisterous assault. Then, ere he quits
His home, or as he enters from the fields,
Lightly the vigorous Peasant at arm's length 65
Tosses his lusty Boy aloft in air
And laughs to see the laughing Child at once
Pleased and half daunted by the dizzy height
Gain'd in a moment, in a moment lost.
A seasonable gladness, a relief 70
Occasional for six laborious days
Is here prepared, and duly this resource
Sweeten[s] the day of leisure and repose
With innocent pastime. In a sheltered vale,
Far from the gross contagion of the world, 75
Thus are the earlier years of wedded life
Adorn'd as spring with flowers, and to uphold
The Pair, and favor them as they advance
In later time along their humble path,
The pitfalls of mistake they shall avoid 80
By prudence guarded whose sure [hand] shall heal
The hurts of unavoidable mischance.
Immoderate labour shall not sap their strength,
Nor sickness overturn their plans, or thwart.
Discord shall find no place by their fire side, 85
Nor shall the dread of Poverty oppress
Their waking thoughts, nor guilt disturb their dreams.

[The Shepherd of Bield Crag][1]

Nor unregarded may I pass thee by,
Thee, poor ill fated Shepherd of BIELD CRAG
Who next dost meet me.— Thou wert longer used
To range the Coves and Heights with different aim,
Far different thoughts, and Thou didst perish there. 5
—There was he doomed to breathe his latest breath:—
More hapless end than his whom we this day
Have given to earth!— But Arthur did not want
House of his own, and lands, and numerous flock,
And wife and children to bewail his loss, 10
And a dumb Friend and Servant, in its kind
Loving as they, and marvellously true.
The Tale with all its moving incidents
Were long to tell.— Behold that smooth blue steep
That perilous descent of shivery stone 15
That sinks abruptly from the grassless Crown
Of yon huge Height.— He, roaming there, in quest
Of some endanger'd Stragglers from his Flock
Slipp'd in the turmoil of a winter storm,
And, far beneath, by next day's light, was found 20
A wounded Corse, with face towards the snow
And raiment by that long precipitous fall
Torn from his back: and there was found his Dog
In mournful posture, o'er the naked part
Couching as if to shield it from the cold! 25
A Bier was brought, and underneath that bier

---

1   The lines editorially titled *The Shepherd of Bield Crag* appear on four leaves in DC MS. 74. The leaves were once removed from the notebook and are now inserted as loose sheets within it. The tale's subject matter and revisions indicate that WW at one time planned to include this narrative in the epitaphic books of *The Excursion*, but he did not carry out the plan.

The afflicted Creature from the fatal spot
Walk'd with his Master's Body, nor withdrew
Nor quitted the forlorn society
Of those remains, till weeping Friends had laid them   30
Beneath this turf.—— Not seldom are we stopp'd
Wandering, through antient churches among tombs,
By sculptur'd image of the buried Man
Recumbent, Knight or Squire, with Sword and Shield,
And, at his feet, armorial Figure couch'd,   35
Lion, or Greyhound, Lamb, or gentle Fawn,
The bold or timid Creature each alike
Resting in duteous quiet, without fear
Of the sword's point and unoffending spurs,
That deck the Warrior in his last repose.   40
So, to assist Tradition, that will long
Preserve in our unvarying solitude
No weak remembrance of that sad event,
So have I sometimes wished that o'er this grave
Like Sculpture might be placed, albeit rude   45
And by some rustic hand uncouthly wrought
A Shepherd imaged in his mountain garb
And at his side the serviceable Staff
With which he lightly bounds o'er brook and crag
And couchant, like a pillow at the soles   50
Of his unarmed feet, the faithful Dog
That loved his Lord and clung to him in death.

Wordsworth's Notes

The Excursion, Book III, l. 116
WW provided the Latin text from Thomas Burnet's *Telluris Theoria Sacra* (2nd ed., 1688–89), I, 89. The translation below comes from *The Excursion* (1814), ed. Bushell, Butler, and Jaye, pp. 388–389:

"If, indeed, anything on this earth gives us a spectacle truly pleasing to and worthy of a philosopher, I can attest that Nature touched me in such a way; when I, looking out from the loftiest cliff, viewed the Mediterranean shore, then the cerulean surface of that sea, and finally certain Alpine regions; nothing truly more disparate and strange, nor of its kind more extraordinary and remarkable. This was a theater I could easily prefer to all the Roman ones and all the Greek ones, and this show put on by nature to all the stage performances or contests in the amphitheater. Nothing here is simply elegant and pretty, but huge and magnificent because it pleases by both its vastness and its immensity. Here I behold the uniform surface of the sea, spread out from end to end, so great a line of sight can be seen; hence to great eruptions on the face of the earth, and immense variegated masses standing high or sinking down: lofty, hanging down, leaning back, heaped together—all placed wild and uneven. The unity and simplicity of Nature, the inexhaustible plains, are pleasing from this vantage point; from another view the diverse complexities of great bodies as well as chaotic debris of all sorts: which, to my eye, seem the rubble not of any given city or town, but of a destroyed world.

"There was something unusual and marvelous on each specific mountain, but above all the rest, that ledge, on which I sat, was most pleasing to me; it was very sheer and high, and when looking up from the ground, disguised its height by a somewhat gradual ascent: looking down to the sea, a fearsome, headlong plunge as if it were a true perpendicular stately wall. Beyond that seaside view, it was smooth and uniform (a situation sometimes noticeable in mountains) and then there was a rupture in that surface from top to bottom rent asunder by either some upheaval of the earth, or by a lightning bolt.

"The bottom portion of the steep was a cave, which had a space containing grottos entering into the hollow mountain; whether made long ago by Nature, or eaten away by the sea and the relentless pounding of the waves. Into these the surgings of the sea entered with great force and noise, and then the cave turned them into foam and thrust them out again as if vomiting them from its deep maw.

"The right side of the mountain was steep, with sharp rock and naked crag; the left was not neglected by Nature, inasmuch as it was adorned by trees: and a stream of clear water rushed toward the foot of the mountain: which irrigated a nearby valley, creeping along slowly, through various twistings, as if attempting to prolong its life, and suddenly disappeared into the great sea. At the highest point of the promontory, pleasantly situated on a rock, I sat in contemplation. Farewell, awesome seat, fit for a king. Majestic rock, forever part of my remembrance!"

Book III, l. 940

"A Man is supposed to improve by going out into the *World*, by visiting *London*. Artificial man does; he extends with his sphere; but alas! that sphere is microscopic: it is formed of minutiæ, and he surrenders his genuine vision to the artist, in order to embrace it in his ken. His bodily senses grow acute, even to barren and inhuman pruriency; while his mental become proportionally obtuse. The reverse is the Man of Mind: He who is placed in the sphere of Nature and of God, might be a mock at Tattersall's and Brookes's, and a sneer at St. James's: he would certainly be swallowed alive by the first *Pizarro* that crossed him:—But when he walks along the River of Amazons; when he rests his eye on the unrivalled Andes; when he measures the long and watered Savannah; or contemplates from a sudden Promontory, the distant, vast Pacific—and feels himself a Freeman in this vast Theatre, and commanding each ready produced fruit of this wilderness, and each progeny of this stream—His exaltation is not less than Imperial. He is as gentle, too, as he is great: His emotions of tenderness keep pace with his elevation of sentiment; for he says, "These were made by a good Being, who, unsought by me, placed me here to enjoy them." He becomes at once a Child and a King. His mind is in himself; from hence he argues, and from hence he acts; and he argues unerringly and acts magisterially: His mind in himself is also in his God; and therefore he loves, and therefore he soars."—From the Notes upon *The Hurricane*, a Poem, *by William Gilbert.*

The Reader, I am sure, will thank me for the above Quotation, which, though from a strange book, is one of the finest passages of modern English Prose.

Book IV, ll. 125–134

The lines quoted in the text are from Daniel's "To the Ladie Margaret, Countesse of Cumberland." The four stanzas from this poem that WW printed in 1814 follow:

Nor is he moved with all the Thunder-cracks
Of Tyrants' threats, or with the surly brow
Of Power, that proudly sits on others' crimes;
Charged with more crying sins than those he checks.
The storms of sad confusion that may grow
Up in the present for the coming times,
Appal not him; that hath no side at all,
But of himself, and knows the worst can fall.

Although his heart (so near allied to earth)
Cannot but pity the perplexed state
Of troublous and distress'd mortality,
That thus make way unto the ugly Birth
Of their own Sorrows, and do still beget
Affliction upon Imbecility:
Yet seeing thus the course of things must run,
He looks thereon not strange, but as fore-done.

And whilst distraught Ambition compasses,
And is encompass'd, while as Craft deceives:
And is deceiv'd: whilst Man doth ransack Man,
And builds on blood, and rises by distress;
And th'Inheritance of desolation leaves
To great-expecting Hopes: He looks thereon,
As from the shore of Peace, with unwet eye,
And bears no venture in Impiety.

Thus, Lady, fares that Man that hath prepared
A Rest for his desires; and sees all things
Beneath him; and hath learn'd this Book of Man,
Full of the notes of frailty; and compar'd
The best of Glory with her sufferings:
By whom, I see, you labour all you can
To plant your heart; and set your thoughts as near
His glorious Mansion as your powers can bear.

Book V, ll. 984

ESSAY UPON EPITAPHS.

It needs scarcely be said, that an Epitaph presupposes a Monument, upon which it is to be engraven. Almost all Nations have wished that certain external signs should point out the places where their Dead are interred. Among savage Tribes unacquainted with Letters, this has mostly been done either by rude stones placed near the Graves, or by Mounds of earth raised over them. This custom proceeded obviously from a twofold desire; first, to guard the remains of the deceased from irreverent approach or from savage violation; and, secondly, to preserve their memory. "Never any," says Cambden, "neglected burial but some savage Nations; as the Bactrians which cast their dead to the dogs; some varlet Philosophers, as Diogenes, who desired to be devoured of fishes; some dissolute Courtiers, as Mecænas, who was wont to say, Non tumulum curo; sepelit natura relictos.

I'm careless of a Grave:—Nature her dead will save."

As soon as Nations had learned the use of letters, Epitaphs were inscribed upon these Monuments; in order that their intention might be more surely and adequately fulfilled. I have derived Monuments and Epitaphs from two sources of feeling: but these do in fact resolve themselves into one. The invention of Epitaphs, Weever, in his discourse of funeral Monuments, says rightly, "proceeded from the presage or fore-feeling of Immortality, implanted in all men naturally, and is referred to the Scholars of Linus the Theban Poet, who flourished about the year of the World two thousand seven hundred; who first bewailed this Linus their Master, when he was slain, in doleful verses then called of him Œlina, afterwards Epitaphia, for that they were first sung at burials, after engraved upon the Sepulchres."

  And, verily, without the consciousness of a principle of Immortality in the human soul, Man could never have had awakened in him the desire to live in the remembrance of his fellows; mere love, or the yearning of Kind towards Kind, could not have produced it. The Dog or Horse perishes in the field, or in the stall, by the side of his Companions, and is incapable of anticipating the sorrow with which his surrounding Associates shall bemoan his death, or pine for his loss; he cannot pre-conceive this regret, he can form no thought of it; and therefore cannot possibly have a desire to leave such regret or remembrance behind him. Add to the principle of love, which exists in the inferior animals, the faculty of reason which exists in Man alone; will the conjunction of these account for the desire? Doubtless it is a necessary consequence of this conjunction; yet not I think as a direct result, but only to be come at through an intermediate thought, viz. that of an intimation or assurance within us, that some part of our nature is imperishable. At least the precedence, in order of birth, of one feeling to the other, is unquestionable. If we look back upon the days of childhood, we shall find that the time is not in remembrance when, with respect to our own individual Being, the mind was without this assurance; whereas, the wish to be remembered by our Friends or Kindred after Death, or even in Absence, is, as we shall discover, a sensation that does not form itself till the social feelings have been developed, and the Reason has connected itself with a wide range of objects. Forlorn, and cut off from communication with the best part of his nature, must that Man be, who should derive the sense of immortality, as it exists in the mind of a Child, from the same unthinking gaiety or liveliness of animal Spirits with which the Lamb in the meadow, or any other irrational Creature, is endowed; who should ascribe it, in short, to blank ignorance in the Child; to an inability arising from the imperfect state of his faculties to come, in any point of his being, into contact with a notion of Death; or to an unreflecting acquiescence in what had been instilled into him! Has such an unfolder of the mysteries of Nature, though he may have forgotten his former self, ever noticed the early, obstinate, and unappeaseable inquisitiveness of Children upon the subject of origination? This single fact proves outwardly the monstrousness of those suppositions: for, if we had no direct external testimony that the minds of very young Children meditate feelingly upon Death and Immortality, these inquiries, which we all know they are perpetually making concerning the *whence*, do necessarily include correspondent habits of interrogation concerning the *whither*. Origin and tendency are notions inseparably co-relative. Never did a Child stand by the side of a running Stream, pondering within himself what power was the feeder of the perpetual current, from what never-wearied sources the body of water was supplied, but he must have been inevitably propelled to follow this question by another: "towards what abyss is it in progress? what receptacle can contain the mighty influx?" And the spirit of the answer must have been, though the word might be Sea or Ocean, accompanied perhaps with an image gathered from a Map, or from the real object in Nature—these might have been the *letter*, but the *spirit* of the answer must have been as inevitably,—a receptacle without bounds or dimensions;—nothing less than infinity. We may, then, be justified in asserting that the sense of Immortality, if not a co-existent and twin birth with Reason, is among the earliest of her Offspring: and we may further assert, that from these conjoined, and under their countenance, the human affections are gradually formed and opened out. This is not the place to enter into the recesses of these investigations; but the subject requires me here to make a plain avowal that, for my own part, it is to me inconceivable, that the sympathies of love towards each other, which grow with our growth, could ever attain any new strength, or even preserve the old, after we had received from the outward senses the impression of Death, and were in the habit of having that impression daily renewed and its accompanying feeling brought home to ourselves, and to those we love; if the same were not counteracted by those communications with our internal Being, which are anterior to all these experiences, and with which revelation coincides, and has through that coincidence alone (for otherwise it could not possess it) a power to affect us. I confess, with me the conviction is absolute, that, if the impression and sense of Death were not thus counterbalanced, such a hollowness would pervade the whole system of things, such a want of correspondence and consistency, a disproportion so astounding betwixt means and ends, that there could be no repose, no joy. Were we to grow up unfostered by this genial warmth, a frost would chill the spirit, so penetrating and powerful, that there could be no motions of the life of love; and infinitely less could we have any wish to be remembered after we had passed away from a world in which each man had moved about like a shadow.—If, then, in a Creature endowed with the faculties of foresight and reason, the social affections could not have unfolded themselves uncountenanced by the faith that Man is an immortal being; and if, consequently, neither could the individual dying have had a desire to survive in the remembrance of his fellows, nor on their side could they have felt a wish to preserve for future times vestiges of the departed; it follows, as a final inference, that without the belief in Immortality, wherein these several desires originate, neither monuments nor epitaphs, in affectionate or laudatory commemoration of the Deceased, could have existed in the world.

Simonides, it is related, upon landing in a strange Country, found the Corse of an unknown person, lying by the Sea-side; he buried it, and was honoured throughout Greece for the piety of that Act. Another ancient Philosopher, chancing to fix his eyes upon a dead Body, regarded the same with slight, if not with contempt; saying, "see the Shell of the flown Bird!" But it is not to be supposed that the moral and tender-hearted Simonides was incapable of the lofty movements of thought, to which that other Sage gave way at the moment while his soul was intent only upon the indestructible being; nor, on the other hand, that he, in whose sight a lifeless human Body was of no more value than the worthless Shell from which the living fowl had departed, would not, in a different mood of mind, have been affected by those earthly considerations which had incited the philosophic Poet to the performance of that pious duty. And with regard to this latter, we may be assured that, if he had been destitute of the capability of communing with the more exalted thoughts that appertain to human Nature, he would have cared no more for the Corse of the Stranger than for the dead body of a Seal or Porpoise which might have been cast up by the Waves. We respect the corporeal frame of Man, not merely because it is the habitation of a rational, but of an immortal Soul. Each of these Sages was in Sympathy with the best feelings of our Nature; feelings which, though they seem opposite to each other, have another and a finer connection than that of contrast.—It is a connection formed through the subtle progress by which, both in the natural and the moral world, qualities pass insensibly into their contraries, and things revolve upon each other. As, in sailing upon the orb of this Planet, a voyage, towards the regions where the sun sets, conducts gradually to the quarter where we have been accustomed to behold it come forth at its rising; and, in like manner, a voyage towards the east, the birth-place in our imagination of the morning, leads finally to the quarter where the Sun is last seen when he departs from our eyes; so, the contemplative Soul, travelling in the direction of mortality, advances to the Country of everlasting Life; and, in like manner, may she continue to explore those cheerful tracts, till she is brought back, for her advantage and benefit, to the land of transitory things—of sorrow and of tears.

On a midway point, therefore, which commands the thoughts and feelings of the two Sages whom we have represented in contrast, does the Author of that species of composition, the Laws of which it is our present purpose to explain, take his stand. Accordingly, recurring to the twofold desire of guarding the Remains of the deceased and preserving their memory, it may be said, that a sepulchral Monument is a tribute to a Man as a human Being; and that an Epitaph, (in the ordinary meaning attached to the word) includes this general feeling and something more; and is a record to preserve the memory of the dead, as a tribute due to his individual worth, for a satisfaction to the sorrowing hearts of the Survivors, and for the common benefit of the living: which record is to be accomplished, not in a general manner, but, where it can, in *close connection with the bodily remains of the deceased*: and these, it may be added, among the modern Nations of Europe are deposited within, or contiguous to their places of worship. In ancient times, as is well known, it was the custom to bury the dead beyond the Walls of Towns and Cities; and among the Greeks and Romans they were frequently interred by the way-sides.

I could here pause with pleasure, and invite the Reader to indulge with me in contemplation of the advantages which must have attended such a practice. I could ruminate upon the beauty which the Monuments, thus placed, must have borrowed from the surrounding images of Nature—from the trees, the wild flowers, from a stream running perhaps within sight or hearing, from the beaten road stretching its weary length hard by. Many tender similitudes must these objects have presented to the mind of the Traveller, leaning upon one of the Tombs, or reposing in the coolness of its shade, whether he had halted from weariness or in compliance with the invitation, "Pause Traveller!" so often found upon the Monuments. And to its Epitaph also must have been supplied strong appeals to visible appearances or immediate impressions, lively and affecting analogies of Life as a Journey—Death as a Sleep overcoming the tired Wayfarer—of Misfortune as a Storm that falls suddenly upon him—of Beauty as a Flower that passeth away, or of innocent pleasure as one that may be gathered—of Virtue that standeth firm as a Rock against the beating Waves;—of Hope "undermined insensibly like the Poplar by the side of the River that has fed it," or blasted in a moment like a Pine-tree by the stroke of lightening upon the Mountain top—of admonitions and heart-stirring remembrances, like a refreshing Breeze that comes without warning, or the taste of the waters of an unexpected Fountain. These, and similar suggestions must have given, formerly, to the language of the senseless stone a voice enforced and endeared by the benignity of that Nature, with which it was in unison.—We, in modern times, have lost much of these advantages: and they are but in a small degree counterbalanced to the Inhabitants of large Towns and Cities, by the custom of depositing the Dead within, or contiguous to, their places of worship; however splendid or imposing may be the appearances of those Edifices, or however interesting or salutary the recollections associated with them. Even were it not true that Tombs lose their monitory virtue when thus obtruded upon the notice of Men occupied with the cares of the World, and too often sullied and defiled by those cares, yet still, when Death is in our thoughts, nothing can make amends for the want of the soothing influences of Nature, and for the absence of those types of renovation and decay, which the fields and woods offer to the notice of the serious and contemplative mind. To feel the force of this sentiment, let a man only compare in imagination the unsightly manner in which our Monuments are crowded together in the busy, noisy, unclean, and almost grassless Church-yard of a large Town, with the still seclusion of a Turkish Cemetery, in some remote place; and yet further sanctified by the Grove of Cypress in which it is embosomed. Thoughts in the same temper as these have already been expressed with true sensibility by an ingenuous Poet of the present day. The subject of his Poem is "All Saints Church, Derby:" he has been deploring the forbidding and unseemly appearance of its burial-ground, and uttering a wish, that in past times the practice had been adopted of interring the Inhabitants of large Towns in the Country.—

>"Then in some rural, calm, sequestered spot,
>Where healing Nature her benignant look
>Ne'er changes, save at that lorn season, when,
>With tresses drooping o'er her sable stole,
>She yearly mourns the mortal doom of man,
>Her noblest work, (so Israel's virgins erst,
>With annual moan upon the mountains wept
>Their fairest gone) there in that rural scene,
>So placid, so congenial to the wish
>The Christian feels, of peaceful rest within
>The silent grave, I would have stray'd:
>. . . . .
>—wandered forth, where the cold dew of heaven
>Lay on the humbler graves around, what time
>The pale moon gazed upon the turfy mounds,
>Pensive, as though like me, in lonely muse,
>'Twere brooding on the Dead inhum'd beneath.
>There, while with him, the holy Man of Uz,
>O'er human destiny I sympathiz'd,
>Counting the long, long periods prophecy
>Decrees to roll, ere the great day arrives
>Of resurrection, oft the blue-eyed Spring
>Had met me with her blossoms, as the Dove
>Of old, return'd with olive leaf, to cheer
>The Patriarch mourning o'er a world destroy'd:
>And I would bless her visit; for to me
>'Tis sweet to trace the consonance that links
>As one, the works of Nature and the word
>Of God."——
>
>>JOHN EDWARDS.

A Village Church-yard, lying as it does in the lap of Nature, may indeed be most favourably contrasted with that of a Town of crowded Population; and Sepulture therein combines many of the best tendencies which belong to the mode practised by the Ancients, with others peculiar to itself. The sensations of pious cheerfulness, which attend the celebration of the Sabbath-day in rural places, are profitably chastised by the sight of the Graves of Kindred and Friends, gathered together in that general Home towards which the thoughtful yet happy Spectators themselves are journeying. Hence a Parish Church, in the stillness of the Country, is a visible centre of a community of the living and the dead; a point to which are habitually referred the nearest concerns of both.

As, then, both in Cities and in Villages, the Dead are deposited in close connection with our places of worship, with us the composition of an Epitaph naturally turns still more than among the Nations of Antiquity, upon the most serious and solemn affections of the human mind; upon departed Worth—upon personal or social Sorrow and Admiration—upon Religion individual and social—upon Time, and upon Eternity. Accordingly it suffices, in ordinary cases, to secure a composition of this kind from censure, that it contains nothing that shall shock or be inconsistent with this spirit. But, to entitle an Epitaph to praise, more than this is necessary. It ought to contain some Thought or Feeling belonging to the mortal or immortal part of our Nature touchingly expressed; and if that be done, however general or even trite the sentiment may be, every man of pure mind will read the words with pleasure and gratitude. A Husband bewails a Wife; a Parent breathes a sigh of disappointed hope over a lost Child; a Son utters a sentiment of filial reverence for a departed Father or Mother; a Friend perhaps inscribes an encomium recording the companionable qualities, or the solid virtues, of the Tenant of the Grave, whose departure has left a sadness upon his memory. This, and a pious admonition to the Living, and a humble expression of Christian confidence in Immortality, is the language of a thousand Church-yards; and it does not often happen that any thing, in a greater degree discriminate or appropriate to the Dead or to the Living, is to be found in them. This want of discrimination has been ascribed by Dr. Johnson, in his

Essay upon the Epitaphs of Pope, to two causes; first, the scantiness of the Objects of human praise; and, secondly, the want of variety in the Characters of Men; or to use his own words, "to the fact, that the greater part of Mankind have no Character at all." Such language may be holden without blame among the generalities of common conversation; but does not become a Critic and a Moralist speaking seriously upon a serious Subject. The objects of admiration in Human Nature are not scanty but abundant; and every Man has a Character of his own, to the eye that has skill to perceive it. The real cause of the acknowledged want of discrimination in sepulchral memorials is this: That to analyse the Characters of others, especially of those whom we love, is not a common or natural employment of Men at any time. We are not anxious unerringly to understand the constitution of the Minds of those who have soothed, who have cheered, who have supported us: with whom we have been long and daily pleased or delighted. The affections are their own justification. The Light of Love in our Hearts is a satisfactory evidence that there is a body of worth in the minds of our friends or kindred, whence that Light has proceeded. We shrink from the thought of placing their merits and defects to be weighed against each other in the nice balance of pure intellect: nor do we find much temptation to detect the shades by which a good quality or virtue is discriminated in them from an excellence known by the same general name as it exists in the mind of another; and, least of all, do we incline to these refinements when under the pressure of Sorrow, Admiration, or Regret, or when actuated by any of those feelings which incite men to prolong the memory of their Friends and Kindred, by records placed in the bosom of the all-uniting and equalizing Receptacle of the Dead.

The first requisite, then, in an Epitaph is, that it should speak, in a tone which shall sink into the heart, the general language of humanity as connected with the subject of Death—the source from which an Epitaph proceeds; of death and of life. To be born and to die are the two points in which all men feel themselves to be in absolute coincidence. This general language may be uttered so strikingly as to entitle an Epitaph to high praise; yet it cannot lay claim to the highest unless other excellencies be superadded. Passing through all intermediate steps, we will attempt to determine at once what these excellencies are, and wherein consists the perfection of this species of composition. It will be found to lie in a due proportion of the common or universal feeling of humanity to sensations excited by a distinct and clear conception, conveyed to the Reader's mind, of the Individual, whose death is deplored and whose memory is to be preserved; at least of his character as, after death, it appeared to those who loved him and lament his loss. The general sympathy ought to be quickened, provoked, and diversified, by particular thoughts, actions, images,—circumstances of age, occupation, manner of life, prosperity which the Deceased had known, or adversity to which he had been subject; and these ought to be bound together and solemnized into one harmony by the general sympathy. The two powers should temper, restrain, and exalt each other. The Reader ought to know who and what the Man was whom he is called upon to think of with interest. A distinct conception should be given (implicitly where it can, rather than explicitly) of the Individual lamented. But the Writer of an Epitaph is not an Anatomist who dissects the internal frame of the mind; he is not even a Painter who executes a portrait at leisure and in entire tranquillity: his delineation, we must remember, is performed by the side of the Grave; and, what is more, the grave of one whom he loves and admires. What purity and brightness is that virtue clothed in, the image of which must no longer bless our living eyes! The character of a deceased Friend or beloved Kinsman is not seen, no—nor ought to be seen, otherwise than as a Tree through a tender haze or a luminous mist, that spiritualizes and beautifies it; that takes away indeed, but only to the end that the parts which are not abstracted may appear more dignified and lovely, may impress and affect the more. Shall we say then that this is not truth, not a faithful image; and that accordingly the purposes of commemoration cannot be answered?—It is truth, and of the highest order! for, though doubtless things are not apparent which did exist, yet, the object being looked at through this medium, parts and proportions are brought into distinct view which before had been only imperfectly or unconsciously seen: it is truth hallowed by love—the joint offspring of the worth of the Dead and the affections of the Living!—This may easily be brought to the test.

Let one, whose eyes have been sharpened by personal hostility to discover what was amiss in the character of a good man, hear the tidings of his death, and what a change is wrought in a moment!—Enmity melts away; and, as it disappears, unsightliness, disproportion, and deformity, vanish; and, through the influence of commiseration, a harmony of love and beauty succeeds. Bring such a Man to the Tombstone on which shall be inscribed an Epitaph on his Adversary, composed in the spirit which we have recommended. Would he turn from it as from an idle tale? Ah! no—the thoughtful look, the sigh, and perhaps the involuntary tear, would testify that it had a sane, a generous, and good meaning; and that on the Writer's mind had remained an impression which was a true abstract of the character of the deceased; that his gifts and graces were remembered in the simplicity in which they ought to be remembered. The composition and quality of the mind of a virtuous man, contemplated by the side of the Grave where his body is mouldering, ought to appear, and be felt as something midway between what he was on Earth walking about with his living frailties, and what he may be presumed to be as a Spirit in Heaven.

It suffices, therefore, that the Trunk and the main Branches of the Worth of the Deceased be boldly and unaffectedly represented. Any further detail, minutely and scrupulously pursued, especially if this be done with laborious and antithetic discriminations, must inevitably frustrate its own purpose; forcing the passing Spectator to this conclusion,—either that the Dead did not possess the merits ascribed to him, or that they who have raised a monument to his memory and must therefore be supposed to have been closely connected with him, were incapable of perceiving those merits; or at least during the act of composition had lost sight of them; for, the Understanding having been so busy in its petty occupation, how could the heart of the Mourner be other than cold? and in either of these cases, whether the fault be on the part of the buried Person or the Survivors, the Memorial is unaffecting and profitless.

Much better is it to fall short in discrimination than to pursue it too far, or to labour it unfeelingly. For in no place are we so much disposed to dwell upon those points, of nature and condition, wherein all Men resemble each other, as in the Temple where the universal

Father is worshipped, or by the side of the Grave which gathers all Human Beings to itself, and "equalizes the lofty and the low." We suffer and we weep with the same heart; we love and are anxious for one another in one spirit; our hopes look to the same quarter; and the virtues by which we are all to be furthered and supported, as patience, meekness, good-will, temperance, and temperate desires, are in an equal degree the concern of us all. Let an Epitaph, then, contain at least these acknowledgments to our common nature; nor let the sense of their importance be sacrificed to a balance of opposite qualities or minute distinctions in individual character; which if they do not, (as will for the most part be the case) when examined, resolve themselves into a trick of words, will, even when they are true and just, for the most part be grievously out of place; for, as it is probable that few only have explored these intricacies of human nature, so can the tracing of them be interesting only to a few. But an Epitaph is not a proud Writing shut up for the studious; it is exposed to all, to the wise and the most ignorant; it is condescending, perspicuous, and lovingly solicits regard; its story and admonitions are brief, that the thoughtless, the busy and indolent, may not be deterred, nor the impatient tired; the stooping Old Man cons the engraven record like a second horn-book;—the Child is proud that he can read it—and the Stranger is introduced by its meditation to the company of a Friend: it is concerning all, and for all:—in the Church-yard it is open to the day; the sun looks down upon the stone, and the rains of Heaven beat against it.

  Yet, though the Writer who would excite sympathy is bound in this case more than in any other, to give proof that he himself has been moved, it is to be remembered, that to raise a Monument is a sober and a reflective act; that the inscription which it bears is intended to be permanent and for universal perusal; and that, for this reason, the thoughts and feelings expressed should be permanent also—liberated from that weakness and anguish of sorrow which is in nature transitory, and which with instinctive decency retires from notice. The passions should be subdued, the emotions controlled; strong indeed, but nothing ungovernable or wholly involuntary. Seemliness requires this, and truth requires it also: for how can the Narrator otherwise be trusted? Moreover, a Grave is a tranquillizing object: resignation, in course of time, springs up from it as naturally as the wild flowers, besprinkling the turf with which it may be covered, or gathering round the monument by which it is defended. The very form and substance of the monument which has received the inscription, and the appearance of the letters, testifying with what a slow and laborious hand they must have been engraven, might seem to reproach the Author who had given way upon this occasion to transports of mind, or to quick turns of conflicting passion; though the same might constitute the life and beauty of a funeral Oration or elegiac Poem.

These sensations and judgments, acted upon perhaps unconsciously, have been one of the main causes why Epitaphs so often personate the Deceased, and represent him as speaking from his own Tomb-stone. The departed Mortal is introduced telling you himself that his pains are gone; that a state of rest is come; and he conjures you to weep for him no longer. He admonishes with the voice of one experienced in the vanity of those affections which are confined to earthly objects, and gives a verdict like a superior Being, performing the office of a Judge, who has no temptations to mislead him, and whose decision cannot but be dispassionate. Thus is Death disarmed of its sting, and affliction unsubstantialized. By this tender fiction the Survivors bind themselves to a sedater sorrow, and employ the intervention of the imagination in order that the reason may speak her own language earlier than she would otherwise have been enabled to do. This shadowy interposition also harmoniously unites the two worlds of the Living and the Dead by their appropriate affections. And I may observe, that here we have an additional proof of the propriety with which sepulchral inscriptions were referred to the consciousness of Immortality as their primal source.

I do not speak with a wish to recommend that an Epitaph should be cast in this mould preferably to the still more common one, in which what is said comes from the Survivors directly; but rather to point out how natural those feelings are which have induced men, in all states and ranks of Society, so frequently to adopt this mode. And this I have done chiefly in order that the laws, which ought to govern the composition of the other, may be better understood. This latter mode, namely, that in which the Survivors speak in their own Persons, seems to me upon the whole greatly preferable: as it admits a wider range of notices; and, above all, because, excluding the fiction which is the ground-work of the other, it rests upon a more solid basis.

Enough has been said to convey our notion of a perfect Epitaph; but it must be observed that one is meant which will best answer the *general* ends of that species of composition. According to the course pointed out, the worth of private life, through all varieties of situation and character, will be most honourably and profitably preserved in memory. Nor would the model recommended less suit public Men, in all instances save of those persons who by the greatness of their services in the employments of Peace or War, or by the surpassing excellence of their works in Art, Literature, or Science, have made themselves not only universally known, but have filled the heart of their Country with everlasting gratitude. Yet I must here pause to correct myself. In describing the general tenour of thought which Epitaphs ought to hold, I have omitted to say, that, if it be the actions of a Man, or even some *one* conspicuous or beneficial act of local or general utility, which have distinguished him and excited a desire that he should be remembered, then of course, ought the attention to be directed chiefly to those actions or that act; and such sentiments dwelt upon as naturally arise out of them or it. Having made this necessary distinction I proceed.—The mighty Benefactors of mankind, as they are not only known by the immediate Survivors, but will continue to be known familiarly to latest Posterity, do not stand in need of biographic sketches, in such a place; nor of delineations of character to individualize them. This is already done by their Works, in the Memories of Men. Their naked names, and a grand comprehensive sentiment of civic Gratitude, patriotic Love, or human Admiration; or the utterance of some elementary Principle most essential in the constitution of true Virtue; or an intuition, communicated in adequate words, of the sublimity of intellectual Power,—these are the only tribute which can here be paid—the only offering that upon such an Altar would not be unworthy!

> What needs my Shakespeare for his honoured bones
> The labour of an age in piled stones,

Or that his hallowed reliques should be hid
Under a star-y-pointing pyramid?
Dear Son of Memory, great Heir of Fame,
What need'st thou such weak witness of thy name?
Thou in our wonder and astonishment
Hast built thyself a live-long Monument.
And so sepulchred, in such pomp dost lie,
That Kings for such a Tomb would wish to die.

Select Bibliography

Bushell, Sally, *Re-Reading the Excursion: Narrative, Response and the Wordsworthian Dramatic Voice* (Aldershot: Ashgate, 2002).

Butler, James A., 'Wordsworth's Tuft of Primroses: "An Unrelenting doom" ', *Studies in Romanticism* 14:3 (1975), 237–48.

Cole, John J., ' "Radical Difference": Wordsworth's Classical Imagination and Roman Ethos', doctoral thesis, University of Auckland, 2008, < http://hdl.handle.net/2292/5677>.

Duggett, Thomas and Jacob Risinger (eds), *The Excursion at Two Hundred*, *The Wordsworth Circle*, 45.2 (Spring 2014).

Finch, John Alban, 'Wordsworth, Coleridge, and "The Recluse", 1798–1814', doctoral dissertation, Cornell University, 1964.

Fry, Paul H., 'The Pedlar, the Poet, and 'The Ruined Cottage' , in *The Oxford Handbook of William Wordsworth*, ed. Richard Gravil and Daniel Robinson (Oxford: Oxford University Press, 2015), 365–78.

Gravil, Richard, 'Is *The Excursion* a 'metrical Novel?', in *Grasmere 2010: Selected Papers from the Wordsworth Summer Conference* (Penrith: Humanities-Ebooks, 2010) 195–217.

———. 'Mr. Thelwall's Ear; or, Hearing *The Excursion*', in *Grasmere 2011: Selected Papers from the Wordsworth Summer Conference* (Penrith: Humanities-Ebooks, 2011), 171–203.

———. 'The "Recluse" Project and its Shorter Poems', in *The Oxford Handbook of William Wordsworth,* ed. Richard Gravil and Daniel Robinson (Oxford: Oxford University Press, 2015), 345–364.

Hartman, Geoffrey, *Wordsworth's Poetry, 1797–1814* (New Haven and London: Yale University Press, 1964).

Hewitt, Regina, *The Possibilities of Society: Wordsworth, Coleridge, and the Sociological Viewpoint of English Romanticism* (Albany, NY: State University of New York Press, 1997).

Jarvis, Simon, *Wordsworth's Philosophic Song* (Cambridge: Cambridge University Press, 2007).

Johnston, Kenneth R., *Wordsworth and The Recluse* (New Haven, CT: Yale University Press, 1984).

——. 'Wordsworth at Forty: Memoirs of a Lost Generation', in *Grasmere 2010: Selected Papers from the Wordsworth Summer Conference* (Penrith: Humanities-Ebooks, 2010) 173–94.

Kroeber, Karl, ' "Home at Grasmere": Ecological Holiness', *PMLA* 89 (1974).

McFarland, Thomas, *William Wordsworth: Intensity and Achievement* (Oxford: Clarendon Press, 1992).

Potkay, Adam, *Wordsworth's Ethics* (Baltimore: Johns Hopkins University Press, 2012)

Reed, Mark, *Wordsworth: The Chronology of the Early Years, 1770–1799* (Cambridge, MA: Harvard University Press, 1975).

——. *Wordsworth: The Chronology of the Middle Years, 1800–1815* (Cambridge, MA: Harvard University Press, 1975).

Risinger, Jacob, '*The Excursion* as Dialogic Poem', in *The Oxford Handbook of William Wordsworth,* ed. Richard Gravil and Daniel Robinson (Oxford: Oxford University Press, 2014), 430–46.

Wordsworth, Jonathan, *The Music of Humanity: A Critical Study of Wordsworth's 'Ruined Cottage'* (London: Nelson, 1969).

Wordsworth, William, *'Lyrical Ballads' and other Poems, 1797–1800*, ed. James Butler and Karen Green (Ithaca NY: Cornell University Press, 1992)

——. *The Excursion*, ed. Sally Bushell, James Butler, and Michael C. Jaye (Ithaca, NY: Cornell University Press, 2007).

——. *The Ruined Cottage and The Pedlar*, ed. James Butler (Ithaca, NY: Cornell University Press, 1979).

——. *The Tuft of Primroses, with Other Poems for The Recluse*, ed. Joseph F. Kishel (Ithaca, NY: Cornell University Press, 1986)

Wordsworth Titles from Humanities-Ebooks

The Poems of William Wordsworth: Collected Reading Texts from the Cornell Wordsworth, 3 volumes, edited by Jared Curtis †

This edition, with an extensive Addendum, is also available as a single PDF Ebook (over 2500 pages) exclusively from Humanities-Ebooks.

The Fenwick Notes of William Wordsworth, edited by Jared Curtis †

The Cornell Wordsworth: A Supplement, edited by Jared Curtis ††

The Prose Works of William Wordsworth, Volume 1, edited by W. J. B. Owen and Jane Worthington Smyser †

Wordsworth's Convention of Cintra, a Bicentennial Critical Edition, edited by W. J. B Owen, with a critical symposium by Simon Bainbridge, David Bromwich, Richard Gravil, Timothy Michael and Patrick Vincent

Wordsworth's Political Writings, edited by W. J. B. Owen and Jane Worthington Smyser. Reading texts of *A Letter to the Bishop of Llandaff*, *The Convention of Cintra*, *Two Addresses to the Freeholders of Westmorland*, and the 1835 *Postscript*. †

Richard Gravil, *Wordsworth and Helen Maria Williams; or, The Perils of Sensibility*

W. J. B. Owen, *Understanding The Prelude*

† Also available in paperback †† hardback (for details see website)

http://www.humanities-ebooks.co.uk

all PDF titles available to libraries from EBSCO, Ebrary and Ingram

www.ingramcontent.com/pod-product-compliance
Lightning Source LLC
Chambersburg PA
CBHW071951220426
43662CB00009B/1082